Lives in Translation

Sikh Youth as British Citizens

KATHLEEN D. HALL

PENN

University of Pennsylvania Press

Philadelphia

Copyright © 2002 University of Pennsylvania Press
All rights reserved
Printed in the United States of America on acid-free paper

10 9 8 7 6 5 4 3 2 1

Published by
University of Pennsylvania Press
Philadelphia, Pennsylvania 19104-4011

Library of Congress Cataloging-in-Publication Data

Hall, Kathleen, 1957–
    Lives in translation : Sikh youth as British citizens / Kathleen D. Hall.
        p. cm.
    Includes bibliographical references and index.
    ISBN 0-8122-3667-X (acid-free paper—ISBN 0-8122-1811-6 (pbk. : acid-free paper)
    1. Sikh youth—Great Britain. 2. Immigrants—Great Britain. 3. South Asians—Great
Britain. 4. Children of immigrants—Great Britain. 5. Great Britain—Ethnic relations. I. Title.

DA125.S57 H35   2002
305.235—dc21   2002020308

For Nana

Contents

I was having a little identity crisis. I'd been greeted so warmly in Pakistan, I felt so excited by what I saw, and so at home with all my uncles, I wondered if I were not better off here than there. And when I said, with a little unnoticed irony, that I was an Englishman, people laughed. They fell about. Why would anyone with a brown face, Muslim name and large well-known family in Pakistan want to lay claim to that cold little decrepit island off Europe where you always had to spell your name? Strangely, anti-British remarks made me feel patriotic, though I only felt patriotic when I was away from England.

—Hanif Kureishi, "London and Karachi"

It is the British, the white British, who have to learn that being British isn't what it was. Now it is a more complex thing, involving new elements.

—Hanif Kureishi, "England, Your England"

1. Introduction: A Different Immigration Story

In Leeds, England, in a house on middle-class Street Lane, locally known as "Sikh Lane," I often spent Sunday afternoons with Amrit.[1] We would talk for hours, drinking tea stretched out in front of an electric fire, an image of a Sikh guru, Guru Gobind Singh, watching us from his garlanded portrait above the fireplace. The aroma of cumin and coriander filtered into the room from the kitchen where Amrit's mother and sister were preparing the evening meal. Amrit, at eighteen, wore her hair in a braid that fell halfway down her back. Her face was free of makeup, but her look was decidedly "modern," the latest in English fashion: Indian-style *pajama* pants with a Marks and Spencers sweater and an Indian-made scarf to match.

Amrit is a second generation British Sikh. Her family's history in Britain has been recounted by numerous narratives of Asian postwar immigration to Britain, narratives that begin with accounts of the "push" or "pull" factors that set her father and his brothers off on a journey, as Lisa Lowe puts it, from "foreign strangeness to assimilation to citizenship."[2] This book is about Amrit, her family, her friends, and other British Sikhs of both her own and her parents' generation.[3] It is about the place they are carving out for themselves in Britain as citizens. This is a story of immigration and of the process of becoming British citizens. It is a story of the children of immigrants who are achieving upward mobility through their educational accomplishments. But in recounting their experiences and the challenges they have faced, my account crafts a radically different type of narrative, one that challenges the conventional assumptions of the traditional immigration "myth."

My central aim in crafting this unconventional account of immigration and social mobility is to demonstrate that the story of immigration is intimately tied to the story of nation formation, particularly in the postcolonial United Kingdom but elsewhere in the Western world as well. Immigrants become citizens through processes of social incorporation. These processes entail complex and multiple forms of cultural politics, which, as I will show, play out across a number of sites within the public sphere of democratic capitalist nations, in law and policy, education and the media, as well as in families and ethnic communities. In the context of these cultural politics, "immigrants" are produced as multiple types of subjects associated with distinctive "minority" statuses that classify those so defined in racial, ethnic, religious, linguistic, generational, and gendered terms. It is here, I argue, within the varied forms of cultural production at work in the public sphere, that identities and subjectivities are "made."

In turning the central focus to cultural processes in the public sphere, my work diverges from traditional ethnographic accounts that have located the dynamics of cultural change within the domestic spaces of immigrant families.[4] Family life is clearly profoundly significant in the lives of the second generation Sikhs whose stories I have the privilege to tell, but the family is only one place where young Sikhs learn about what it means to be Sikh, Indian, Asian, and British, in Britain and in the diaspora more broadly. The cultural lessons their families teach them, explicitly and tacitly, take on new meaning and deeper levels of significance in relation to lessons they learn in other contexts about Sikh tradition, racial identity, and gender differences. In this reconfigured immigration story, then, the family becomes one social field among many in which second generation Sikh identities and subjectivities are made. The journey to citizenship, from this perspective, is the story of how migrant people come to know themselves and others through profound experiences of solidarity, contest, and contradiction as they move across different social fields.

I begin by considering the way Sikh young people, in describing the dilemmas they face growing up in Britain, often use a dominant trope in traditional immigration studies. These young people say they feel "caught between two cultures," though their everyday lives are saturated with a wide range of cultural influences and styles, sets of normative expectations, and imaginative possibilities. There is a sense of ethnographic irony here that provides a stepping off point for considering the dynamics of power and cultural production that lie beneath. Next I consider the broader context of social incorporation and nation formation in the United Kingdom, within which the experiences of British Sikhs have been shaped. The book's analysis begins here, taking a radical step away from more conventional ethnographies of Sikh populations abroad. To emphasize the constitutive role of cultural politics in the public sphere on processes of immigrant identity formation, I look first to the public sphere to portray the social and political terrains in relation to which Sikhs have crafted lives for themselves as British citizens. In this way the account moves down levels of social scale from cultural politics and subject formation in national legal and policy debates, to the school, the media, Sikh communities and families, and, finally, to the everyday lives of Sikh young people themselves.

The Master Narrative of Sikh Immigration

The stories of Asians who immigrated to Britain after World War II are richly varied, yet in fact they share some historical commonalities. Amrit's father came to Britain, as did many Sikh men, in the late 1950s from a village in the Indian state of the Punjab where his family, as members of the Jat caste, were landowning farmers. Amrit's father and uncles were part of the first phase of ex-colonial immigration into Britain, exclusively men to begin with, mainly semiskilled or unskilled workers, who came to fill a demand for laborers needed to rebuild Britain in the aftermath of the war. Amrit's mother joined her husband in the early 1960s, and they have lived in Leeds ever since.

Amrit and her family moved to the middle-class area of Moortown from the predominantly black "inner city" area of Chapeltown, both as a sign of their social mobility and in an effort to be nearer to Amrit's high school, Grange Hill. Most of the Sikh youths at Grange Hill High either were born in England to parents, like Amrit's, who migrated in the 1950s and '60s from villages in the Punjab, or came with their parents from East Africa during the late 1960s and early '70s at a very young age. They are British citizens.

In British India the Sikhs had enjoyed a privileged relationship with their colonial rulers. After the British were nearly defeated in the Anglo-Sikh Wars, they designated the Sikhs a "martial race," giving them a privileged status in the British Indian Army. For the next hundred years, the Sikhs distinguished themselves as soldiers in far greater proportion than their relative numbers. Sikhs, together with other groups from India, also enjoyed a position of privilege in East Africa. In this racially stratified colonial society, Asians served as middlemen, occupying administrative positions that gave them power and authority over indigenous Africans who were excluded from government positions and relegated to the bottom of the colonial social hierarchy.

Within the empire, the Sikhs had achieved status and stature. But when Sikh immigrants arrived on British soil they encountered a wall of racism and discrimination. Regardless of their qualifications or colonial contributions, Sikhs found themselves grouped together with other Asians, Africans, and Afro-Caribbeans collectively as "black," foreign, and inferior. Teachers found that their colonial qualifications did not apply in Britain and took jobs in factories next to illiterate and unskilled fellow immigrants. These experiences were painful ones and made them determined to make life better for their children. Parents share stories of the racism they experienced to encourage their children to study and do well in school. Through these stories a sense of a collective past enters the present to shape the imagined futures of the next generation. Devinder, a Sikh girl in her early twenties who was completing a dentistry course at Leeds University, spoke of how her father's stories had given her a sense of academic purpose.

Well I always used to say to Dad that he was overreacting whenever he used to talk about it. Because he went through hell when he started off. He started off working in the factories. And the whole reason he went on his own into business was because of the racism. He couldn't stand the way he was being treated in the factories. I mean, Dad has got a lot of pride and he just can't stand being talked to like that.... So he always used to talk about how important it was that we should not work in factories, which was the whole reason that we studied—that I studied, it's the only way out.

Families like Amrit's and Devinder's, who were members of the first phase of immigration, showed me photo albums with pictures that provided clues to the disjointed cultural adjustment the first generation experienced in coming to terms with British racism. These pictures, as well as their stories, vividly disrupt the classic narrative of unidirectional stages of cultural assimilation, showing how these men have reappropriated and reinvented "tradition." Photos of the early settlers captured images of very English-looking young men, their short hair slicked back, posing in an English version of a James Dean-esque stance. A number of these men will now be wearing a turban (covering their now unshorn hair) and a neatly trimmed beard. While the trimmed beard is actually a compromise, they have chosen to keep the five symbols of the Sikh faith (the Five Ks): *kes* (uncut hair), *kanga* (a comb worn in the hair), *kara* (a silver bracelet), *kachh* (underwear traditionally worn by soldiers), and *kirpan* (a sword or dagger worn on the side of the body in a holster that wraps diagonally around one shoulder).[5] Keeping the symbols is one way of signifying their commitment to the Sikh faith and identifying themselves publicly as Sikh.

Sikh identity, I argue throughout this account, has many meanings and referents and corresponds to a wide range of social statuses. At the most basic level, people can identify as Sikhs in terms of the ethnicity they embrace, the religion they practice, or family ties (for those for whom neither ethnicity nor religion hold personal meaning). Some who practice Sikhism choose to keep the symbols of the faith, while others do not, and, of course, not all those who *could* identify as Sikh, ethnically or religiously, actually *do*—in Britain, in India, or across the diaspora. But for many among the first generation whom I met in the *gurdwaras* (Sikh temples), the experience of racism and the recognition of the boundaries of belonging in Britain have reaffirmed the value of their traditions and communal ties.

These processes of cultural change cannot be captured adequately by classic theories of cultural maintenance or assimilation. The forms of cultural production that lead British Sikhs to reembrace or move beyond their traditions are far more complex. Migrant people live their lives through acts of cultural translation within what Homi Bhabha has termed the cultural "third space" (1994). Within this "third space," cultural orientations and identities are continually being made, and, hence cannot in any simple sense be "lost" or "passed on" as "given" (S. Hall 1996: 629). As Bhabha explains, if

the act of cultural translation (both as representation and as reproduction) denies the essentialism of a prior given originary culture, then we see that all forms of culture are continually in a process of hybridity. But for me the importance of hybridity is not to be able to trace two original moments from which the third emerges, rather hybridity to me is the "third space" which enables other positions to emerge. (Bhabha 1990: 211)

Through everyday acts of translation people negotiate what are often contradictory cultural influences in their lives. In the process, "tradition" becomes an object of reflection and reinvention just as new lifestyles, cultural practices, and identities come to be created. As they reach adulthood, they fashion lifestyles that reflect a vast range of cultural orientations, from Rushdie-esque expressions of global cosmopolitanism to reassertions of a deep connection to their Sikh religious and Punjabi cultural heritage.

This account portrays the experiences of British Sikhs as acts of translation, "immigrant acts" which—drawing on Lisa Lowe's (1996) dual delineation of this term—involve both being "acted upon" by discourses that produce identities and "acting" or performing—and therein producing—forms of self-identification. Yet immigrant acts are "staged" in specific public spheres within distinct nations. British Sikh identities, more particularly, have been fashioned within a postcolonial British nation unsettled by the winds of change.

"The End of Britain"?

On the front page of the *New York Times Magazine* on February 21, 1999, a classic image of Queen Victoria, a tear newly etched on her cheek, gazed up toward a caption reading, "The End of Britain" (the title of the week's lead article). The legacy of Britain as grand dame of imperial power has been gently fading into the mists of history. "This precious stone set in a silver sea" that once ruled a vast empire is once again simply an island nation.

In the years that have transpired since the beginning of the end of Empire, the colonial ties between ruler and subject have been transformed into "race relations" between purportedly "equal citizens." The exotic colonial subject of worlds far beyond has become the ethnic citizen-stranger residing within, often in the house next door. The migration of ex-colonial subjects of color to the imperial motherland in the aftermath of Empire represents a final chapter in the history of British colonialism, a chapter some have cynically entitled, "The Empire Strikes Back" (Centre for Contemporary Cultural Studies 1982).

The story of Britain after Empire is one of a nation struggling to come to terms with itself as a multiracial society as its ex-colonial citizens of color challenge the basis of national identity and fight the battle to truly belong (Goulbourne 1991).[6] Immigration has hardly been the only force to test the nation's foundations, however. Economic globalization, European political unification, and Scottish and Welsh nationalist movements as well as the establishment of a Scottish Parliament and a Welsh assembly have undermined Britain's political sovereignty. The imagined cultural "purity" of the nation since World War II has become part of Britain's sacred past, available now largely in commodity form as "heritage" sold to tourists. This, however, is hardly Britain's destiny alone. In this era of

identity politics, contests over culture and claims to rights based on the principles of cultural recognition (Gutmann 1992; Kymlicka 1995) are testing
the traditional notion of the homogeneous nation throughout the democratic
world. While the politics of plural publics challenge the nation-state from
within, the forces of global capitalism defy these boundaries from beyond.

This account chronicles the experiences of Sikh students attending a
racially mixed comprehensive high school, Grange Hill High, in a middle-
class neighborhood in Leeds. It follows these adolescents as they move
across the social worlds that make up their everyday lives. The young people are continuing to write their family's immigration stories by challenging a central paradox of modernity: the contradiction between the liberal
ideology of meritocracy and the collective boundaries of race, nationality,
gender, and class. Their efforts to achieve social mobility and create identities as "black" British citizens provide a window to the workings of social
inequality, nationalism, and education in Britain.[7]

Ethnographic research for this project was carried out from 1986 to
1995, during the height of Thatcherism. Though Thatcher stepped down on
November 22, 1990, Prime Minister John Major carried on the Thatcher
legacy to a great degree until 1997, when Tony Blair's landslide victory
brought the Labour Party back to power after eighteen years of Tory rule.
That period had culminated, during the late 1980s and early '90s, in a period
of profound political, economic, and social change, typified by heated debate, radical innovation, and retrenchment by "the new right" into "little England" nationalism. "New times" were on the horizon, and they arrived with
Tony Blair and his political "third way." London has become a jewel in
the crown of global capitalism, a phoenix rising powerfully from the ashes
of empire to become a truly global city, a center of multinational finance,
and an icon of cosmopolitan consumer culture, hybrid fashion, music, art,
and style. Yet at the historical moment this ethnography captures Britain
was in the throes of a last valiant surge of nationalist fervor, one fueled by
fears about and ambivalence toward the prospect of cultural change.

Globalization and the Politics of Difference

Since World War II, shifts in global political and economic relations have
disrupted the taken-for-granted authority, centrality, and assumed imperme-
ability of modern nation-states across the industrialized world. Transnational

corporations and international market forces have undermined the ability of national governments to control, protect, and regulate their own economies (Reich 1992). The emergence of supranational political and military units has weakened the basis of national political sovereignty and autonomy (Sassen 1996). Advances in communication technology and media production, as well as the expansion of commodity markets have contributed to the spread of a culture of global capitalism. The accessibility of international travel has paved new paths for labor migration, bringing increased numbers of people of color as well as religious "others" to the old colonial motherlands, such as France, Germany, and Britain.[8]

We are, in short, living in an age in which national boundaries are increasingly cross-cut by global financial networks, shifts in the geopolitical order, and the fast-paced transnational movements of people, commodities, ideas, and media images (King 1997; Appadurai 1996; J. L. Comaroff 1996; Featherstone 1990; Hannerz 1990, 1996). The decentering of the nation-state and the declining geopolitical dominance of the West have created spaces for new forms of cultural politics to emerge. Advances in global communication and media technology together with the expanding forces of commodification and consumerism have also created new environments for and influences on local processes of collective and self-identity formation. Whether one views our present predicament as representing a transition from modernity to a postmodern condition (Lyotard 1984), postmodernity (Harvey 1989), or simply the emergence of a new "reflexive" stage of modernity (Beck, Giddens, and Lash 1994), in this era of globalization cultural politics are becoming ever more common, significant, and complex (K. Hall 1999).

In the politics of the public sphere, debates about social justice increasingly have "a notably cultural face" (Smelser and Alexander 1999; see also Wuthnow 1999). Calls for redistributive justice have been silenced by demands for recognition legitimated by claims to identity based in assertions of cultural authenticity (N. Fraser 1997). In the age of multiculturalism, "anthropologists no longer 'own' culture" (Dirks, Eley, and Ortner 1994: 4; see also Turner 1994). Concepts of "culture," "tradition," and "identity" are being invoked in myriad ways, by a diverse range of peoples, across social contexts and for any number of political purposes (Dominguez 1992). "Culture" has developed a popular currency within the public sphere of late capitalism; it has taken on new meanings, connotations, and relevance. Within discursive contexts as varied as nationalist political movements, controversies over educational curriculum, multinational advertising, and critiques of aesthetic production and consumption are found debates that highlight the tension between assertions of cultural authenticity and essentialized identities and the celebration of new forms of cultural hybridity.[9] "Culture" has become an object that people increasingly reflect on, talk about, negotiate, and attempt, consciously and intentionally, to control—to teach, pass on, improve, package, protect, as well as challenge, subvert, and reject—or, in the end, consume.

This, of course, is not an entirely new phenomenon. Coming to see one's culture from the outside or developing double-consciousness in W. E. B. Du Bois's (1903/1969) sense, has probably always been an aspect of the experiences of migrants and peoples defined as "other." What seems new, however, is the extent to which it happens and the vehicles through which these dialogues are taking place (Appadurai 1991). Within modernity, particularly in response to forms of globalization, there are "unprecedented resources provided by the industrial, scientific, and most especially the communications revolutions which provide new technologies of objectification" (Miller 1995: 4). As "culture" circulates—across networks of migrant peoples and the circuits of media technology—"tradition" becomes increasingly "deterritorialized," detached from the immediacy of mundane sensory experience. Modernity has become increasingly reflexive as "social practices are constantly examined and reformed in the light of incoming information about those practices," information that is disembedded from local contexts and "restructured across indefinite spans of time and space" (Giddens 1990: 21). What this suggests is that "tradition" plays a new role as it is ruptured from its safe location in time and space. "Tradition" has not lost its "authority" in the Weberian sense, its power to justify or legitimate social practice, but people increasingly reflect on "tradition" as a disembedded cultural form and in relation to information that circulates into daily life from outside a particular local setting.

What was once assumed to be an immutable link between people, place, and culture within the anthropological imaginary, has been ruptured and replaced with an emphasis on processes that are "cultural"—global as well as local, deterritorialized as well as situated within historically specific social spaces (Gupta and Ferguson 1997; Ong and Nonini 1997; Lavie and Swedenburg 1996; Kearney 1995; Appadurai 1991). In the era of globalization, anthropologists are being challenged to develop theoretical frameworks and ethnographic approaches that will allow them to capture adequately the influence of large-scale processes on subjectivities, identities, and communities "in a way that demonstrates the specific and evolving nature of local responses" (Moore 1999: 10).[10]

The postmodern turn in anthropology, and in cultural theory more generally, has sounded the death knell to cultural holism and has given primacy instead to frameworks that stress cultural displacement, fragmentation, and pluralization. Substantialist or essentialist theories of social identity have also effectively been taken to task for adopting categories of practice as categories of analysis (Brubaker 1996).[11] Identity is not grounded in a static state of being but is continually being produced within ongoing processes of becoming. Never an already accomplished fact, identity is always in the making, "a 'production,' which is never complete, always in process, and always constituted within, not outside, representation" (S. Hall 1990/1996: 210).

While the postmodern turn has contributed more complex and dynamic frameworks for understanding cultural production and identity formation, postmodern critiques of the totalizing "master narratives" of traditional theories of class and social status have not generated more powerful frameworks for analyzing social stratification. But as many have noted, a critique of the reductionist tendencies in classic Marxist formulations of class relations should not blind social theorists to the crucial role that class or resource distribution plays in structuring people's life chances.[12] In the aftermath of the postmodern turn, we must develop analytic frameworks that account for the different forms and relations of inequality and oppression that coexist in society. Social actors in their everyday lives find themselves positioned as subjects, their identities represented or their life choices constrained by very different social hierarchies that classify difference in relation to contradictory types of distinctions—such as race, class, caste, gender, sexual orientation, and age. These social relations and identities are constituted through the operation of distinctive forms of power that are also located across various institutional and social settings in any social order. Capturing the interworkings of these constitutive forces in social actors' lives calls for a complex map of power that accounts for the multiplicity as well as the interrelationships between various technologies and relations of power and privilege, authority and control.

In this study I provide a framework for analyzing multiple types of power in the public sphere. I draw on the contributions of postmodern and poststructuralist theory to revisit classic questions concerning the basis of class inequality and status group ranking. My analysis considers the cultural, discursive, and structural or social organizational aspects of inequality.

I move away from the class determinism of traditional Marxist analyses to examine the way multiple markers of inequality are symbolically constructed, represented, and circulated through discourse. Discourse about difference informs and legitimates practices that enact asymmetrical structural relations that support the unequal distribution of and access to wealth and prestige, power and privilege—or forms of "durable inequality" (Tilly 1998). Subjects are formed in discourse, or power-knowledge configurations in the form of systems of ideas and practices. Discourses are not about objects, according to Foucault, but are "practices that systematically form the objects of which they speak" (1972: 49).

Feminists in particular have brought Foucault to task for not giving adequate attention to resistance or to mechanisms through which individuals may maneuver against or contest the productive power of discourse. Individuals, they insist, are not molded into "unitary subjects uniquely positioned," but "are produced at a nexus of subjectivities, in relations of power which are constantly shifting, rendering them at one moment powerful and at another powerless" (Walkerdine 1990: 3). This provides "room for maneuver" (Chambers 1990), for negotiating, performing, and playing with multiple identities (Butler 1990; see Morris 1995). In this way, power is always partial: "the discursive production of self ... is always incomplete and fragmented because of the multiple and contradictory discourses to which each person is subject" (Davies 1990: 346).

In their everyday lives, British Sikhs are subject to multiple forms of power that position them in relation to national/racial, caste status-group, class, and generational differences. British Sikh lives are lived at the intersection of different relations of inequality, relations that in turn inform their various struggles to belong and to become middle class, British, and adult Sikhs.

In a study of the cultural politics of race, ethnicity, and nationalism in Guyana, Brackette Williams proposes that in unraveling the workings of inequality in culturally plural nations we should not give analytic priority to race, class, or ethnicity, but "we must produce ethnographic accounts of the manner in which race, class, and culture have been entangled in the historical development of particular ideological fields" (1991: 29). She goes on to frame the workings of racial, class, and ethnic inequalities as contained within the ideological field that she associates with a national process of integration, a process "aimed at homogenizing heterogeneity" or "assimilating elements of that heterogeneity through appropriations that devalue them or that deny the source of their contribution" (30).[13] The framework for this study also locates various forms of cultural politics in Britain within an overarching consideration of nationalist dilemmas of pluralism and integration; but my analysis diverges from hers in that the process of national integration is not defined as the central organizing mechanism or force informing all other contests over culture and power. My analysis does not privilege nationalism over other ideological fields, but aims to show how different forms of power and relations of inequality overlap as they enter into and are negotiated by social actors in their everyday lives.

The central contribution of this study, perhaps, is its concern to understand forms of power, inequality, and difference as people experience them, as they shape their understandings of themselves and each other in deeply human ways. The account focuses on these forms of power and sources of inequality—in schools, peer groups, caste communities, and dominant forms of media and political discourse. Across these multiple sites of power, these various discourses about difference, and in ongoing situated practice or social interactions, Sikhs are creating new cultural orientations and identifications that challenge the boundaries of belonging and the basis of inequality in Britain.

Cultural Politics and the Production of Culture

The book moves away from classic British studies of Sikhs as an already existing ethnic group (James 1974; Ballard and Ballard 1977; Bhachu 1985; Helweg 1986, 1999) to consider the forms of cultural production and the social relational dynamics that engage British Sikhs in creating a range of identities and lifestyles at different life stages (K. Hall 1995). This approach builds on the work of other South Asian diaspora scholars who have described how South Asian populations overseas come to be "relationally positioned" or "'situated' in and through a wide variety of discourses, economic processes, state policies, and institutional practices" in a given context of settlement (see, in particular, Brah 1996: 182–83). These studies have paved the way for my own in describing the forms of cultural politics that emerge in culturally plural societies and how they condition the meanings South Asians come to give to ethnic and religious traditions as well as to the hybrid cultural forms they create in these new national settings, in the "articulation of nation and migration" (van der Veer 1995).[14]

The tendency in these recent studies has been to focus on particular forms of cultural politics that emerge in a specific discursive field, emphasizing the role of either political, media, or youth culture discourse in local processes of cultural production and identity formation. Studies such as Verne Dusenbery's (1997) comparative analysis of Sikhs in Singapore and Canada, and Gerd Baumann's (1996) work with South Asians in Southall outside London have considered the power of dominant forms of political discourse to exercise "taxonomical control over difference" (Appadurai 1990: 13), to impose categories of identity on local residents that represent the relationship between culture, community, and identity in ethnic reductionist terms. The dominant national discourse about difference, they argue, sets the terms for nationalist politics of identity between groups within these plural societies. Yet, as each case shows, alternative local discourse provides South Asians with the "creative power ... to resist, deflect, or work with these social and political categories ... to play the politics of recognition in terms not of their own making" (Dusenbery 1997: 739).

Religion, predictably, is frequently privileged in national politics of recognition within plural nation-states, as Aisha Khan's (1995) study of Muslims in Trinidad and Steven Vertovec's (1995) work with Hindus in Trinidad as well as in Britain have demonstrated. In these contexts, ideologies asserting the authenticity and legitimacy of particular religious traditions, they argue, have been "shaped and marshaled in struggles over representation" (Khan 1995: 93). In national contexts structured by ethnic and religious heterogeneity, migrants and their children are required to reflect on what their religion is and who may legitimately belong. This type of reflection, Vertovec argues, in turn "is catalyst to processes of 'symbolic disarticulation' and reification affecting ethnic identities, social forms, and cultural practices" (1995: 151).

Media discourse and youth popular cultural forms also become sources for reflection and resources for fashioning identities among South Asian diaspora populations (see Gopinath 1995). Marie Gillespie's (1995) research on television consumption among Punjabis, again residing in Southall and Suraina Maira's (1999) analysis of the dance club scene among "Indian American youth" in New York City both point to the significant role of cultural consumption as a site of cultural transmission, negotiation, and change (see also Bakrania 2002). Gillespie and Maira, each in distinctive ways, show how actors appropriate popular culture's semiotic resources both to reinforce conservative orientations toward "traditional" forms of culture and to embrace cosmopolitan views and tastes. "Social actors," Maira suggests, "are able to draw on models of personhood that are based on stability and authenticity of cultural elements in some situations, and to embrace identities that emphasize fluidity and multiplicity at other moments" (1999: 53).

As these studies collectively portray, identities are produced in relation to multiple forms of discourse that circulate into peoples' lives through various channels and in relation to distinctive forms of cultural or identity politics. My project builds on this body of research by incorporating what has been learned about these separate discursive fields and corresponding forms of cultural production into a more comprehensive framework for considering their interrelationship, or how they intersect in the everyday lives of social actors. Actors engaging with popular culture, political debates, or religious identities encounter multiple identities, forms of identification, reified constructs of "culture" and "tradition," as well as structural relations of inequality. The complexity of the social and cultural worlds necessarily involves individuals in processes of cultural translation, everyday acts of interpretation, negotiation, and situational performance through which, over time and across social settings, they fashion identities, create lifestyles, and pursue imagined futures. My analysis, then, offers a framework for studying identity as relational and reflexive, as *produced* through multiple forms and forces of discourse in relation to distinctive forms of power, and as *performed* as individuals negotiate multiple identifications across contexts of situated practice. It is, in other words, a story of British Sikh lives in translation.

Lives in Translation

Growing up in England, British Sikhs imagine their futures in relation to numerous possible identities, potential communal ties, and alternative life paths. Their sense of self is molded by contradictory cultural influences in contrasting social settings and transmitted through multiple forms of media. In their homes, at the gurdwara, as well as in religious education classes in British schools, "their culture," "their heritage," and "their religion" are represented in distinctive ways. As members of the South Asian diaspora, their sense of what it means to be "Asian," "Indian," or "Sikh" is shaped by ideas and images, film narratives, and artistic forms circulating across networks linking Leeds, Vancouver, New York, and Amritsar. As teenagers in a capitalist culture, British Sikh youths also consume youth culture commodities providing myriad cultural styles and subcultural orientations to use in creating adolescent identities.

Simply to celebrate the creative potential within processes of cultural production and identity formation, however, would be to overlook a profound aspect of their lives: the cultural constraints as well as the social barriers they, as the children of immigrants and as racial minorities, frequently face.[15] Social actors, particularly those defined as different, do not produce new cultural forms or make identity choices freely, independently, or in isolation from one another. Identity and lifestyle choices have social consequences in terms of how the dominant society, family members, neighbors, teachers, peers, and coworkers evaluate one another's everyday conduct in relation to particular cultural distinctions, moral codes, and normative standards.[16] To choose to be traditional or cosmopolitan can have significant social and personal consequences, in terms of one's status in British society and within British Asian communities.

These constraints are evident in the way young people make sense of their everyday life choices. Although their lives are rich in cultural influences, they consistently feel pulled between two ways of life or caught between two cultures. To make sense of the disjuncture between the choices in their lives and the way they perceive these choices, the choices need to be considered in relation to the normative pressures that inform them. Many accounts of second generation South Asians in Britain and in the United States have noted the powerful influence familial demands for loyalty to traditional cultural ideals can have in young people's lives. Yet this, I argue, is only part of the picture.

As the first generation to grow up in Britain, second generation British Sikhs are subject to two explicit projects of social reproduction.[17] They are the focus of attempts on the part of two "imagined status communities"—the dominant British national community and the caste status communities within the Sikh population—to socialize the next generation. Relations of power and inequality in these status communities are legitimated by the dominant values and beliefs inscribed within two contrasting ideological formations.[18] The first ideological formation, the ideology of family honor, supports status rankings of prestige and honor within Sikh caste communities, influencing, most significantly, the arranging of marriages. The second, the ideology of British nationalism, represents British identity as primordial or given, an identity that cannot be chosen or achieved and must, to survive, be protected and preserved. This construction of Britishness as rooted in time and territory excludes Britain's citizens of color and serves to legitimate racialized boundaries of national belonging.[19]

Second generation British Sikhs live between the forces of these two ideological formations. As they negotiate the boundaries, social expectations, and constraints supported by the ideologies of British nationalism and family honor, they develop a sense of living between two worlds they frequently refer to as "English" and "Indian." They associate things "Indian" with being "traditional" and things "English" with being "modern." Yet in their everyday lives these young people enact a much broader range of lifestyles. Their lives embody a creative tension that engages the dialectics of power and inequality as well as the dynamics of cultural improvisation and transformation. They negotiate these fields of power and meaning through acts of translation. These acts of cultural translation emerge from a "third space," a position from which they can observe and reflect on different cultural influences, forms of oppression, and future opportunities. From this interstitial perspective, individuals create hybrid lifestyles that are traditional, cosmopolitan, and often a mixture of both.

British Sikhs find themselves objects of dominant discourses about difference, they consume and appropriate a wide range of mediated semiotic resources, and, over time, they are producing new forms of culture and identity. Taking the perspective of these young people, considering how they perceive and negotiate the messages in their everyday lives, provides unique insight into how individuals experience and actively participate in processes of identity formation. In other words, subjects are not only "made" within the contexts of discursive formations, but actors, through processes of negotiation, situated performances, and symbolic "play," are actively making themselves.

The Ethnographic Study

The central focus of my research was the social mobility experiences of Sikh young people growing up in Leeds, England. I became involved in the everyday worlds of Sikh teenagers as they went to school, as I attended rituals and other events at the gurdwara and sat with families as they socialized, entertained, or simply watched television at home. I wanted to understand and appreciate the rich and varied cultural influences in their lives from their perspectives, to learn as much as I could about the people and places that were significant to them. As my approach to understanding identity formation was to consider its relational production, it was also important to gain some understanding of the everyday worlds of white, Afro-Caribbean, and other Asian teenagers.[20] Participant observational research was carried out over more than a decade in many different social settings, including a number of schools, homes, religious institutions, community organizations, shopping malls, sports facilities, and other leisure activity locations.

The initial fieldwork project involved fourteen months of ethnographic research. Much of my time was spent in a comprehensive high school I call Grange Hill High, a site I selected because it was situated in a middle-class neighborhood, yet its student body was mixed by race, ethnicity, and class. I began fieldwork in the middle of one school year and continued work until the middle of the next, a total of eleven months. I attended school at least three and often four days a week, moving from the classroom to the staff room, the playground to the smoking hideouts. I followed and grew to know well a range of students who were in different academic sets and from varying cultural and class backgrounds. I chose not to teach or take on an institutional role at Grange Hill High. Instead, I observed life at school from the multiple vantage points of someone who is "role-less" and, being an American, quite "the other." On the first day school, in my second school year there, I was given a nametag designating me "Kathy Hall, Anthropological Researcher."

The arrival at the school of an American anthropologist interested in race relations and the experiences of Asian students was quite out of the ordinary. The school had little contact with researchers generally and with Americans more particularly; I was paving a very new path. As time passed, my unusual presence, my California brand of friendliness, perhaps, and my genuine concern and intense curiosity opened the way for frank conversation. People became willing and often seriously interested in discussing or debating sensitive topics, such as the nature of race relations at the school or what should qualify as "fair play" or equitable treatment in a diverse school community such as Grange Hill High.

The overarching objective of my work was to understand the social organization of the school, to obtain—to the degree that it is possible—a "god's eye" view of the social relations, normative expectations, and multiple orientations and perspectives of staff and students in order to understand how all of these forces interacted to shape the patterns of everyday life at Grange Hill High. I spent time in classrooms, covering all of the subject areas from languages to maths, computer to cookery classes, but I focused most on the curriculum and discussions that took place within religious education, history, and English literature classes.

I sat in on classes in each of the five "sets" (academic levels) and in all five "forms" ("grades" in the United States). The forms at Grange Hill High ranged from third through upper and lower sixth (the two years spent in sixth form). At the time, the old exam structure of O-level/CSE and A-levels was still in existence. Students took their O-level/CSE exams at sixteen, after which many students went on to work or to a certificate course at a college of further education. The top students academically stayed on and entered the sixth form, where for two years they took classes and studied for their A-level exams. After their exams, most of these students went on to some form of higher education.

I spent a great deal of my time socializing informally with students and teachers. I "hung about" with white, Afro-Caribbean, and Asian students both inside and outside school in order to gain insight into the nature of peer relations and dynamics. To better understand the way teachers viewed the school, other teachers, their own professional identities, and their relations with students and parents, I engaged individual teachers in conversation, attended teacher meetings, and relaxed with groups informally in the teachers' lounge and during social activities after school. I also became active in the Leeds University Indian and Pakistani Student Associations and visited local colleges that a number of Asian students attended.

During my initial year of fieldwork, I became deeply involved in the lives of the students and staff at Grange Hill High. I developed the closest ties, however, to a number of Sikh families who were active in the two major gurdwaras, the "main" Sikh gurdwara and the Ramgarhia Board. My involvement with people in Leeds drew me into a wide range of social activities, which included celebrating at Sikh weddings and births; taking Punjabi language classes with Sikh children at a temple; watching television with groups of white or Asian friends; attending a Chris De Burgh rock concert with teachers from Grange Hill High; going on school fieldtrips to museums; scavenging in Indian shops and record stores for material on British Asian popular culture; taking care of teens (seldom Asians) who had drunk too much alcohol at parties; picnicking with Sikh families on the grounds of estate homes; shopping, shopping, and shopping; "hanging out" in front of fish and chip shops at lunch with giggling teenage girls;

tagging along on a trip to Blackpool Pleasure Park with the Leeds University Pakistani Society; attending academic conferences on racism and education; and listening, during a youth conference held in a local Sikh temple, as a "white" Scottish Sikh, a follower of Yogi Bhajan, lectured Punjabi Sikh youth on the health benefits of practicing Sikhism.

My data are also drawn from interviews—150 hours of discussions with students, teachers, parents, community leaders, local government administrators, and other academics. The majority of my interviews were with teenagers. I interviewed seventy Asian, thirty white English, and seven Afro-Caribbean youth (the majority were Grange Hill High students).[21] Interviews were conducted individually, in pairs, and in groups, some made up of students of the same race, religion, and gender, others mixed. Collective interviews brought together different combinations of students to discuss their lives, interests, and identity issues in an open-ended interactive way. Teachers generously allowed me to take students out of class to be interviewed (which made me quite popular with the students). Sixth formers also had free study periods during which they would congregate in the sixth form lounge. This provided a wonderful context and opportunity for engaging in discussions with whichever students happened to appear on any particular day.

In years that followed, I spent shorter periods of time in Leeds as well as in London and in the south of Wales. During these visits I interviewed politicians and community leaders in Leeds and in Southall, continued to celebrate births, weddings, and other communal events, visited clubs and youth centers in London, and gathered information about media programming and youth culture. Their stories and my research are ongoing.

The Setting

Leeds, in West Yorkshire in northeast England, is the setting of this story. Leeds provides a particularly rich context for studying immigration, race relations, and class mobility, for it has been the place of settlement for a range of immigrant groups, from Jewish immigrants in the early twentieth century to Polish refugees, Afro-Caribbeans, and South Asians after World War II. Leeds has been one of the central sites of Sikh immigration, and the population now includes groups who vary according to caste background, socioeconomic status, religious orientation, and country of origin. During the Thatcher economic revolution, Leeds, unlike other cities, did not experience a deep recession. With deindustrialization, Leeds has successfully made the transition to a service industry center. Therefore, unlike the situation in other more economically depressed areas of Britain, social mobility in 1980s Leeds continued to be imaginable.

Leeds, according to the city's official guide, "is a strangely unpompous city." Historically Leeds has played second city to Manchester in the north. More recently it has achieved a rise in stature as a center for finance and the arts. Located along the River Aire and on the Leeds-Liverpool canal (a coast-to-coast link), the city is the gateway to charming towns nestled in the beautiful countryside of the Yorkshire moors and dales. Southeast of Leeds is the coal mining area of Yorkshire, and to the north and east stretch the rural countryside of the Yorkshire Dales and the stark hilly Moors better known to tourists as "Brontë Country." Designated the "Motorway City of the Seventies" (Broadhead 1990: 1), the city sits at the intersection of the M62 (which crosses over the Pennine mountain range, the island's spinal cord, into Manchester), and the M1 (which connects London to Edinburgh). Leeds is two hours by train from London. A regional airport, Yeadon, shared with neighboring Bradford, connects Leeds by air to Europe and to other provincial cities within Britain.

Some historians of Leeds trace its origins back to the beginnings of the island's history—to Roman times perhaps, to the days of the Norman Conquest clearly. The first written record of the city is found in the Doomsday Book of 1086. Two of its traditional industries, cloth-making and dyeing, had their origin in early Norman times (Broadhead 1990: 4). The earliest map of Leeds dates from the Tudor period, in 1560. In 1626 the city received its borough charter. Leeds is best known, however, as a Victorian manufacturing city.

Leeds rose to prominence during the industrial revolution as a center for the woolen and worsted cloth industries, parallel to the development across the Pennine way of the cotton industry in Manchester. The population and wealth of both cities grew during Queen Victoria's reign. Bradford, Leeds's closest neighbor, was described as "one of the most striking phenomena in the history of the British Empire," due to its rapid and consistent growth after 1815 (A. Briggs 1968: 140; see also D. Fraser 1980). After 1851 industry in Leeds diversified. In 1871 three industries dominated its economy: cloth-making, engineering, and tailoring. Although Leeds is known as a center for ready-made clothing, engineering "established itself as the backbone of the city's industrial economy" (A. Taylor 1980: 392). Workers in the engineering workshops produced textile machinery, agricultural implements, railway locomotives, and machine tools. Deindustrialization has resulted in the closing of many factories over the past two decades.

The economic recessions of the 1970s and '80s did not have a serious impact on Leeds. The Leeds economy again diversified and kept pace with the growth in service industries. The city is a center for large insurance companies, international and national banks, legal firms, and accountants and management consultants. The town center boasts several indoor malls and a great maze of Victorian arcades lined with shops.

Leeds's significant role in the industrial revolution and its more recent revitalization as a service industry center are visibly inscribed in its architecture and the design of its urban space. The prominence and wealth of Victorian Leeds is memorialized in the great size and grandeur of the structures that give the city center its character. The power and glory of this era of Empire are still palpable, embodied in the ornate ironwork, giant columns, and elaborate frontage decorating the municipal buildings, banks, churches, theaters, markets, and shopping arcades. From hills in Leeds one looks down on a landscape blanketed with red brick industrial skeletons, smokestacks, and abandoned factories interwoven with long winding rows of back-to-back terrace houses that conjure images of working-class life in Dickensian days. These urban icons live together with the less romantic yet equally emblematic architectural expressions of the 1960s economic boom—modern concrete boxes standing in stark contrast to the opulent decor and splendor of their Victorian neighbors. Around the periphery of Leeds are further signs of economic change: in the shadows of the towering brick factories are the makeshift structures of modern manufacturing, small nondescript two-story buildings identified only by company names such as "Nanak Textiles" (Guru Nanak was the founder of Sikhism).

Like that many Victorian cities, Leeds's history is written across its urban landscape. Historical time is represented architecturally as one travels from the civic monuments in the city center through streets lined with stately Victorians out to Britain's version of the suburbs, middle-class neighborhoods filled with semi-detached homes complete with double-glazed windows. Driving up Chapeltown Road, an old thoroughfare through Leeds, one finds rows of shops. Signs posted on old storefronts tell the story of postwar immigration: "Jyoti Video Centre"—with its poster-filled windows,

Hindi film starlets gazing out to passersby—"Warsaw Stores," "The Bamboo Leaf," and "Sharma and Sons, LTD" all claim for the present architectural structures from the past. Chapeltown Road is home to three gurdwaras. An old gothic church was the site of the first gurdwara. It is marked by a yellow flagpole behind a fence with a placard reading "Sikh Temple" in English and Punjabi. A new Sikh Temple complex has recently been built across the road. A second, Gurdwara Shri Kalgidhar Sahib Ji, is a small temple attended largely by members of the Bhatra caste. The third is a large temple and sports center complex known as the Ramgarhia Board. This complex was built in the 1980s by Sikhs of the Ramgarhia caste who migrated to Leeds from East Africa. Two other smaller gurdwaras have been established in other sections of Leeds.

Leeds has a long and rich history of immigrant settlement. During the nineteenth century two major ethnic populations—Irish and Jews—established themselves in Leeds. There were a substantial number of Irish in Leeds before 1841 (5,000, or 6 percent of the population), but the greatest influx occurred between 1841 and 1861, particularly after the Famine in 1846. The total estimated number of Irish in Britain in 1851 was 727,326, or 2.9 percent of the population (Anwar 1998: 2). The Jewish community in Leeds dates back to the eighteenth century. In 1841 the number of Jewish families was estimated at 10. By 1877 there were 500. The largest increase, however, came after 1881, when immigrants fled the Russian pogroms (Morgan 1980: 62). Between 1875 and 1914 an estimated 120,000 came to Britain from Russia and Eastern Europe (Anwar 1998: 2). By 1909, there were some 20,000 Jews residing in Leeds, working largely in the tailoring and shoemaking industries. Restrictions were placed on immigration in 1905, and by 1914 Jewish immigration had ceased (Morgan 1980: 62). Like the Irish before them, the Jews were concentrated in the Leylands district, an area south of what is now the inner city area of Chapeltown; the area has been leveled and today is criss-crossed by motorways.

Sikh migration into Leeds, along with the immigration of ex-colonial people of color in Britain generally, is largely a postwar phenomenon. It is estimated that in 1939 there were only five or six Sikh families in the city (Agnihotri 1987). The numbers gradually grew during the 1950s as men arrived to meet the demand for laborers in clothing and engineering factories. Sikh women and children traveled from India to join their husbands in the 1960s.[22] In the late 1960s and early '70s, a large number of Sikhs came to Leeds as refugees from Uganda and Kenya. The current population is divided between the earlier immigrants from villages in India and the "twice-migrants" (Bhachu 1985) from cities in East Africa. As I explain in Chapter 6, this division reflects class differences between these communities as well.

Sikh immigration to Leeds mirrors patterns of immigration to Britain more generally. During the depression years of the late 1930s, Britain became the destination for a relatively small "chain migration" of Sikh men. This was part of broader large-scale patterns of migration that brought Sikhs to places throughout the Empire, including Burma, Thailand, Hong Kong, and East Africa. By the end of the 1930s, "most of Britain's ports and many of its major industrial cities had small Sikh colonies" (R. Ballard 1989: 206). Early Sikh migrants to Britain were primarily men from the Jat or landowning farming caste. They were recruited into the army in large numbers, and as landowners possessed the capital to finance the venture. They were joined by substantial numbers of Sikhs from the Bhatra caste, peddlers and fortune-tellers who settled in Cardiff as well as in Leeds. The population as a whole included fewer than 5,000, mostly male Jats and Bhatras.

Immigration was halted for the duration of World War II, but resumed shortly after it ended. Postwar migration brought men from India and other colonies (primarily the Caribbean) to meet the demand for laborers. The greatest number of immigrants from the Caribbean arrived between 1955 and 1964, while the majority of Indians and Pakistanis came during the years 1965 to 1974. Bangladeshi immigration, in contrast, was at its highest from 1980 to 1984 (see Figure 1).[23]

Ethnic census data were collected for the first time in Britain in 1991.[24] According to these figures, ethnic minorities make up 5.5 percent of the population. People of Indian ethnicity totaled 840,255, making them the largest ethnic category listed in the census (see Table 1).[25] The next largest population is Black-Caribbeans, followed by Pakistanis. Indians comprise 27.7 percent of the ethnic minority population in Britain and 1.5 percent of the total British population. Of those with Indian ethnicity, 41.2 percent were born in the UK, 36.8 percent in India, 16.9 percent in the East African Commonwealth countries, 0.7 percent in South East Asia, 0.5 percent in Pakistan, and 3.9 percent elsewhere (see Robinson 1996: 98).

The greatest numbers of South Asians (or Indians, Pakistanis, and Bangladeshis) in Britain live in the Greater London region. Other areas with large Asian populations include the West Midlands, South East England, the East Midlands, West Yorkshire, and Greater Manchester (see Figure 2).

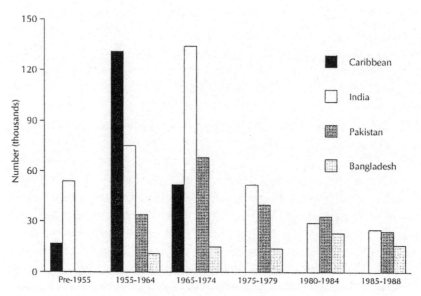

Figure 1. Arrival dates of the Caribbean, Indian, Pakistani, and Bangladeshi population, Great Britain, 1988. Source: Labour Force Survey, 1990, 1991; from Peach (1996: 9).

Table 1. Comparison of Ethnic Categorization Used in 1991 Census and Labour Force Survey

1991 Census	1991	Labour Force Survey	1989/91
White	51,873,794	White	51,808,000
Black-Caribbean	499,964	West Indian	
		(inc. Guyanese)	455,000
Black-African	212,362	African	150,000
Black-Other	178,401		
Indian	840,255	Indian	792,000
Pakistani	476,555	Pakistani	485,000
Bangladeshi	162,835	Bangladeshi	127,000
Chinese	156,938	Chinese	137,000
Other-Asian	197,534		
Other-Other	290,206		
		Arab	67,000
		Mixed	309,000
		Other	154,000
		Not stated	495,000
Persons in household with head born in Ireland	1,089,603		

Source: OPCS/GRO(S) (1993), vol. 2, Tables 6, 11; Labour Force Survey 1990, 1991 (HMSO, 1992: 34); from Peach (1996: 6).

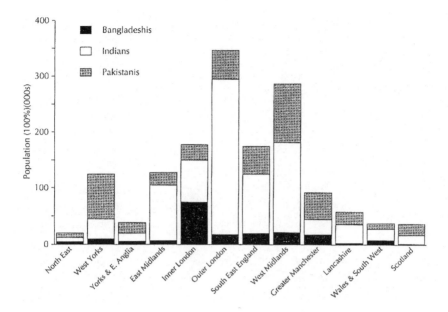

Figure 2. Regional distribution of South Asian population, Great Britain, 1991. Source: R. Ballard (1996: 132).

Variation is evident, however, among the settlement patterns of Indians, Pakistanis, and Bangladeshis (see Figure 2). Bangladeshis, similar to Afro-Caribbeans, have primarily settled in urban areas and less frequently reside in smaller or rural districts. The largest Pakistani communities are not in London but in the West Midlands and West Yorkshire metropolitan areas, with smaller populations in the North West, Greater Manchester, South Yorkshire, and central Clydeside (Robinson 1996: 103–5). The greatest concentration of Indian communities is in Outer London, but large populations also reside in the West Midlands, Inner London, the East Midlands, and the West Yorkshire metropolitan area.

Robinson's comparison of data from 1981 and 1991 shows changes in the regional distribution of the Indian population in Britain, particularly growth in the population in the South East and East Midlands, and a decrease in the West Midlands, the South West, Yorkshire and Humberside, and the North West (1996: 99).

The 1991 census figures show Leeds with a total population of 717,400.[26] The city is home to 6,475 Black-Caribbeans, 2,887 "Black-Other" and 1,268 "Black-Africans" (see Table 2). The total British Asian population of 20,914 includes an Indian community of 9,871, a Pakistani population numbering 9,292, and 1,751 Bangladeshi residents (see Table 3). The population also includes 2,021 ethnic Chinese and 1,527 who identified themselves as "Other-Asians" (see Table 4).

Data from the 1991 census supports prior research on social class among British Asians that has shown a bipolar profile, particularly among Indians (Robinson 1990). Figures suggest that members of the Indian population are highly represented in the "upper echelons of white collar work" (social classes I and II) and also among semiskilled manual laborers (class IV) (Robinson 1996: 109). A smaller proportion of Indian citizens are found in the intermediate level or in nonmanual and manual jobs (class III), as well as in the least skilled jobs (class V). According to Robinson's analysis, between 1981 and 1991 there appears to have been an increase in the number of Indian men and women in white-collar work, at least at the level of social class II (see Table 5).

When occupational social class data are broken down by age and by gender, this same bipolar pattern remains evident (see Tables 6 and 7). When the data are differentiated by gender and type of employment, two

Table 2. Minority Ethnic Communities of 1,000 Persons or More in Northern England, 1991: Black

District	Black total	Black-Caribbean	Black-Other	Black-African
Manchester	18,672	10,329	5,015	3,328
Leeds	10,630	6,475	2,887	1,268
Sheffield	7,892	4,965	1,866	1,061
Liverpool	7,052	1,448	3,230	2,374
Kirklees	6,544	4,428	1,743	373
Bradford	5,272	3,299	1,392	581
Trafford	4,040	2,878	952	210
Oldham	1,789	1,051	596	142
Bolton	1,523	680	476	367
Preston	1,505	890	501	114
Doncaster	1,248	771	379	98
Stockport	1,096	487	388	221
Total	67,263	37,701	19,425	10,137
Northern England	84,622	42,959	27,034	14,629
% of Northern England	79.5	87.8	71.9	69.3

Source: 1991 Census, Local Base Statistics; from Rees and Phillips (1996: 275).

Table 3. Minority Ethnic Communities of 1,000 Persons or More in Northern England, 1991: Indian, Pakistani, Bangladeshi

District	Indian	District	Pakistani	District	Bangladeshi
Bolton	13,329	Bradford	45,227	Oldham	5,130
Kirklees	11,885	Kirklees	17,456	Bradford	3,651
Bradford	11,676	Manchester	15,314	Manchester	1,993
Blackburn	10,470	Rochdale	11,035	Leeds	1,751
Leeds	9,871	Leeds	9,292	Rochdale	1,641
Preston	8,188	Oldham	8,914	Tameside	1,599
Manchester	4,339	Sheffield	8,855	Newcastle	1,300
Tameside	3,327	Blackburn	8,030	Sheffield	1,081
Trafford	2,678	Pendle	8,008		
Oldham	1,552	Calderdale	6,271		
Sheffield	1,393	Bolton	4,235		
Stockport	1,372	Hyndurn	3,778		
Liverpool	1,247	Middlesbrough	3,636		
Doncaster	1,177	Rotherham	3,241		
		Bury	3,239		
		Burnley	3,138		
		Newcastle	2,913		
		Wakefield	2,170		
		Trafford	2,082		
		Tameside	1,888		
		Preston	1,717		
		Stockport	1,575		
		Stockton	1,218		
		Doncaster	1,017		
Total	82,514		174,249		18,146
Northern England	101,406		179,955		26,320
% of Northern England	81.4		96.8		68.9

Source: 1991 Census, Local Base Statistics; from Rees and Phillips (1996: 275).

patterns emerge that have particular significance in relation to occupational and academic developments I explore. First, the percentage of Indian males who are self-employed is nearly twice that of white males (with employees; see Tables 8 and 9). Second, a higher percentage of the Indian population (15 percent) have also achieved qualifications beyond A-level exams, compared to whites (13.3 percent), Pakistanis (7.0 percent), and Bangladeshis (5.2 percent); only the Chinese show higher levels of academic achievement (Robinson 1996: 108).

Table 4. Minority Ethnic Communities of 1,000 Persons or More in
Northern England, 1991: Chinese, Other-Asian, Other-Other

District	Chinese	District	Other-Asian	District	Other-Other
Liverpool	3,246	Manchester	1,788	Manchester	5,432
Manchester	2,885	Bradford	1,579	Leeds	4,242
Leeds	2,021	Leeds	1,527	Sheffield	3,540
Sheffield	1,295			Liverpool	3,386
Newcastle	1,114			Bradford	2,993
Wirral	1,013			Kirklees	2,068
				Trafford	1,201
				Stockport	1,085
Total	11,574		4,874		23,947
Northern					
England	28,070		17,872		44,662
% of Northern					
England	41.2		27.4		53.6

Source: 1991 Census, Local Base Statistics; from Rees and Phillips (1996: 276).

Table 5. Social Class Profiles, 1981, 1991: Indian

	Male		Female	
Class	1981	1991	1981	1991
I	8	8	5	5
II	17	25	15	23
III	12	11	21	18
III	29	27	12	11
IV	27	23	42	38
V	8	5	5	5

Source: Robinson (1996: 109).

At the time of the 1991 census, the vast majority of British residents at the time of the census, were choosing marriage and cohabitation partners from within their own ethnic group. Only 1.3 percent of unions reported were inter-ethnic, the majority between ethnic minority and white individuals (Berrington 1996: 198; see Tables 10 and 11). The census found little intermixing among the Asian (e.g., Indian with Pakistani) or Black ethnic groups (e.g., Black-Caribbean with Black-African; see Table 10). More male than female ethnic minority group members were in inter-ethnic partnerships

Table 6. Percentage Distribution by Social Class and Ethnicity, 1991: Men

	18–19				30–44				45–59			
Class	White	Pakistani	Indian	Bangladeshi	White	Pakistani	Indian	Bangladeshi	White	Pakistani	Indian	Bangladeshi
Professional	5.8	6.5	11.1	2.8	8.2	6.8	12.0	4.2	7.3	7.2	14.8	10.5
Manager	20.4	19.2	25.4	7.2	33.3	23.4	30.4	14.3	32.3	25.2	30.8	14.7
Skilled non-manual	14.8	18.3	21.1	14.0	9.5	9.7	10.3	21.2	8.5	10.8	12.0	20.5
Skilled manual	32.7	23.7	20.9	31.7	31.3	32.7	25.6	33.0	32.3	27.0	20.2	21.0
Semi-skilled	17.1	23.3	15.9	37.3	11.9	20.2	16.8	22.2	14.0	20.6	16.3	22.5
Unskilled	5.5	4.8	3.0	2.5	3.4	4.3	2.8	1.9	4.2	6.4	3.8	7.1
Armed forces	2.7	0.1	0.2	0.1	1.4	0.1	0.1	0.1	0.4	0.0	0.0	0.0
Inadequately specified	0.9	4.1	2.5	4.3	0.9	2.9	2.0	3.0	1.1	2.7	2.1	3.6

Source: OPCS/GRO(S) (1993) vol. 2, Table 16; from R. Ballard (1996: 141).

Table 7. Percentage Distribution by Social Class and Ethnicity, 1991: Women

Class	18–19				30–44				45–59			
	White	Pakistani	Indian	Bangladeshi	White	Pakistani	Indian	Bangladeshi	White	Pakistani	Indian	Bangladeshi
Professional	2.4	3.2	5.6	0.9	2.2	3.7	4.0	7.3	1.0	6.2	4.4	17.3
Manager	25.5	20.1	20.2	14.0	32.2	34.3	26.1	27.4	27.5	35.3	26.1	34.6
Skilled non-manual	45.1	42.7	49.9	37.9	36.2	23.0	28.6	17.7	35.4	14.5	19.0	17.3
Skilled manual	7.7	6.2	3.7	10.3	6.1	6.4	6.3	8.1	7.3	6.5	6.7	5.8
Semi-skilled	15.2	22.9	17.1	28.0	15.8	25.8	30.0	27.4	16.9	28.7	35.3	15.4
Unskilled	3.0	1.2	1.5	0.9	6.8	2.2	3.2	2.4	11.1	4.0	6.0	7.7
Armed forces	0.4	0.0	0.0	0.0	0.1	-0.0	0.0	0.0	0.0	0.0	0.0	0.0
Inadequately specified	0.7	3.6	2.0	7.9	0.7	4.5	1.9	9.7	0.8	4.7	2.5	1.9

Source: OPCS/GRO(S) (1993), vol. 2, Table 16; from R. Ballard (1996: 141).

Table 8. Percentage Distribution Among Socioeconomic Groups by Ethnicity, 1991: Men

Class	18–29				30–44				45–59			
	White	Pakistani	Indian	Bangladeshi	White	Pakistani	Indian	Bangladeshi	White	Pakistani	Indian	Bangladeshi
Employer (large scale)	0.0	0.0	0.1	0.0	0.0	0.0	0.2	0.1	0.1	0.2	0.1	0.0
Professional self-employed	0.3	0.2	1.2	0.0	1.8	1.4	3.6	1.0	1.9	3.3	6.0	4.0
Employer (small scale)	1.4	5.0	4.4	9.2	4.4	10.3	8.5	21.2	5.0	10.9	7.9	17.2
Non-professional self-employed	7.5	11.7	8.2	2.4	9.9	17.9	13.4	6.1	10.3	14.6	12.1	6.3
Total self-employed	9.2	17.0	14.0	11.6	16.1	29.6	25.6	28.5	17.3	29.0	26.0	27.5
Manager (large scale)	3.3	1.5	2.4	0.5	7.9	1.9	3.4	1.3	8.0	2.0	3.3	1.8
Professional employed	5.5	6.3	9.9	2.8	6.4	5.3	8.4	2.7	5.3	4.0	8.8	6.5
Manager (small scale)	6.7	5.7	7.6	3.4	10.8	5.5	7.7	7.2	10.1	5.3	7.1	5.4
Semi-professional	8.8	4.7	8.3	2.5	10.7	4.0	6.2	4.5	8.7	4.2	6.9	3.8
Supervisor	2.4	1.6	2.1	0.6	4.3	1.8	2.8	0.4	4.8	2.6	2.7	0.0
Junior non-manual	13.8	15.9	19.5	5.4	7.3	6.9	7.8	3.6	6.2	6.5	9.1	5.4
Personal service	2.5	3.7	1.8	56.6	0.8	1.8	1.0	34.3	0.6	1.0	0.7	17.4
Skilled manual	24.3	15.6	15.1	2.7	19.3	18.8	17.3	3.7	20.0	18.1	14.4	6.9
Semi-skilled manual	13.2	19.0	13.6	6.8	9.3	17.2	14.9	8.7	11.3	18.3	15.1	14.7
Unskilled	4.7	4.8	2.9	2.5	2.8	4.2	2.7	1.9	3.6	6.3	3.7	7.1
Agricultural	2.1	0.0	0.1	0.0	1.9	0.0	0.0	0.0	2.5	0.1	0.1	0.0
Armed forces	2.7	0.1	0.2	0.1	1.4	0.0	0.1	0.1	0.4	0.0	0.0	0.0
Inadequately described	0.9	4.1	2.5	4.3	0.9	2.9	2.0	3.0	1.1	2.7	2.1	3.6

Source: OPCS/GRO(S) (1993), vol. 2, Table 16; from R. Ballard (1996: 139).

Table 9. Percentage Distribution Among Socioeconomic Groups by Ethnicity, 1991: Women

Class	18–29				30–44				45–59			
	White	Pakistani	Indian	Bangladeshi	White	Pakistani	Indian	Bangladeshi	White	Pakistani	Indian	Bangladeshi
Employer (large scale)	0.0	0.0	0.0	0.0	0.0	0.0	0.1	0.0	0.0	0.0	0.0	0.0
Professional self-employed	0.1	0.3	0.5	0.0	0.5	1.2	1.0	0.8	0.2	4.4	1.5	5.8
Employer (small scale)	0.6	2.6	1.6	1.9	2.1	8.5	4.4	2.4	2.5	9.1	4.0	0.0
Nonprofessional self-employed	1.8	5.6	2.7	3.3	3.4	12.1	8.4	3.2	3.1	13.1	8.3	5.8
Total self-employed	2.5	8.5	4.8	5.1	6.0	21.8	13.9	6.5	5.8	26.5	13.9	11.6
Manager (large scale)	3.4	2.1	2.6	0.5	3.6	1.3	1.6	2.4	2.7	0.0	0.9	1.9
Professional employed	2.3	2.9	5.1	0.9	1.7	2.5	3.0	6.5	0.8	1.8	2.9	11.5
Manager (small scale)	6.3	3.7	4.1	1.9	6.2	3.9	3.6	2.4	5.0	3.3	3.3	3.8
Semi-professional	15.1	9.3	10.3	10.7	19.8	15.1	10.8	19.4	16.2	15.6	11.6	28.8
Supervisor	2.1	1.6	2.0	0.0	2.3	0.7	1.6	0.8	2.3	1.1	0.8	0.0
Junior non-manual	42.9	41.3	48.4	36.0	33.6	20.9	26.9	17.7	33.2	12.4	17.9	17.3
Personal service	8.5	3.9	2.8	15.0	8.0	6.3	3.5	14.5	8.4	5.8	3.4	5.8
Skilled manual	3.1	3.1	1.8	3.7	2.3	3.0	4.0	2.4	2.6	2.5	4.8	3.8
Semi-skilled manual	9.2	18.6	14.5	16.8	8.3	17.5	26.0	15.3	10.2	21.5	31.8	5.8
Unskilled	3.0	1.1	1.5	0.9	6.7	2.2	3.2	2.4	11.0	4.0	6.0	7.7
Agricultural	0.6	0.4	0.1	0.5	0-7	0.3	0.1	0.0	0.9	0.7	0.3	0.0
Armed forces	0.4	0.0	0.0	0.0	0.0	0.0	0.0	0.0	0.0	0.0	0.0	0.0
Inadequately described	0.7	3.6	2.0	7.9	0.7	4.5	1.9	9.7	0.8	4.7	2.5	1.9

Source: OPCS/GRO(S) (1993), vol. 2, Table 16; from R. Ballard (1996: 140).

Table 10. Inter-Ethnic Unions, All Married and Cohabiting Men and Women, Resident Population, Great Britain, 1991

Ethnic group of male partner	Ethnic group of female partner										
	White	Black-Caribbean	Black-African	Black-Other	Indian	Pakistani	Bangladeshi	Chinese	Other-Asian	Other	Total
White	126,150	102	41	63	71	10	0	79	148	139	126,803
Black-Caribbean	225	559	8	10	4	2	0	2	3	12	865
Black–African	48	16	208	4	2	1	0	0	0	2	281
Black–Other	76	3	2	62	1	0	0	0	2	1	147
Indian	134	2	4	1	1,762	18	0	5	4	5	1,935
Pakistani	42	0	0	1	6	775	0	0	4	3	831
Bangladeshi	7	0	2	0	4	1	217	0	0	2	233
Chinese	34	0	0	0	2	0	0	234	0	0	270
Other-Asian	55	4	1	1	4	4	1	2	296	6	374
Other	218	2	1	2	7	4	0	2	5	191	432
Total	126,989	688	267	144	1,863	815	218	324	462	361	132,171

Source: 1991 Census One Per Cent Household SAR; from Berrington (1996: 199).

with whites (Table 11), and inter-ethnic unions were more common among Black ethnic minorities than among Asian groups. The exceptions were Chinese and "Other-Asian" women, who partnered with white men more frequently than Chinese or "Other-Asian" men partnered with white women. There appears to be an increase in ethnically mixed couples among younger people (see Table 11). Berrington's comparison of white/ethnic group unions among "first" and "second" generations men and women, however, showed inconsistencies. "Among men, inter-ethnic unions seemed to be more likely among those born in the UK ($p < 0.05$ only for Pakistani, Bangladeshi, and Other men). There is no difference among Indian, Pakistani and Bangladeshi women according to generation" (1996: 198–99).

These demographic data set the stage for the stories I am about to tell. They point to patterns of increased social mobility among those who claim to be ethnically "Indian" (including Sikhs) in a context of continued racial and ethnic segregation. They reflect the tensions I saw in the lives of the people I grew to know.

The lives of teenagers tell us a great deal about the tensions within modern capitalist formations. Teenagers are subject to projects of social reproduction at school, at home, and in their ethnic and religious communities. They are also prime targets of the market forces of consumer capitalism and the commodification of mass culture. In this way, the central

Table 11. Number and Percentage of Married and Cohabiting Men and Women Living with a White Partner, Resident Population, Great Britain, 1991

	16–34		35–39	
	Men	Women	Men	Women
Black-Caribbean	263/39.5	187/20.9	420/21.9	385/15.1
Black-African	104/19.2	90/8.9	162/13.0	163/17.8
Black-Other	80/60	77/51.9	57/42.1	56/33.9
Indian	556/7.0	537/4.1	1,141/7.6	1,089/3.8
Pakistani	273/6.2	271/2.2	477/3.6	470/0.6
Bangladeshi	75/4.0	68/0.0	122/1.6	116/0.0
Chinese	76/15.8	89/22.4	169/11.8	207/26.1
Other-Asian	89/18.0	115/38.3	258/13.6	316/30.4
Other	149/57.7	117/44.4	234/48.3	201/37.3

Source: 1991 Census One Per Cent Household SAR (ESRC/JISC purchase); from Berrington (1996: 200).

ideological forces within a social order can be seen to converge in the lives of adolescents. I frame my ethnographic account of social mobility and identity formation among British Sikhs within a broader analysis of the workings of social stratification, forces of social reproduction both within the public sphere and within the Sikh communities. The study focuses on the dynamic tensions in the lives of Sikh adolescents between the normalizing power of these mutually determining status systems and the possibilities that other cultural influences provide for interpreting and negotiating these normative expectations. It is at this site of intersection that young British Sikhs pave distinctive paths to social mobility.

2. From Subjects to Citizens

I have always thought it extremely paradoxical to speak of the
need to "integrate" people who have been an integral part of the
social structure of our country for one, two or even three
generations. The question is how to confront or to minimize
particular conflicts but not how to integrate those who are already
inside social structures.

—Balibar (1991a: 82)

The problem of world history appears in a new light. At its core
is no longer the evolution and devolution of world systems, but
the tense, ongoing interaction of forces promoting global
integration and forces recreating local autonomy. This is not a
struggle for or against global integration itself, but rather a
struggle over the terms of that integration.... At the center of this
study is the question of who, or what, controls and defines the
identity of individuals, social groups, nations and cultures.

—Bright and Geyer (1987: 69–70)

The final chapter in the history of British colonialism is the
story of imperial subjects becoming national citizens. Over
the past forty years, lines dividing colonizer from colonized
drawn in centuries of lawmaking, institution building, and
civilizing missions abroad have been challenged in courts, in
schools, and on cricket fields at home. The postwar British
public sphere has been a contested terrain on which the politics of cultural pluralism have been debated across institutions from law to policy, the media to the school. Considered
in concert, as will be the case here, these forms of public
discourse and debate tell the story of the making of a multicultural British nation.

   In this chapter I examine the political processes associated with what Yasemin Soysal has referred to as an

"incorporation regime," the processes through which host societies come to define, delineate, and, therein, produce collective identities and statuses that configure the possibilities and the limitations of citizenship and national belonging. Basing her analysis in large part on a comparative review of the membership status of guest workers across different national contexts, Soysal formulates, in her words, "an emergent model of membership that I call 'postnational'" (1994: 12).[1] She explains that "national citizenship is no longer the main determinant of individual rights and privileges," for "these rights are now codified in a different scheme, one that emphasizes universal personhood rather than nationality" (12). "Postnationalism," as Randall Hansen explains, is founded on a set of assumptions about the evolving nature of citizenship in a globalizing world.

Postnationalism, to summarize briefly, holds, first, that universal personhood has decoupled rights, on the one hand, and citizenship and identity, on the other (one can enjoy many of the rights of German citizenship without being German) and, second, that this development resulted from the "internationalization" and "universalization" of human rights legislation and discourse. (2000: 22, n. 72)[2]

Recognition of the impact of global political and economic forces on national politics has led many, like Soysal, to privilege global over national dynamics in defining the nature of citizenship. What I will argue instead, is that, although "postnational" influences clearly have played an important role in unsettling the British nation and in shaping responses to postwar immigration, British immigration and citizenship have been and remain very much a national matter. British ex-colonial immigrants, for the most part, arrived as citizens. Processes of incorporation have been shaped by liberal discourse centering on the nature of British national identity, the rights of individual citizens, and the responsibilities of the nation toward "all" its citizens.[3] The story of British postwar immigration, then, is best framed as a story of nation formation, a story that as this book goes to press is still being written.

I consider the cultural politics of immigration and citizenship across several domains within the public sphere where discourses of difference open horizons of possibility for particular forms of politics. These processes of nation formation and public management produce political imaginaries, statuses, and identities that configure the fields of possible action for "immigrants" in this nation. The institutional practices that define citizenship statuses and rights constitute what Aihwa Ong refers to as "a cultural process of 'subject-ification,'" in the Foucauldian sense, "a dual process of self-making and being-made within webs of power linked to the nation-state and civil society" (1999: 263–64). "Subject-ification" is an effect of "governmentality" or, "the ensemble formed by the institutions, procedures, analyses and reflections, the calculations and tactics that allow the exercise of this very specific albeit complex form of power" (Foucault 1991a: 102).

I begin this chapter with an analysis of political discourse that has emerged as Britain has struggled to define the nature of nationalism and the rights of and the nation's responsibilities with respect to its citizens of color. I consider legal and political discourse about national incorporation that centers on British national identity in immigration and race relation legislation and in educational policy.

An Island Story

Since the end of the Empire, Britain has been obsessed with the future of the nation. This island nation has felt under siege, threatened by the presence of ex-colonial citizens within and the pressures of European unification from without. Ironically, perhaps, in their obsession with Britain's future, many have turned their attention to the past where they bask in the ancient essence of their greatness, in the "continuity-with-progress" of a very English British heritage.[4]

Gazing backward, nationalists recount a highly nostalgic national story, an origin myth of sorts, expressing powerfully the symbols and values of British patriotism. Versions of this island story were captured vividly in a volume of *The Field: Magazine for the Country* published in Britain in the early 1990s. Luminary figures of the time responded to the topic "Being British, What It Means to Me" in a collection of essays subtitled a "Fanfare on Being British." The collection portrayed a people "proud of all that our British race [has] done for the world" by sharing its language, law, and government. In the words of the eminent historian A. L. Rowse,

As for continuity, I think of it when I see St. Augustine's chair at Canterbury, in which the Archbishops are enthroned: that rite goes back to before, a little before, the coronation of the *Anglo-Saxon* kings. We do not need to make Chaucer's pilgrimage to Canterbury—though when I went for the service of re-dedication after the German bombing during the war, I read *The Canterbury Tales* on the way down and back in the train. With any imagination we can see an *image of the continuity of our country* when we look at our local church—inside, we can feel the history, and with gratitude. (1990: 79)

The metaphor depicting "British" history for this historian is continuity. Events, architecture, and artifacts are joined as "heritage" from a point of origin to the present, a view that extends a sense of peoplehood over a great expanse of time. Heritage is a historical continuity that "we can feel"; given the heritage he invokes, it is an English "we" who feel this history and envision this image of "our country."

This historical portrait is inherently problematic. It speaks of unity and consensus where difference and conflict have typically reigned. What feel for Anglo-Saxon heritage might other long-term residents in Britain possess? The history of the Celts (the Welsh, Scots, and Northern Irish)—particularly the battles they fought against their Anglo-Saxon enemies—is not included in Rowse's version of "British" history.[5] The Celtic peoples of Britain do not possess the same sense of heritage, nor have they always shared a single language or common laws. And they hardly constitute a unitary "race." This primordial construction of a "Britishness," rooted in time and territory, excludes not only British Celts but Britain's more recent citizens as well.

The heightened celebration of continuity in these pages is a clarion call in a battle to preserve the British status quo in the face of inevitable change. Resonating from these nostalgic musings on the greatness of (English) national heritage is an underlying sense of impending doom. Words like those of Norman Tebbit (then a Tory MP) depict a Britain at war with the invasion of change and pay homage to the insularity of the island nation. Tebbit's tone is foreboding. With florid rhetoric he argues that the boundaries that historically have protected English culture and institutions against "rabid dogs and dictators" and "the political virus which brings on the sick fever of dictatorship" are under threat. Captioned to the right of a striking panoramic picture of the white cliffs of Dover towering over the deep blue Channel sea are Mr. Tebbit's words of warning to the readers of *The Field*, "We must learn how to stay an island." He continues:

"Desert Island Discs" is one of Britain's longest-running radio programmes. Not least of its attractions is the wonderful sense of insularity which it engenders. Perhaps its charms are lost on our continental neighbours who use "insular" as a word of near abuse, but we in Britain enjoy the programme and have every reason to be thankful for our insularity. Our boundaries (that troublesome one in Ireland apart) are drawn by the sea—some may say by Providence.... Sadly what has been almost an age of innocence is ending. Our gentle nationalism, more a sense of nationality, *was never built on any sense of racial purity*.... But in recent years our sense of insularity and nationality has been bruised by large waves of immigrants resistant to absorption, some defiantly claiming a right to superimpose their culture, even their law, upon the host community. All this in an era when the great Euro legal and cultural magimixer of Brussels is trying to blend us into a Continental culture.... The race relations industry tells us that British pride is offensive but the patriotism of others is virtuous. The Euro-fanatics intent on the arbitrary creation of a Euro-superstate in which nations of great antiquity would become mere provinces, tell us that the day of the nation state is over. Let them tell that to Hungarians, Romanians, Poles or Lithuanians. *Nationality is deeply rooted in ties of blood, kith, kin, language and religion and it is about more than Morris dancing on the English village greens or wearing a kilt in Scotland.* (1990: 76–78; emphasis mine)

Tebbit's words express a profound contradiction at the heart of postwar British nationalism. He denies that British nationality was "built on any sense of racial purity" but insists that it is "deeply rooted in ties of blood, kith, kin, language and religion." It does not derive from simply "acting" British (doing a Morris dance or wearing a kilt). This view of nationality is tied to a particular notion of ethnic heritage. It evokes a primordial sense of peoplehood, a collective identity that is given, cannot be chosen or achieved, and must to survive be protected and preserved.

During the late 1960s, Enoch Powell in his infamous "Rivers of Blood" speech introduced many of these same themes.[6] Powell represented black migration as a dangerous "threat" to the "national character" and to the social and cultural fabric of British society (Solomos 1993: 182). Powell, of course, was by no means the only source of provocative political rhetoric. Margaret Thatcher, in a television statement in 1978, gave voice to the collective fears of the British people as she perceived them:

people are really rather afraid that this country might be swamped by people of another culture. The British character has done so much for democracy, for law, and done so much throughout the world that if there is any fear that it might be swamped, then people are going to be rather hostile to those coming in.... We are a British nation with British characteristics. Every nation can take some minorities, and in many ways they add to the richness and variety of this country. But the moment a minority threatens to become a big one, people get frightened.[7]

In the political rhetoric of the "New Right" and of Thatcher's Tory Party leadership, fears of a national crisis were expressed through metaphors of invasion and transgression. Immigrants and the European Union were enemies threatening the stability and the sanctity of the nation and its heritage (in the past few years, refugees and asylum seekers have been represented in similar terms). Yet an ever-expanding American "invasion"—the arrival in the 1980s of hamburger and pizza chains, military personnel and their bombs, American football, prime time "soaps," and Reagan economics, followed in the '90s by Starbucks, Madonna, and Clinton's "third way"—has been ignored, largely, by the soothsayers of cultural doom.

Many scholars have characterized "right-wing" nationalist discourse as a new form of "cultural racism" legitimated by the belief that it is natural—human nature—for individuals to want to live with "their own kind," separate from those who are culturally different (Barker 1981). Scientific racism with its focus on innate differences has been replaced by a racism that stresses the incompatibility of different cultures—in Etienne Balibar's words, "racism without race" (1991a: 23).

The new racism is a racism of the era of "decolonization," of the reversal of population movements between the old colonies and the old metropolises, and the division of humanity within a single political space.... It is a racism whose dominant theme is not biological heredity but the insurmountability of cultural differences, a racism which, at first sight, does not postulate the superiority of certain groups or peoples in relation to others but "only" the harmfulness of abolishing frontiers, the incompatibility of life-styles and traditions. (1991a: 21)[8]

Social inclusion is based on feelings for one's own kind; therefore excluding others stems not from "racial" antipathy but from a "natural" response to "cultural" others.

The English elite have long felt a cultural aversion to those they define as "other"—from the undeserving poor of Victorian London to the subordinate racial subjects of the empire (see Miles 1993). What does seem new, however, is the vulnerability, the fear of cultural erosion. In the postcolonial era, belief in the insurmountability of cultural differences has strengthened, while faith that cultural others will remain separate or assimilate has weakened, generating fears that nonwhite ex-colonial "others" threaten the dominant (white) British way of life. This sense of national crisis, as Paul Gilroy suggests, has produced a deep nostalgic longing for a Britain imagined in the past, a homogeneous and pure national community untainted by the cultural presence of ex-colonial peoples of color.

It would appear that the uncertainty the crisis has created requires that lines of inclusion and exclusion that mark out the national community be redrawn. Britons are invited to put on their tin hats and climb back down into their World War II air raid shelters. There, they can be comforted by the rustic glow of the homogeneous national culture that has been steadily diluted by black settlement in the postwar years. (1990: 266)

As Britain enters the new millennium, controversies over "Britishness" rage on. In the fall of 2000, patriotic passions once again were ignited by statements published in a major report, "The Future of Multi-Ethnic Britain," sponsored by the Runnymede Trust, an independent think tank devoted to promoting racial justice. For weeks after the report was published, British newspapers were saturated with commentary about the "race row" the report had incited.

The report, referred to as the "Parekh Report"after the committee chair Lord Bhikhu Parekh, is an impressively comprehensive document covering issues ranging from policing and employment to education and the arts. The report makes numerous recommendations and outlines detailed strategies for addressing racial injustice through government leadership, legislation, and organizational change. Yet, despite this breadth, a single issue became emblematic of the report as a whole. These words fueled the flames of public controversy:

Does Britishness as such have a future? Some believe that devolution and globalisation have undermined it irretrievably. Many acknowledge that ideally there needs to be a way of referring to the larger whole of which Scotland, Wales and England are constituent parts. But the nation-state to which they belong is the United Kingdom, not Britain.... Where does this leave Asians, African-Caribbeans and Africans? For them Britishness is a reminder of colonization and empire, and to that extent is not attractive.... For the British-born generations, seeking to assert their claim to belong, the concept of Englishness often seems inappropriate, since to be English, as the term is in practice used, is to be white. Britishness is not ideal, but at least it appears as acceptable, particularly when suitably qualified—Black British, Indian British, British Muslim, and so on. However, there is one major and so far insuperable barrier. *Britishness, as much as Englishness, has systematic, largely unspoken, racial connotations.* Whiteness nowhere features as an explicit condition of being British, but it is widely understood that Englishness, and therefore by extension Britishness, is racially coded.... Unless these deep-rooted antagonisms to racial and cultural difference can be defeated in practice, as well as *symbolically written out of the national story*, the idea of a multicultural post-nation remains an empty promise. (Parekh 2000: 38–39, emphasis mine)

The report exploded into highly politicized pieces when sections of the right-wing press linked Home Secretary Jack Straw directly to these words, proclaiming that "Straw wants to rewrite our history."[9] Straw responded with a "scathing attack" on members of the "political left" as well as those among the "nationalist right" who, he argued, had "turned their backs on the concept of patriotism" by promoting the notion that "Britain as a cohesive whole is dead."[10]

The significance of the report was largely overshadowed by the controversy about Britishness and patriotism that the report's narrow reading produced. The *Daily Telegraph*, a conservative paper, characteristically denounced the report's findings as "sub-Marxist gibberish." Other commentators, like this one—with his touch of "traditional British irony"—alluded to the deeper undercurrents of insecurity that characterize this period in the nation's history:

Far from being trapped in a stereotype of Britishness, people are no longer certain what Britain stands for. The old identities have crumbled, but nothing has emerged to replace them. The result is a profound confusion and insecurity. In a sense, the commission's call for a celebration of this diversity amounts to celebrating the fact that we are all rather confused.[11]

The most disturbing responses to the report, however, were those that took members of the commission to task not simply for voicing an ideological view of Britishness but for voicing a view at all.[12] Lord Parekh, a member of the House of Lords, is an honored citizen as well as a respected scholar, but his Britishness became a focus of discussion, for he is Hindu and was born in India. A letter submitted to the *Daily Telegraph* suggests that the heated reaction to the report, for this reader, had as much to do with the messenger as with the message. "One might have thought that Lord Parekh's 40-year connection with this country would at least have taught him that presuming to tell *your hosts* what to call themselves is an act of atrocious bad manners" (emphasis mine). To this Lord Parekh responded, "I'm not a tenant. I've put down my roots here. As somebody who has been in Britain for 40 years and raised his children and grandchildren here, I have as much right as that person to take part in a national conversation about what Britain should be like."[13]

In the months following publication of the Parekh Report, the nation became caught up in election campaigning in which the national conversation about Britishness continued to figure centrally. Tory and Labor politicians each clamored to capture the public's patriotic spirit. Labor leaders, in particular, spoke of "reasons for being optimistic about the future of Britain and Britishness" and called citizens to celebrate British values.[14] MP Michael Willis acknowledged in a radio program that the prime minister had given him the task of encouraging members of government to give special attention to celebrating the national identity, prompting Roy Hattersley to quip, "Tony Blair wants our nationality to be celebrated. But what is it?"[15]

This popular political discourse concerning the nature of Britishness, past and future, represents only one among the political debates about citizenship and social incorporation to circulate through political channels during the past forty years. The history of the transformation of ex-colonial subjects into British citizens is a history configured through multiple layers of cultural politics fought across the boundaries of various state and public institutional settings. In the context of these legal, political, and policy debates, Britain's citizens of color find themselves represented and positioned in various ways within distinctive political imaginaries. These political imaginaries produce and regulate both the statuses "ethnic minorities" are granted and the possibilities for political action that they possess in a multicultural Britain.

The Political Construction of Minority Statuses

The political construction of minorities in democratic nations positions minority groups in different discursive formations, formations associated with various techniques of governance (Foucault 1991a, b).[16] The process of defining political statuses and determining minority rights is often a matter of heated political, legal, and policy debate; yet these statuses, when designated, invoke identities, inscribe social positions, and confer privileges that are officially recognized, legitimated, and accepted by the state and its institutions. Legal discourse and social policies, in other words, constitute group identities and statuses and, in the way these are constituted, forge the terrain on which rights and resources can be claimed and contested (Benhabib 1999: 298). Minority statuses are the vehicles through which the politics of recognition are fought, rights determined, and needs claimed.

Legal and political discourse, in demarcating minority statuses also mark groups so designated as different, identifying them in ways that serve to marginalize and exclude them from fully belonging in mainstream society. These collective identities include while they exclude; they provide legal protection while reinscribing relations of subordination, setting up the possibilities for as well as the limitations on political action. Political constructions of minority statuses, in this way, are inherently contradictory.

British Sikhs have found themselves subject to a range of discursive formations and governing institutions granting them distinctive types of minority statuses corresponding to contrasting political possibilities and restrictions. Their status as immigrants and citizens has evolved in the midst of decades of political debate and controversy that resulted in the passage of a series of increasingly restrictive nationality and immigration acts. Their status as a racial or ethnic minority has been constructed in discrimination cases fought under the auspices of the Race Relations Acts. And, finally, Sikhs have found themselves positioned as culturally and linguistically different in education policies aiming to increase educational equity. Across these political sites, racial, ethnic, and national identities are articulated in distinctive ways within the construction of each official minority status: immigrant/citizen, racial/ethnic minority, and bilingual/bicultural student. In this chapter, I look across these different forms of legal, political, and educational discourse about difference to consider the relationship between the making of minority statuses and processes of nation formation.

Creating Citizens

The successive nationality and immigration laws enacted in Britain since World War II chronicle a progressive narrowing of notions of British belonging from the expansionist vision of Empire to the exclusionary practices of the postcolonial nation.[17] Under the Empire, the relation between rulers and ruled was captured by the principle of *Civis Britannicus sum*, "I am a British Citizen," an imperial notion (resonating with *Civis Romanus sum*, upheld across the Roman Empire) premised on the belief that all British subjects were joined in an allegiance to the monarch and through this allegiance enjoyed the full privileges and protection subjects were granted, including the right to enter the UK. This imperial vision was to provide the basis for the citizenship status defined in the British Nationality Act of 1948, a status that future immigration and nationality legislation would slowly dismantle. Yet in postwar Britain the tradition of "Civis Britannicus sum" was still a powerful source of British pride, for in the words of

Minister for Colonial Affairs Henry Hopkins during a 1954 Parliamentary debate, "We still take pride in the fact that a man can say *Civis Britannicus sum* whatever his colour may be, and we take pride in the fact that he wants and can come to the Mother country" (quoted in Bevan 1986: 77).

The British Nationality Act of 1948, passed at the beginning of the end of the Empire, was the first step on a legislative path that reconfigured the boundaries of British belonging. Its contents reflect the contradictions inherent in Britain's position in the world at that time. Prior to this act, legislation had divided the world into two categories, British subjects and aliens. A single British nationality was conferred on all subjects of the Empire (with the exception that people from certain foreign territories over which the British extended "protection" were defined as British protected persons—BPPs). Yet, by the end of World War II many of the former colonies had become independent states, Commonwealth nations with their own citizenship laws. In response to these developments, the British government was forced to readjust its own nationality laws.[18]

Relations between Britain and the Old Dominions, particularly Canada, Australia, and New Zealand, were at that time of utmost importance politically to a British nation in the throes of decolonization. During the 1950s, the United Kingdom had demonstrated its continued allegiance to the Commonwealth by rejecting European integration in the name of Commonwealth solidarity. The passage of the British Nationality Act of 1948 should be interpreted in this light, and hence, Hansen suggests, "the story of New Commonwealth/colonial migration in the 1950s is the story of the Old Commonwealth's place in British politics" (Hansen 2000: 64).

The British Nationality Act of 1948 confirmed that citizens of the newly independent Commonwealth nations together with those who lived in the remaining colonies would remain subjects of the British Crown. The act created two main categories of citizenship—Citizens of the Independent Commonwealth Countries (CICCs, Commonwealth Citizens) and Citizens of the United Kingdom and Colonies (CUKCs). CICC status, at the time of the act's passage, applied only to subjects in Canada, but it was envisioned to apply eventually to subjects in New Zealand, South Africa, Newfoundland, India, Pakistan, Southern Rhodesia, and Ceylon. Individuals possessing either status continued to enjoy nearly identical citizenship rights. Their status as British subjects granted them the right to enter, settle, and work in the UK, vote in elections, stand for Parliament, and work for the British government.

In the years that followed, as the numbers of black immigrants increased, their legal rights to enter and work in the UK were taken away in a series of increasingly restrictive immigration acts that progressively restricted entry to all but British citizens connected to the UK through descent or ancestry. Between 1948 and the passage of the British Nationality Act of 1981 (which redefined the status of British citizenship), citizenship rights and immigration rights were decoupled. The passage of the Commonwealth Immigration Act of 1962 was the first step in this decoupling process. The act retained the status of CUKCs (citizens residing in Britain and in the colonies continued to hold the same citizenship status), but their right to enter Britain was now determined by where their passports had been issued. Only citizens with passports issued in Britain possessed full rights of citizenship, or the right to enter and work freely in the UK.

Commonwealth Citizens, moreover, were for the first time denied what had under colonialism been theirs by right—free entry into Britain.[19] The act established an employment voucher scheme, a quota system for work permits for Commonwealth Citizens. Three categories of workers were designated: category A, people who were coming to take a job; category B, those with skills, training, or educational attainments in demand in Britain; and category C, unskilled workers without a job in the UK. The category C quota was 10,000 vouchers per year; for categories A and B combined, 20,800 (Hansen 2000: see also Hayter 2000: 47). Although the scheme differentiated people according to occupational skills not color, recently released cabinet papers show that the act's intent was to restrict black immigration. In a cabinet meeting, Rab Butler, then home secretary, presented the work voucher scheme to colleagues with these words: "The great merit of this scheme is that it can be presented as making no distinction on grounds of race or colour. . . . Although the scheme purports to relate solely to employment and to be non-discriminatory, the aim is primarily social and its restrictive effect is intended to, and would in fact, operate on coloured people almost exclusively" (quoted in Hayter 2000: 47).

When the Labour government came to power in 1964, it undertook policies directed toward "integration and immigration control." In the words of the Mountbatten Report on Commonwealth Immigration, immigration was further restricted in order to provide the "breathing space needed for assimilation" (quoted in Hansen 2000: 147). In 1965, C vouchers for unskilled workers without job offers were formally abolished.[20] Vouchers in the first two categories were reduced first to a maximum of 8,500 a year and in 1969 to only 4,010. This policy closed the door to British immigration for most Commonwealth members outside the Old (and white) Dominions (Hayter 2000: 51).

The Commonwealth Immigrants Act of 1968 was and remains one of the most controversial pieces of legislation enacted in British history. The act was passed at a moment of heightened racial hysteria, prompted by the threat of a mass immigration of Asian British citizens in Kenya who were being forced to leave in the face of new nationality legislation associated with the "Africanization" of the recently independent Kenyan nation.[21] In the midst of widespread panic over a continued "flood" of Kenyan Asians into Britain, the Labour government, at record speed, pushed through an act that restricted their right to enter the UK.[22]

The Commonwealth Immigration Act of 1968 curtailed the rights of Asian British citizens to enter the UK by restricting free entry to British citizens with British passports issued under the authority of London or Dublin (or those exempted from control) who *also* possessed an ancestral connection to the UK. Free entry was restricted to holders of British passports who had a father or grandfather who had acquired citizenship by birth, naturalization, or adoption.[23] The act introduced the concept of belonging into British immigration law. More precisely, it racialized the boundaries of national belonging by restricting the entry of British citizens who were not connected to the nation through ties of blood or descent. The law created first- and second-class citizens among Citizens of the United Kingdom and Colonies.

The kith-and-kin connection restricted the automatic entry of East African Indians, since their ancestral connections led back to the Commonwealth country of India. Their entry was now regulated by the quota system set in place by the 1962 Commonwealth Immigration Act. The 1968 act provided an additional 1,500 vouchers per year for Kenyan Asian heads of households and their dependents. As British was the only citizenship many Kenyan Asians possessed, those who did not receive vouchers were rendered stateless. This was not the case, however, for the white civil servants in Kenya who could trace their ancestry back to Britain.

In 1972 the British government's responsibility toward CUKCs in independent ex-colonies was once again brought into question. A year after coming to power in a military coup, Idi Amin announced that there was no longer room in Uganda for Asians. After living for generations in East Africa, Ugandan Asians were given only three months to leave. Many of those with Ugandan citizenship had it taken away and all were disposed of their property, savings, and businesses. The British government in this instance accepted full responsibility for its Asian citizens. Britain accepted large numbers of refugees into the UK and encouraged several other nations to accept smaller numbers of refugees as well.

The Immigration Act of 1971, which came into force in 1973, brought an end to primary immigration from Africa, the Indian subcontinent, and the Caribbean (though it temporarily increased the number of vouchers granted to Kenyan Asians to 3,000). The legislation replaced the separation between British subjects and aliens with a distinction between "patrials" and "nonpatrials." Only patrials were free from immigration control. Patrials were (1) British or Commonwealth citizens born in the UK; (2) British Commonwealth citizens who had a father or British citizens who had a grandfather who had been born or naturalized in the UK; or (3) British and Commonwealth citizens and their wives who had resided in the UK for five years and had applied to register for citizenship. The act abolished category A and B work vouchers, replacing them with temporary work permits that did not carry the right to permanent residence or to bring one's family members to the UK (Hayter 2000: 54).[24]

The creation of the status of patrial, though implicitly a marker of race, was defended on more neutral grounds as affirming connections based on ancestral links, shared culture, and sentiment. The act did nothing to address the disjunction between nationality and immigration rights. British nationals were no longer equal, as some now possessed British passports that did not allow them to cross their nation's boundaries freely. The act's obvious bias toward whites received strong criticism from the European Human Rights Commission.

Citizenship and immigration rights were brought in line once again with the passage of the British Nationality Act of 1981, which repealed the British Nationality Act of 1948 and redefined the status of British citizen. The act abolished the status CUKC, replacing it with three main categories of citizenship: British Citizenship, British Dependent Territories Citizenship (BDTC), and British Overseas Citizenship.[25] Those who had been CUKCs with the right of abode were granted the status of British Citizenship. Following passage of this legislation, the Immigration Act of 1971 was amended to state that all British citizens had the right of abode. People possessing British Dependent Territories Citizenship or British Overseas Citizenship could only be granted right of abode by acquiring British citizenship.

The final chapter in the evolution of Empire to nation played out during the negotiations between Britain and China over the transference of Hong Kong sovereignty. The Hong Kong British Nationality Order of 1986 granted the status British National (Overseas) (BNO) to Hong Kong BDTCs if they registered before sovereignty reverted to China on July 1, 1997. BNOs were to enjoy only restricted rights, such as the ability to travel on a UK-endorsed passport and to obtain consular protection while abroad. Concern over human rights in China, fueled by the massacre in Tiananmen Square, opened the way for the British Nationality (Hong Kong) Act of 1990, which provided full British citizenship to 50,000 nationals and their dependents (Hansen 2000: 217–19). The act was not passed without opposition, but in the end Hong Kong BDTCs found the United States, Canada, and Australia more inviting and this quota was barely filled.

Since 1962 the legal status of British nationality has been transformed from a concept of belonging founded on connections of subjecthood in the British Empire to a notion of nationality based on a "genuine connection" to Britain—a "natural bond" of kinship and culture. The passage of increasingly restrictive nationality and immigration legislation has articulated an ideology of national belonging, delineated national boundaries, and determined new criteria for who could qualify as a "citizen." Through defining national identity, however implicitly, in racial terms, the law has positioned Britain's citizens of color outside these boundaries of national belonging.[26]

As the government sought to control entry to the nation through increasingly rigid immigration controls, other laws were passed in the 1970s aimed at bringing about the harmonious "integration" of those who had already arrived. Under the auspices of the Race Relations Acts, legal statuses have been constructed that protect and provide special rights to groups who meet particular status criteria. These criteria have been defined and further refined in legal deliberations over cases that have been brought before the court. Particular peoples have been recognized and thereby produced as "racial" or "ethnic" groups.

Designating Racial and Ethnic Minorities

During the past fifty years, legal cases have been brought, political battles fought, and legislation passed in the struggle to integrate minority groups into the British nation. Under the auspices of the British Race Relations

Acts, integration came to be associated in part with fighting racial discrimination and protecting the civil rights of those granted the legal status of racial or ethnic minority.

During the 1960s the government took action to address concerns about an increase in racial tensions. The government's approach combined antidiscrimination legislation with restrictions on immigration. The overall aim was to keep the number of black colonial immigrants down while working to create a "social order" in which, to quote then Labour Home Secretary James Callaghan, "every citizen shares an equal right to the same freedoms, the same responsibilities, the same opportunities and the same benefits."[27] The fear of "social disintegration" was appeased with policies designed to promote equal opportunity and harmonious racial integration.

In 1965 the first of the three Race Relations Acts was passed. Modeled on legislation in Canada and the United States, the first Race Relations Act targeted racial discrimination in "places of public resort" such as hotels, restaurants, places of entertainment, and public transport, but did not address discriminatory practices in areas of housing or employment. A Race Relations Board was created to deal with complaints and to bring legal action according to the act's provisions.

A second Race Relations Act, passed in 1968, defined "discrimination" carefully, stating: "For the purposes of this act a person discriminates against another if on the ground of color, race or ethnic or national origins he treats that other ... less favorably than he treats or would treat other persons." The authority of the act was extended to "the provision of goods, facilities and services; employment; trade unions, employers' and trade organizations; housing accommodation, business premises and other land" (Macdonald 1969: 10). The Community Relations Commission was created to promote "harmonious community relations."

In 1976 a third Race Relations Act established the Commission for Racial Equality (CRE), assigning to it the combined roles of the Race Relations Board and the Community Relations Commission. The legal powers of the CRE were increased; it was granted the authority to initiate its own investigations and to issue nondiscrimination notices. Influenced by antidiscrimination laws in the United States, this act extended the definition of discrimination to include indirect or unintentional forms, but it retained the same categories or "grounds" for discrimination and the same conception of a "racial group." Section 3(1) states that a "'racial group' means a group of persons defined by reference to color, race, nationality or ethnic or national origins." The jurisdiction of the act did not extend to groups defined by religion, language, sex, or political belief or status (Macdonald 1969: 11). Numerous court battles have ensued to determine whether particular peoples qualify for protection under the law as racial or ethnic groups.

Among British Sikhs, discrimination cases have largely been fought over the right of men and boys to wear the turban. *Mandla v. Dowell Lee* set a precedent for cases that came after. The headmaster of a private school had refused to admit to the school an orthodox Sikh boy (who wore long hair under a turban) unless he removed the turban and cut his hair. The headmaster wanted to minimize religious and social distinction in the school, which he thought would be accentuated by the boy's wearing the turban with his school uniform. The boy's father, acting for the boy, brought a case to court in 1982, declaring that the "no turban" rule mounted to discrimination under the auspices of the Race Relations Act of 1976. This set in motion a series of court disputes articulating a range of arguments regarding the nature of Sikh ethnic identity. The case was appealed twice and finally decided in the House of Lords. In the first decision, the county court judge concluded that the outstanding distinction differentiating Sikhs from other groups from South Asia was their religion, Sikhism. Therefore Sikhs could not be "defined by reference to ... ethnic origins" (though Punjabis or Indians might be so defined). The court of appeal upheld this decision. The judgment stated that a group could be defined as "ethnic" "only if the group could be distinguished from other groups by a definable racial characteristic with which members of the group were born." This decision, however, was overturned in the House of Lords on the basis that, in Lord Templeman's words:

The Court of Appeal thought that the Sikhs were only members of a religion or at best members of a religion and culture. But the evidence of the origins and history of the Sikhs which was adduced by the parties to the present litigation disclosed that the Sikhs are *more than a religion and a culture....* The Sikhs ... are *more than a religious sect,* they are *almost a race* and *almost a nation.*

The abstruseness of this assessment reflects the ambiguous nature of Sikh identities. Problems arise whenever an attempt is made to attribute an unambiguous and singular group identification—either purely religious or purely ethnic—to Sikhs. As the judges acknowledged in their debates, the

Sikh community accept converts who do not share their "racial or ethnic origins." But at the same time many people who consider themselves Sikh do not keep the signs of the faith (the five Ks) or practice the Sikh religion. They are considered Sikh, the judges determined, because they share the same history and culture. The Lords found that Sikhism had "evolved into a political movement as well" and that the "religious and political features of the movement then bred distinctions in social customs, including in particular the wearing of the turban as a symbol of defiance."[28] This shared history, they concluded, qualified the Sikhs as "more than a religion" and "almost a race," "almost a nation," a status that granted them protection from discrimination under the terms of the Race Relations Act.

The Lords decision in *Mandla v. Dowell Lee* set requirements that had to be met in future cases before a group could qualify as "ethnic." Lord Fraser, in his leading speech, proposed that to be granted the status of ethnic group a group should

regard itself, and be regarded by others, as a distinct community by virtue of certain characteristics. Some of these characteristics are essential; others are not essential but one or more of them will commonly be found and will help to distinguish the group from the surrounding community. The conditions which appear to me to be essential are these: (1) a long shared history, of which the group is conscious as distinguishing it from other groups, and the memory of which it keeps alive; (2) a cultural tradition of its own, including family and social customs and manners, often but not necessarily associated with religious observance, as well as other relevant, yet not essential characteristics related to geographical origin, language, literature, and religious and minority status as either an oppressed or dominant group.[29]

However, determining whether it was discriminatory to require a Sikh to remove his turban called for additional deliberation. In interpreting the "can comply" rule set down in the act by Parliament, Lord Fraser argued that a religiously observant Sikh could not comply with the requirement to remove his turban and stay true to his religious beliefs. Therefore, he deduced, the "no turban" rule was a form of indirect discrimination and thus illegal.

When *Mandla v. Dowell Lee* came to court, there was already a long history of political controversy centering on a Sikh's right to wear the turban. Disputes over turbans arose as early as 1959, when Mr. G. S. S. Sagar applied to the British Transport Department for a job as a bus conductor. His application was rejected because his turban "did not conform to the existing conditions of service"—meaning it could not replace the conductor's cap as an acceptable part of the uniform.[30] He was offered a job in the garage instead. Mr. Sagar galvanized the Manchester Sikh community. He actively sought to educate the local council and the Transport Committee concerning the historical significance of the Sikh turban, reminding them that the British had made special exceptions for the Sikhs in another place and time. The turban had been an important part of the uniform worn by the 82,000 Sikhs in the British Army who had been killed in battle during the two world wars. "If they could die for Britain in their turbans, could they not also be allowed to work in them?" (Beetham 1970: 21). Mr. Sagar prepared a lengthy document providing further evidence and sent it to the city councillors. He quoted authorities on the Sikhs, statements "showing the origin and importance of the turban, and its effect in building up the Sikh character," and others that documented "lavish praise for the Sikhs from British generals and ex-servicemen" (30). After seven years of political struggle, Mr. Sagar won his battle. The council voted in favor of allowing turbans and the Transport Committee was forced to follow suit. By that time, however, Mr. Sagar had passed the maximum age and could not apply for the job.[31]

The Race Relations Acts are concerned with discrimination on the grounds of color, race, ethnicity, or national origin. To be protected by this legislation an individual must prove her- or himself to be a member of a "group," one that regards itself and is regarded by others as a distinct community with a cultural tradition of its own—a tradition, moreover, with a long history. The legislation protects an individual's right to practice cultural difference, but in so doing defines cultural difference in ethnic or racially absolute terms.

Legal discourse constitutes minority statuses in efforts to determine who belongs to a nation and to protect the rights of those who do. These forms of political discourse designate minority status in ethnic reductionist terms that assume a homology between a community and a culture. These essentialist constructs, in contradictory fashion, provide the basis for challenging discrimination while simultaneously defining the boundaries of national belonging in racial terms.

Processes of social incorporation, however, are shaped not only by the designation of legal statuses and the provision of particular rights. They are founded on and informed by visions of national unity that provide the

rationale for different types of integration efforts. What is assumed to preserve the social fabric of a nation or, contrastively, to tear it apart? And how
are cultural differences imagined to contribute to either of these social
ends? These questions lie at the heart of educational policy debates over
how educational experiences might contribute to achieving greater justice
and equity for all. These debates in turn configure additional statuses for
those who, like British Sikhs, find their culture and language objectified
within educational discourse about difference.

Education and the Paradox of Pluralism

The politics of difference in culturally plural nations bring into focus a fundamental contradiction inherent in modern liberal democracies: How can
nation-states protect the moral community of the nation while accommodating the diverse and sometimes conflicting cultural beliefs and practices
of members of its citizenry? What has been referred to as "the challenge
of multiculturalism and the politics of recognition" (Gutmann 1992) strikes
at the heart of some of the central presuppositions of liberal democracy.
It has stimulated a great deal of debate about the relationship between
individual and collective rights, the fundamental basis of forms of civic solidarity, the value of different modes of social integration, and the legitimacy
of "minority cultural rights" to financial support and legal protection for
their languages and practices, particularly in the field of education.

Over the past twenty years, the cultural politics of education in Britain
have produced distinct positions concerning education's role in forging
national unity, bringing about social integration, and furthering social justice. At the heart of these debates is a classic tension between positions that
privilege efforts to nurture national solidarity and provide for the "common
good" and those aimed at protecting individual (and group) rights to practice different cultural traditions. The contradictory relationship between these
positions derives, as Habermas notes, from their grounding in a particular view of the common good, one he refers to as "communitarian," a view
that assumes "a necessary connection between the deliberative concept of
democracy and the reference to a concrete, substantively integrated ethical
community" (1996: 24).[32] Educational approaches to diversity are often
founded on an assumption that education should aim to realize this ethical

integration in order to prevent ethnic conflict and national fragmentation. In the case of two educational proposals for addressing diversity, Honeyford's integrationist view and the Swann Report's vision of "education for all," the paradox of pluralism is assumed to be resolved by invoking a liberal delineation of public and private cultural realms—"differences are treated as matters of private, but not public interest" (Calhoun 1997: 83).[33]

Honeyford and Integration

During the late 1980s Ray Honeyford became a leading spokesperson on race and education for the New Right.[34] He first came into the public eye in 1984, when the then Labour Council in Bradford (a city located next to Leeds) asked him to accept early retirement from his position as headmaster of an elementary school that had a majority of Asian students. A heated controversy had erupted over the racially prejudicial views he expressed in essays he published in a right-wing journal, the *Salisbury Review*. When he was forced to step down, the media transformed him into an icon of white victimization. What the media coined "the Honeyford Affair" created a popular "moral panic" over "Honeyford's censorship."[35] In the aftermath, Honeyford wrote a book titled *Integration or Disintegration: Towards a Non-Racist Society* (1988). His goal was to clarify his position—which calls for "integration" and denounces "multiculturalism"—and stimulate public debate about the nature of Britain's multi-ethnic society.

In his argument in support of social integration, Honeyford employs rhetoric of incorporation based on liberal principles regarding the relationship between the democratic nation-state and minority cultures. This position is founded on a liberal defense of state neutrality. The state should not sponsor any particular "substantive" view of "the good life." Instead, a liberal democracy requires that its citizens agree that cultural and historical differences be subordinated to "more general and binding political and constitutional principles." Cultural minorities must be absorbed into "the broader majority consensus regarding such things as civil liberties, the role of law, parliamentary democracy, the Welfare State and the separation of state and society" (1988: 48). Only then, Honeyford insists, can minority groups and individuals "successfully integrate commitment to public principles and private behavior, an arrangement that threatens neither national solidarity nor individual freedom" (39). The practice and maintenance of minority cultures are viewed as a "private" or individual matter, separate from the "culture of public institutions."

One of Britain's greatest assets is the tradition of keeping separate the private and public domains. It is a guarantee of that freedom of the individual we take for granted. Crucial to our understanding of ourselves is the notion of the reasonable person who lives and lets live, who believes that such matters as the language of the home, dress, diet and, indeed, that range of prejudices we all carry around with us are essentially private matters. The culture of public institutions is a function of history, tradition and the broad cultural consensus which, until very recent years, the citizens took for granted. There is no question of such things being imposed. Those who seek to do so would be regarded as extremists or fanatics—types detested by the great majority of British people. Keeping society and the state separate is vital to this view of the world. It is this principle of private choice and public consensus—which the notion of officially sponsored versions of culture violates. (1988: 45–46)

Honeyford's formulation is founded on two problematic assumptions: first, that there is "public" consensus; and, second, that the British state is a neutral player in the politics of difference. In the first instance, the invocation of an authoritative public consensus must be viewed with suspicion, for as Craig Calhoun has argued, "all attempts to render a single public discourse authoritative privilege certain topics, certain forms of speech, and certain speakers" (1997: 81).[36] The rhetorical use of "the public" in Honeyford's writings illustrates a discursive shift that was also common within the political rhetoric of "Thatcherism." A significant source of Thatcher's power, Stuart Hall contends, stemmed from the construction of ideological consent under the rubric of "authoritarian populism" (1990b: 7). The notion of "the popular" articulated and condensed different, often contradictory discourse within the same ideological formulation. In this way, divergent positions were silenced through the remaking of a hegemonic "common sense" (8).[37]

Second, the assignment of culturally different practices to the private domain, while legitimated by a principle of state neutrality, simply sidesteps moral dilemmas at the heart of cultural differences. As Honeyford's words illustrate in this depiction of Islamic practice, the liberal concern to protect a minority's right to its private cultural practices does nothing to address the moral dilemmas of pluralism or the misunderstandings, misrecognitions, and prejudices that divide Britain.

If culture is difficult to pin down, how much more difficult will be the notion of a multiculture to define?... For instance, if the concept is to work there would need to be some understanding of which items of ethnic minority culture should enter into the new version.... Would the public, for instance, approve of ritually slaughtered halal meat in school dinners, as Moslem citizens insist? There is good evidence that public opinion regards this practice as cruel and primitive. (1988: 43)

Minority interests—regardless of their legitimacy as collective needs or citizenship rights—are signified as offensive, "primitive," or simply inappropriate. Honeyford warns that accommodating such interests will inevitably lead to a decline in public confidence and ultimately to a state of national disintegration.

The discourse of public consensus is rhetorically persuasive and powerful. Honeyford characterizes the public through the metaphor of the melting pot. But in his metaphor "melting" is a one-directional process involving the assimilation of difference to consensus and the neutralization of potential sources of contestation and resistance. Alternative publics are denied legitimacy, their oppositional voices silenced. Minority cultures and concerns are relegated to the private domain, beyond the realm of political power and authority.

The position of the New Right, however powerful it became in the popular imagination, did not go uncontested. The Swann Report was to support a position quite different from Honeyford's. The report emphasizes the achievement of *diversity within unity* in British society through a policy defined as "education for all." The Swann Report does not explicitly invoke the dichotomy between public and private domains, but it implicitly relies on this distinction to create a veneer of unity in the face of heated controversy over minority needs and rights in British education.

The Swann Report: "Diversity Within Unity"

The Swann Report was presented to Parliament in March 1985. Titled "Education for All," it is 800 pages long and bears the seal of government authority stamped on what was then the standard green government document cover. The document contains the research, conclusions, and proposals of the Committee of Inquiry into the education of children from ethnic minority groups. The origins of this inquiry date back to 1977 and to a recommendation by the Select Committee on Race Relations and

Immigration that the government should institute a "high level and independent inquiry" into "the causes of underachievement of children of
West Indian origin." The government responded to this recommendation in
1979 by setting up the Rampton Committee, whose members included
academic experts, government officials, minority leaders, businesspeople,
and members of the clergy.

The title of the report reflects its primary contention that "the education of West Indian children cannot be seen in isolation and must be
considered as part of the education of *all children*."[38] Racism was found to
be a central factor in the "underachievement" of West Indian children, and
this prompted a consideration of how schooling might counter racism in
British society. The committee concluded that the needs of ethnic minority
and majority pupils require that education reflect the multiracial nature of
British society. The report supports state intervention and a "multicultural
approach" to "lay the foundations for a society based on genuinely pluralist principles." In defining what it means by "pluralism," it adopts a communitarian approach. It envisions a British society founded on a common
core of shared "values, practices and procedures" believed necessary for
the maintenance of a democratic social order. Within this unity, diversity
must also be protected, ensuring the right of minorities to maintain distinct
identities.

We consider that a multiracial society such as ours would in fact function most
effectively and harmoniously on the basis of pluralism which enables, expects and
encourages members of all ethnic groups, both minority and majority, to participate fully in shaping the society as a whole within a framework *of commonly
accepted values, practices and procedures*, whilst also allowing and, where necessary, *assisting the ethnic minority communities in maintaining their distinct ethnic
identities within this framework*. Clearly the balance between the shared common
identity of society as a whole and the distinct identities of different ethnic groups
is crucial in establishing and maintaining a pluralist society. (Swann 1985: 5; emphasis mine)

The Swann Report explicitly distances its proposals from those that
support unidirectional assimilation. In calling for a "genuinely plural society," the report deploys rhetoric of incorporation quite different from that
of Ray Honeyford. Its vision of a harmonious multiracial Britain would
not require minority communities to "melt" into an "unchanged dominant
way of life," one that is "relatively homogeneous in language, religion and
culture." Rather, it would seek "the 'assimilation' of *all* groups within a

redefined concept of what it means to live in British society today." The "mould" of British society must be recast into one that, while not "in all senses 'foreign' to our established way of life," does in fact retain "the fundamental principles of the original but within a broader pluralist conspectus—diversity within unity" (1985: 8). This vision can only be achieved, they conclude, if both majority and minority cultures accept that neither will remain untouched or unchanged.

The ethnic majority community in a truly pluralist society cannot expect to remain untouched and unchanged by the presence of ethnic minority groups—indeed the concept of *pluralism implies seeing the very diversity of such a society ... as an enrichment of the experience of all those within it.* Similarly, however, the ethnic minority communities cannot in practice preserve all elements of their cultures and lifestyles unchanged and in their entirety—indeed if they were to wish to do so it would in many cases be impossible for them then to take on the *shared values of the wider pluralist society....* [E]thnic minority groups must nevertheless be free within the democratic framework to *maintain those elements which they themselves consider to be the most essential to their sense of ethnic identity*—whether these take the form of adherence to a particular religious faith or the *maintenance of their own language for use within the home and their ethnic community*—without fear of prejudice or persecution by other groups.... We would thus regard a democratic pluralist society as seeking to achieve a *balance* between, on the one hand, the maintenance and active support of the essential elements of the cultures and lifestyles of all the ethnic groups within it, and, on the other, the acceptance by all groups of a set of shared values distinctive of the society as a whole. This then is our view of a genuinely pluralist society, as both socially cohesive and culturally diverse. (Swann 1985: 5–6; emphasis mine)

Beyond its support for multicultural education, however, Swann has little to say about the mechanisms that might bring about unity in diversity. Its support for a "genuinely plural society" invites "public" *recognition* of cultural diversity, but in the end its proposals relegate the *practice* of diversity, particularly with regard to language and religion, to the homes and communities of ethnic minorities—to the "private" domain.

The Committee of Inquiry's original objective—to address concerns *identified by the ethnic minorities themselves*—resulted in proposals encased in the comfortable rhetoric of "education for all." In carrying out its mission, the committee was required to reconcile contradictory, deeply conflicting interests and needs within a single conciliatory statement. The report exemplifies an effort to construct unity without denying diversity; yet its failure to represent adequately any radical minority position reflects, ironically perhaps, the incommensurability of the diverse values and views the writers of the report would seek to "unify."

Multiculturalisms

The Swann Report, however contradictory, represented a major advance over earlier educational responses to the presence of ethnic minorities in British schools. Initial policies had taken a more singularly assimilationist view toward ethnic minority cultural differences. Educational reforms were directed toward preparing ethnic minority children to integrate into the existing educational system (primarily through programs for developing English language skills).

Multicultural education, in validating cultural diversity, represents a step toward a greater appreciation for cultural difference. The term "multiculturalism," of course, has never corresponded to a single philosophy or pedagogic method. At the most general level, however, multicultural approaches can be separated into two basic orientations that have been referred to as "difference" and "critical" multiculturalism.

Difference multicultural initiatives typically have sought to broaden student awareness of cultural differences through curricular "enrichment." These programs assume that social tolerance can be enhanced through teaching and talking, by giving students knowledge that will encourage a greater appreciation for minority cultures and for the diverse origins of and influences on British culture and history. Characterized as the "Three S" or "steelbands, saris, and samosas" curricula, difference multiculturalism materials have tended to locate "difference" in ethnic folk culture—in artifacts, cuisine, musical styles, and ritual practices abstracted from the complex meanings and varying significance that people give to these cultural forms in their everyday lives.

This "Three S" orientation is similar to the difference multiculturalism Turner (1994) finds in the academy. In each case, difference multiculturalism has viewed the received curriculum as "an instrument for reproducing the hegemony of the dominant group" (412). To challenge this dominance, difference multiculturalists have sought to "decenter" the canon and to incorporate the (selectively appropriated) knowledge of subordinate peoples into the curriculum. As Turner points out, however, the additive method of "decentering" reasserts dominant schematic categories and aesthetic criteria.

The focus of the multiculturalist challenge to these aspects of the traditional curriculum ... has ironically led many academic multiculturalists, even as they call for a decentering of the dominant Eurocentric notion of high culture, to adopt much of its schematic content as the form of their own oppositional conception of minority "cultures." The result is that the ideological forms and values of established hegemonic notions of culture and history have tended to be carried over into multiculturalist challenges to these forms.... [M]ulticulturalists ... have formulated these challenges by revaluing minority cultural productions in terms of the sorts of aesthetic criteria employed to define the value of canonical "high cultural" forms of art, literature, or music. The hegemonic Eurocentric categories (literature, art) in which the canonical notion of culture as high culture is framed thus go unchallenged. (1994: 412)

The goal of difference multiculturalism has been the neutralization of prejudice through the eventual acceptance of difference. Yet, here again, difference has been defined in essentialist terms, as culture possessed by bounded homogeneous ethnic groups. This approach to difference soon digresses into a form of cultural apartheid, with society envisioned as a mosaic of bounded cultural groups differentiated according to reified forms of cultural difference (Rex 1989). As Turner concludes,

multiculturalism tends to become a form of identity politics in which the concept of culture becomes merged with that of ethnic identity. From an anthropological standpoint, this move, at least in its more simplistic ideological forms, is fraught with theoretical and practical dangers. It risks essentializing the idea of culture as the property of an ethnic group or race; it risks reifying cultures as separate entities by overemphasizing their boundedness and mutual distinctness; it risks overemphasizing the internal homogeneity of cultures in terms that potentially legitimize repressive demands for communal conformity; and by treating cultures as badges of group identity, it tends to fetishize them in ways that put them beyond the reach of critical analysis. (1994: 407)

What has been called "critical" multiculturalism, on the other hand, questions the relationship between power and knowledge, or how a society selects and recognizes, evaluates and elevates certain kinds of information to the rank of "public knowledge." Critical approaches have moved beyond the celebration of diversity to question the basis of social inequality and racism and to look more critically at the politics of difference. They have problematized the valorization of all forms of difference (what Mouffe refers to as extreme pluralism), emphasizing that difference is inherently antagonistic, deeply embedded in relations of power, and therefore inevitably political.[39]

Anti-Racist Education

The Race Relations Act of 1976 made racial discrimination in school a legal offense. Anti-racist Education (ARE), correspondingly, has sought to eradicate racism from schools and eventually, through educational projects, from society. In contrast to multicultural education policies, or what the late Barry Troyna labeled "deracialized forms of discourse and intervention," anti-racist education has offered a "benign (meaning non-malevolent) racialization of educational policy and debate" (Troyna and Carrington 1990: 23). While multicultural perspectives have focused on the lifestyles and cultures of ethnic minorities, anti-racist education has been concerned with white institutions and white forms of racism (prejudice) as well as racialism (discrimination), as Troyna (a white male) put it, with "us" rather than "them."

Anti-racists have been critical of multiculturalism on several counts. While acknowledging the value of celebrating cultural diversity, anti-racists have taken multiculturalists to task for ending the debate here, thereby impoverishing the notion of culture and its relationship to inequality. Multiculturalists have tended to ignore social class and to reduce racism to prejudice, to intolerant attitudes located in individuals—a position that ignores discriminatory practices, institutionalized forms of racial injustice, or structural inequality.

Anti-racist education, in contrast, has directed its attention to the structures that "produce, sustain, and legitimate values and practices which help maintain racial inequality" (Troyna 1989: 176). These programs have targeted the social context of instruction as well as the content of what is taught. Advocates have called for a rewriting of the "hidden curriculum," a restructuring of relations of authority and the democratization of forms of social interaction in schools. More specifically, proponents have supported

the recruitment of more black teachers (especially to promoted positions); more effective measures to counter cultural bias in assessment and selection procedures; initiatives to extend parental and pupil involvement in decisions about the organization and priorities of schooling; and the development of strategies and policies to deal with racist harassment. Anti-racists have also stressed the need for the democratization of schooling and for changes in the formal curriculum to include explicit teaching against racism and other forms of injustice. (Troyna and Carrington 1990: 1–2)

In these programs explicit teaching against racism and injustice has often taken the form of service or experiential learning. Students in all-white schools have been given the opportunity to meet with students of color to share and explore their different perspectives on racism. White students have been challenged to confront negative images and stereotypes—about the inner city, for example—through research projects or direct involvement in community life. Proponents have assumed that the cumulative effects of these types of educational interventions will transform existing relations of power and create a more just, democratic, and equitable nation for "all."

Anti-racist education has also attracted criticism. While the New Right challenged anti-racist programs for politicizing schooling, others have questioned whether its politics have in fact been misplaced and misconceived.[40] Paul Gilroy, in an article "The End of Anti-Racism," faults anti-racist education strategies such as Race Awareness Training (RAT) for addressing racism in isolation from other forms of social inequality. This view of racism, he argues,

trivializes the struggle against racism and isolates it from other political antagonisms—from the contradiction between capital and labor, from the battle between men and women. It suggests that racism can be eliminated on its own because it is readily extricable from everything else. Yet in Britain, "race" cannot be understood if it is falsely divorced from other political processes or grasped if it is reduced to the effect of these other relations. (1992: 50–51)

The privileging of racism over other relations of inequality is reductive and essentialist. Moreover, early anti-racist approaches tended to focus nearly exclusively on "color racism" or the "black-white dichotomy" and, hence failed to address the multiple forms of racism that have existed both across time and at particular moments in history (May 1999: 2–3).

While supporting Troyna and Carrington's formulations of democratic and collaborative anti-racist pedagogies as "a step in the right direction," Ali Rattansi has cautioned against adopting simplistic notions of racism and naive theories of learning in creating anti-racist education policies. Multicultural and anti-racist proposals alike, he suggests, are founded on a rationalist approach to education, one that may be quite inappropriate for dealing with the irrationalities of racism.

The rationalism of their educational project is contingent on the supposed irrationalism of the racist subject—often conceptualized as a collective, class subject. In the context of schooling one significant issue that is paradoxically neglected is the "rationality" of the working-class students' resistance to anti-racist curricula and

classroom discussions in so far as this resistance is bound up with a more general-
ized opposition to the degrees of surveillance, discipline, authoritarianism and class
domination involved in conventional forms of schooling. (1992: 33)

Rattansi's critique raises two related issues. First, students, particularly working-class students, often resist the authoritarian discipline of the
school and in so doing interpret and respond to the knowledge "taught" in
contradictory and ambiguous ("irrational") ways. Second, white racist attitudes, practices, and ideologies are themselves contradictory, inconsistent,
and ambiguous. Rattansi reminds us that

Racialized discourses are always articulated in context: in an English or history
class; in a school corridor, dinner queue or playground; at work or on the streets; in
one neighborhood or another. These different sites can yield complex and shifting
alliances and points of tension. The ambivalences generated for many white youth
by the attractions of Afro-Caribbean, Afro-American and African music forms, and
their admiration for some aggressive forms of Afro-Caribbean masculinity, have
resulted in alliances in particular schools and neighborhoods between white and
Afro-Caribbean youth against Asian youth. (1992: 27)

In recent years, the dichotomy between multicultural and anti-racist education approaches has begun to break down as British anti-racists have
attempted to draw from multiculturalism in order to develop more complex
frameworks for understanding racism, ethnicity, and culture (May 1999: 3;
see Gillborn 1995).

Within academic circles, and particularly in schools of education, debates over the political possibilities of pedagogy carry on, despite the powerful setback these progressive education programs encountered in the late
1980s and early '90s. At the height of the anti-racist education controversy,
the alternative educational voices of the 1980s were rendered momentarily
mute by the conservative reforms of the 1988 Education Reform Act. As
anti-racist radicals, Swann moderates, and New Right conservatives were
battling over local authority education policies, Margaret Thatcher and Secretary of State for Education Kenneth Baker were drafting legislation that
erased the battlefield. The act was officially announced in Parliament on
June 11, 1987. The introduction and passage of this legislation were swift
and shocking to those who did not share the Thatcher/Baker vision.[41]

Only attentive observers of educational affairs, and not many of these, fully grasped
the emergence of Tory policy and its implications: for these there was always the
possibility that it might never be implemented. That is why, when very shortly after

their victory, the new government announced its educational policy in a series of seemingly hurriedly concocted "consultation papers," they were generally received with shocked amazement by the educational—and wider world. (Simon 1991: 535)

The structural implications of this policy were radical and far-reaching, though its aim was simple: "to diminish the role of local government in education" so as to "liberate the schools from what was perceived as an ossifying, and in some cases malign control" (538). The reform's ideological rationale reflected the assumptions of classic Thatcher/Reagan economics. Consumer "choice" was introduced into the domain of education to stimulate competition between schools, which, it was believed, would improve the quality of education available to "customers" (the parents). Market forces would drive the production of an improved educational product. Local management and budgetary control were granted to individual schools, allowing them to compete better as "semi-independent corporations" for these customers. Schools were given the opportunity to "opt out" of their affiliation with local authorities and could choose instead to become part of a new system of schools financed directly by the state. The reform that was most damaging to multicultural and anti-racist initiatives, however, was the statutory setting of a national curriculum and the institution of a corresponding schedule of national examinations at ages seven, eleven, fourteen, and sixteen.

In the mid-1980s a number of local authorities in Britain instituted anti-racist policies in their schools. At that period in British history, the power to designate local educational policies still resided in local governments. With the passage of the 1988 Education Reform Act, much of the authority of the education departments of local authorities was taken away and delegated to schools and to the national government. The Reform Act dissolved the Inner London Educational Authority, the most progressive and controversial local authority in England at that time. The Education Reform Act gained royal assent on July 29, 1988. And with its implementation the politics of difference in British education policy entered a new era. Thatcher's Reform Act reasserted central government dominance in matters of educational policy.

The challenge of cultural pluralism in democratic nation-states will not be easily resolved. Policies infused with rhetoric of incorporation, tropes like "education for all" and "unity in diversity," cannot resolve the contradictions at the heart of the politics of difference. Contests over culture, discourses of difference, and politics of identity will continue to test traditional notions of the homogeneous national "social order" as the forces of capitalism deepen relations of inequality on a global scale. The paradox of pluralism in democratic nations is no longer simply a national concern, as issues of social integration are influenced by structural inequities grounded increasingly in the workings of global political and economic relations.

However, to end on this note with an acknowledgment of the ultimate hegemony of the state would misrepresent the cultural politics of education and more generally would ignore the potential of local campaigns to effect social change. Legal rights discourse provides avenues for minorities to make claims against the state; it creates opportunities for groups to assert their interests under the cloak of liberalism's principles of fairness and equity for all. The creation of educational policies directed toward protecting the rights of minorities to equal schooling opportunities generates a unique form of cultural politics. To better understand local democratic approaches to resolving dilemmas of cultural diversity, we must look more closely at the nature of this form of cultural politics. What do subordinate groups attempt to achieve in their struggles to reconfigure the way needs are defined and political claims legitimated? How are their claims subverted and their potential power defused by the reassertion of dominant and authoritative definitions of the social situation and corresponding assumptions about the "needs" of minority students? How do the needs and problems constituted in the politics of needs interpretation correspond, if at all, to the way people experience these "problems" in their everyday lives? And what does this tell us about the potential for as well as the limitations of using rights discourse to achieve social justice and greater equality?

I turn now to consider these issues from the perspective of a campaign that was organized by Sikh parents to demand that their heritage language, Punjabi, be incorporated into the curriculum at Grange Hill High.

3. The Politics of Language Recognition

The struggle to adopt minority languages within dominant institutions such as education, the law, and government, as well as the struggle over language rights, constitute efforts to legitimize the minority group itself and to alter its relationship to the state. Thus while language planning reflects relationships of power, it can also be used to transform them.

—Tollefson (1991: 202)

Processes that act to incorporate immigrants like British Sikhs socially into a particular nation formation, as we have seen, work through a range of forms of cultural politics across different domains in the public sphere. But questions of citizenship rights and national responsibilities are not simply negotiated at the level of top-down policymaking and legislative actions. To understand the dynamic nature of processes of social incorporation, one must examine not only the political imaginaries defined by a nation, but how groups so defined as ethnic or racial or immigrants make use of the possibilities these political imaginaries provide for making claims and asserting their rights as citizens. Cultural politics in the public sphere involve forms of power that both act on and are enacted by immigrant citizens. I turn now to consider a particular form of citizen action, the politics of recognition.

Whether associated with the "post-socialist condition" (N. Fraser 1997) or the rise of multiculturalism (C. Taylor 1992), the late twentieth century witnessed a dramatic shift in paradigms of political conflict. What Nancy Fraser has characterized as "the eclipse of a socialist imaginary centered on terms such as 'interest,' 'exploitation,' and 'redistribution'" has brought to light a new political imaginary, a politics founded in notions of "identity," "difference," "cultural domination," and "resistance" (1997: 11). Strategies for addressing socioeconomic inequity have been supplanted by politics targeting cultural domination—forms of disadvantage and disrespect, misrecognition and social exclusion rooted in attributions of difference. This emphasis on cultural injustice, in the words of Charles Taylor, assumes that "nonrecognition or misrecognition . . . can be a form of oppression, imprisoning someone in a false, distorted, reduced mode of being. Beyond simple lack of respect, it can inflict a grievous wound, saddling people with crippling self-hatred. Due recognition is not just a courtesy but a vital human need" (1992: 25).

Across this political terrain, "cultural recognition has displaced socioeconomic redistribution as the remedy for injustice and the goal of political struggle" (C. Taylor 1992: 11). The political discourse of cultural recognition differentiates people into "members of discrete ethnic, linguistic, and other cultural groups" in need of "public recognition and preservation of particular cultural identities" (Gutmann 1992: 9). Within this political imaginary, subordinate peoples gain the power to claim rights on the basis of cultural, religious, or linguistic authenticity in conflicts ranging from battles over indigenous land rights to contests over language education policies (Turner 1994).

The 1980s in Britain, as in other Western industrial nations, witnessed the expansion of liberal politics of recognition galvanized in the name of multicultural principles. The rise of politics of recognition, in Britain as elsewhere, both challenged the traditional hegemony of the culturally homogeneous nation and prompted the invocation of objectified cultural and linguistic forms in arguments for awareness and valuation of the linguistic and cultural practices of "ethnic" others.

Politics of recognition have become an important vehicle for asserting claims to linguistic rights in language policy debates (see Heller 1999). Discourse calling for linguistic recognition produces language as a reified object associated with essentialist constructs of discrete linguistic, ethnic, or national groups. The process of invoking language as a symbol, as a reified object within a politics of recognition, separates "language as object" from "language in use." This, in turn, produces a paradoxical situation in which a reified construct of language in contexts such as educational policy debates comes to stand for what are much more complex and changing patterns of language use.

This chapter looks more deeply into this disparity between political and practical constructions of language, culture, and identity in the lives of British Sikhs. I consider this question from the perspective of a language rights campaign organized by Sikh parents at Grange Hill High. The parents mobilized this effort to challenge what they perceived as the administration's "ghettoization" of Punjabi language classes by scheduling them after school. The parents felt that it was their right to have Punjabi recognized and respected, that it should be taught with the other modern languages during regular school hours. In analyzing this event, I contrast the discourse about learning Punjabi that circulated during the campaign with the meanings Sikh students gave to Punjabi in their everyday lives. This contrast brings into relief the complex and multiple ways relations between language, culture, and identity come to be constructed in the lives of "linguistic minorities."

Language and Power in Modern Nations

In the modern era of nation-states, language has played a complex role in political processes of nation formation and legitimation (Heller 1999). Language is central to the imagining of national communities (Anderson 1983), and in multilingual nations "linguistic minorities" have been created "by nationalisms which exclude them" (Heller 1999: 7).[1] Boundaries dividing linguistic communities are the product of national politics of representation that "involve massive projections of power, status, values, norms onto the linguistic phenomenon at hand" (Blommaert 1999: 431). Through these processes, languages are identified, labeled, and ranked according to criteria of quality that attribute status and value to particular languages relative to others within an overarching hierarchy of languages.[2]

The concept of language as "a discrete, finite entity defined by standard grammars" is a European cultural artifact fostered by processes such as literacy and standardization associated most directly with the theories, values, and methods of positivist linguistic paradigms (Ricento 2000: 201; see also Pennycook 1998: 80). Yet assumptions about the nature of language and its relationship to national identity have brought linguistic issues to the forefront of efforts to develop or reinforce cohesion and stability within the modern nation-state (May 2000: 369; Ricento 2000). Language planning and policy are contested terrains on which imagined nations and corresponding nationalist agendas are articulated and debated. Language ideological debates, then, provide a powerful window on the politics of difference within modern nation-states (Blommaert 1999: 427–28).

Noam Chomsky once wrote that "questions of language are basically questions of power" (1979: 191), and questions of national language policy are no different. Across national contexts the politics of linguistic difference and corresponding language ideological debates have reflected a variety of power relations associated with distinctive forms of nation formation. These debates vary along a number of dimensions (see Blommaert 1999); two are most relevant to the case I consider here, namely, contrasts between ideological visions for the nation and variations in the way rights are allocated to those who come to be defined as linguistic minorities.

Language policies reflect contrasting ideological visions for the future of multicultural nations and about the place of difference—cultural and linguistic—within these imagined communities. As Nancy Hornberger (2000) has noted, an ideological tension has permeated dominant language policy discourse in multilingual nations around the globe. Whereas assimilationist ideologies equating "one language-one nation" have called for standardizing monolingual policies to ensure national unity and social cohesion (Bourne 1997; Woolard and Schieffelin 1994), pluralist ideologies envision a national unity founded on the recognition of linguistic diversity. Pluralist ideologies support multilingual policies in the name of "minority" rights or needs, or, alternatively, by defining multilingualism as a valuable national resource or social good (Phillipson 2000; Coulmas 1998; Ó Riagáin and Shuibhne 1997). While globalization is giving greater symbolic currency to multilingualism in many Western nations (see Heller 1999), a countervailing resurgence of ethnic conflict and nationalist movements at the same time is reinforcing the traditional congruence between nationalism and cultural and linguistic homogenization (May 2000: 371).[3]

Projects of nation formation also create different types of linguistic minorities depending on the historical relationship subordinate peoples have to that nation's territory. As Stephen May has suggested (following Kymlicka 1995), linguistic minorities can be differentiated into two general groups: national minorities, "who have always lived in a particular territory but have been subject to conquest, colonization, or confederation" (including both indigenous and subnational populations such as the Québécois in Canada and the Welsh in the United Kingdom); and ethnic minorities, who have voluntarily migrated to and settled in a particular host nation, one already dominated by a particular cultural/linguistic population (May 2000: 380). The two types of linguistic minorities are similarly subject to processes that position them within a particular system of stratification, but they differ in terms of the resources they can draw on in asserting their linguistic rights. While national minorities can make legitimate demands on the basis of alternative national identities, ethnic minorities must work within the constraints of rights allocated on the basis of citizenship (when, that is, immigrants are granted citizenship).

Here I consider a specific moment in recent English history when a particular alignment of language educational policies provided the opportunity for Sikh immigrants to exercise citizenship rights and to challenge the dominant language hierarchy at Grange Hill High. As Jan Blommaert suggests, "there are crucial moments in history during which languages become targets of political, social and cultural intervention, and there are moments in which very little in the way of drama and crisis seem to happen" (1999: 425). The late 1980s, during the height of Thatcherism in Britain, reflects one such moment in British language history when ideological shifts brought linguistic as well as cultural and racial differences into the center of educational policy debates. This as noted was a time of great political transition, one in which a cacophony of voices were articulating a wide range of educational visions, from liberal varieties of multicultural education to more radical forms of anti-racist programming. At this moment in 1986—a little more than a year before passage of the 1988 National Education Act would silence many of these voices—politics of recognition mobilized in the name of "ethnic minority rights" became possible. The efforts of these parents in Leeds were part of a broader social movement to have "community languages" validated and incorporated as exam level subjects in British schools.

Blommaert notes, "language is being changed by debates. Political-linguistic debates intervene in sometimes brutal ways in the histories of languages and speech communities, and their effect can overrule 'spontaneous' effects of language contact or of language evolution" (1999: 435). Hence, he proposes, researchers need to look somewhat deeper into "the precise mechanisms by means of which political factors intervene in language change." This analysis of the Sikh parents' campaign provides a deeper look into a mechanism for politically asserting linguistic claims.

Claiming "Needs" and Legitimating Value

Language education policy debates are struggles over the social valuation of cultural and linguistic difference and, consequently, over the way cultural and linguistic minorities are defined and positioned within asymmetrical structural relations. They are deeply embedded in the politics of inequality in a nation and bring into play social dynamics that both challenge and reproduce unequal relations of power within plural societies (Gal 1989). In the words of Marilyn Martin-Jones and Monica Heller,

> multilingual educational practices and ideologies will be shaped by the interests of certain groups who, because of the control they exert over a particular set of highly valued material or symbolic resources, are in a position to assign value to other forms of culture and linguistic capital and to influence the operation of educational institutions that produce and distribute the most highly valued resources. (1996: 129)

This, they conclude, is how the "production and reproduction of relations of power and inequality are legitimized through ideologies of language and accomplished through local social and discursive practices in specific historical locations and in a number of institutional sites" (129).

Assigning social value to majority and minority languages entails ideological cultural politics situated in historical developments in a specific nation at a particular point in time. But locating these claims ideologically and historically does not explain how particular claims come to be viewed as legitimate by educators, parents, policymakers, or students, or, in the end, by sociolinguists. What provides the basis for legitimating claims about the value of teaching particular languages in schools? What gives authoritative power to particular ideological positions? One would imagine that in the context of educational policy debates the social value of a language would be closely tied to assessments of the educational value of learning such a language. Yet, as many sociolinguists have pointed out, those arguing for and against monolingual or multilingual policies have not always substantiated their positions with evidence from research findings (Rampton, Harris, and Leung 1997). Rather, the social value of particular types of language teaching and learning is often calculated, asserted, and legitimated through forms of discourse invoking other officially recognized idioms.

In the contested terrain of education language policy debates, "needs talk" and "rights talk" serve as powerful vehicles for asserting the value of particular linguistic policies. These idioms provide vocabularies for instantiating claims and for interpreting the legitimacy of these claims on the basis of shared assumptions about the common good (N. Fraser 1989). The political vocabulary of "rights" and "needs" is inscribed within particular paradigms of argumentation, paradigms which, as Fraser explains, are accepted as "authoritative in adjudicating conflicting claims" (1989: 164–65). In late capitalist welfare-state societies, argues Fraser,

> needs-talk functions as a medium for the making and contesting of political claims: it is an idiom in which political conflict is played out and through which inequalities are symbolically elaborated and challenged. . . . It coexists, albeit often uneasily, with talk about rights and interests at the very center of political life. Indeed, this particular juxtaposition of a discourse about needs with discourses about rights and interests is one of the distinctive marks of late capitalist political culture. (1989: 161–62, emphasis mine)

Needs and rights talk in language policy debates, as forms of recognition politics, invoke essentializing categories of group identity and assumptions about the simple correspondence of ethnic identity and language affiliation and use. The traditional equation of language, culture, and identity, in educational language policies as well as in local campaigns, as many have suggested (Collins 1999; Leung, Harris, and Rampton 1997; Hornberger 2000), relies on a form of ethnic reductionism that reifies ethnic identities (or national identity, as in the case of English-only or English standardization policies), abstracting them from the processes through which actors negotiate identities across varying social situations and over time (Gilroy 1987; S. Hall 1992; Baumann 1996). In their everyday lives, bilingual youth actively construct their own linguistic practices, identities, and relationships to "their culture" and "their language" in ways that directly contradict the reified language patterns and ethnic identities attributed to them implicitly within educational language policies (Rampton 1995; Leung, Harris, and Rampton 1997). The relationship between language and identity is further complicated by processes of cultural hybridization, processes of cultural production that occur in the spaces where cultural differences meet and are mixed in "acts of translation" (Bhabha 1994; S. Hall 1996). What this suggests is that minority languages—such as Punjabi in England—in everyday contexts of linguistic practice acquire social value in relation to a range of forces, social relational dynamics, and forms of cultural production.

The juxtaposition between the use of language as a political symbol and as enacted in everyday use brings into relief two different processes through which the social value of a minority language, Punjabi, is asserted, contested, and negotiated for different purposes and to distinctive ends. Viewing language education policy from this perspective complicates our understanding of the relationship between language education and identity. The analysis that follows demonstrates, once again, that language education policy decisions have significance in the lives of ethnic minorities that reaches beyond academic concerns into the realm of identity politics and struggles over equity and justice (Ricento 2000; Hornberger 2000; Martin-Jones and Heller 1996).

In the first section of the chapter I provide a brief overview of the educational rights and needs of ethnic minority groups as expressed in policy discourse about community language teaching in England.[4] My aim is not to provide a comprehensive analysis of the policies and debates themselves but to describe how claims instantiated within national education language policy discourse at a particular moment in British history created the possibility for minority parents to mobilize a language campaign at Grange Hill High. Next, I turn to the case study itself to explore how rights talk and needs talk were used as idioms for making political claims within this local campaign. I examine how needs and rights were alternatively invoked in dialogue about the relative value of teaching and learning Punjabi at school. The chapter concludes with an analysis of contrasts between the construction of Punjabi and its value in political discourse and the way Sikh young people related to the language across different situations in everyday life. I end with a discussion of developments in the field of community language education policy that have arisen since the parents staged their campaign. Locating the campaign in this way brings into relief the historically specific nature of identity politics within the contested field of language education policy, suggesting once again how language policy debates are deeply influenced by the political and economic concerns that become salient in the public sphere of specific nations at particular points in time.

Purposes of Language Learning: Assimilation, Access, Awareness, or Asset?

Widespread discussion of the language needs and rights of ethnic minorities in Britain began in the 1960s with the arrival of ex-colonial immigrants from Commonwealth countries, particularly India, Bangladesh, and Pakistan.[5]

Over the past forty years, language education policies in England have shifted from assimilationist to integrationist to multiculturalist or pluralist orientations and objectives. Within each of these policy orientations, arguments claiming the value of language teaching have been articulated through rhetoric of rights and needs that assumes a shared sense of the common good.

In the 1960s, language education policies represented immigrant youth as a problem that education needed to address. Their presence—and the cultural and linguistic pluralism they represented—was perceived as a threat to the purported harmonious homogeneity of the English-speaking British nation. To protect the common good—in this instance, the unity and cohesion of the nation—immigrants had to be absorbed, assimilated into the imagined national culture. Teaching English as a Second Language was the vehicle for achieving assimilation. Arguments stressing the need for intensive ESL teaching prevailed, paving the way for the passage of Section 11 of the Local Government Act of 1966 (Thompson, Fleming, and Byram 1996: 108–9).[6] Assimilationists also couched their arguments in rhetoric claiming the rights of ethnic minorities to equal access. ESL teaching, they asserted, would give immigrant children greater access to the curriculum and, therefore, to more equal educational opportunities.

The 1960s and '70s witnessed an increase in racial tensions as expressions of racist hostility were met with acts of black resistance and urban uprisings. In this era, the focus of language education debates shifted from assimilation to integration, opening the way for positions supporting the value of "mother-tongue" teaching. In 1975, a Commission of Inquiry Report, "A Language for Life" (the Bullock Report), argued that community languages were national assets. "Their bilingualism," the report stated,

is of great importance to the children and their families, and also to society as a whole. In a linguistically conscious nation in the modern world we should see it as an asset, as something to be nurtured, and one of the agencies which should nurture it is the school. Certainly the school should adopt a positive attitude to its pupils' bilingualism and wherever possible should help maintain and deepen their knowledge of their mother tongues. (DES 1975: 293–94)

The Swann Report further embraced the multiculturalist view that had gained support during the late 1970s and '80s. A central theme in the report was the value of linguistic diversity: "Within the concept of 'Education for All' there is also a need to broaden pupils' concept of language so that they no longer see it solely in terms of 'English,' and come to appreciate the positive aspects of living in a linguistically diverse society" (Swann 1985: 419). This call for greater language awareness was prompted by the Swann Report's finding that there was widespread ignorance among ethnic majority teachers about the languages and cultures of ethnic minority students. This ignorance, they assessed, contributed to the perpetuation of racist attitudes and pointed to the need for attitude change in the majority community. Changes in attitude, they concluded, would come from a deepening of the dominant populations' awareness of and appreciation for diversity.

The Swann Report gave further support for linguistic diversity by suggesting that ethnic minority languages "be given their rightful status and ... acceptance ... both as media of communication and as subjects for academic study of relevance to all pupils in multilingual Britain" (1985: 411). Hence, the report concluded, "we would expect to see community languages being built into the school timetable ... as an integral part of the curriculum" (410). In an interesting twist, however, the report argued that community language provision at the secondary level not be offered in the form of bilingual or language maintenance programs.

We would regard mother tongue maintenance, although an important educational function, as best achieved within the ethnic minority communities themselves rather than within mainstream schools. We are however wholeheartedly in favor of the teaching of ethnic minority community languages, within the languages curriculum of maintained secondary schools (state-supported schools), open to all pupils whether ethnic minority or ethnic majority.... It is important that schools should *not* assume that the demand for such provision will come solely from "mother tongue" speakers of the languages. We would hope to see a growing number of other pupils, and perhaps more importantly their parents and teachers, seeing these languages as realistic options for them. (Swann 1985: 406, 410)

Offering community languages in secondary schools would meet a national need and achieve a common good—the broadening of awareness of and appreciation for linguistic diversity. Language awareness would benefit "all"; it would contribute to creating a more tolerant and just multicultural Britain.

The Swann Report's proposals set the stage for demands that community language teaching be provided. The report provided the political capital and a vocabulary that members of ethnic minorities could use to instantiate their educational claims, in this case the right to request that Punjabi be included in the main timetable at Grange Hill High.

The Politics of Recognition at Grange Hill High

On a Monday night in early fall, Sikh parents were invited to a school meeting to discuss their proposal to introduce Punjabi classes into the school's main timetable. I arrived at the school at seven o'clock just as the meeting was about to begin. The student lounge, which earlier in the day had been full of teenagers stretched out across shabby sofas, was packed, largely with fathers, many in turbans, seated in rows of folding chairs. My eyes met those of people I knew, men who seldom occupied the same room as their worlds were separated by caste factions and class divisions.[7] The symbolic importance of this campaign, the possibility that the school would recognize Punjabi, had created a sense of solidarity.

The teachers were surprised by the turnout. They knew education was important to Sikh families, but Sikh parents seldom visited the school. The all-white teaching staff had little contact with the Sikh community; they had presumed that the lobbying effort was a pet project of one or two community activists and had no way of knowing it was so widely supported.

Teachers and administrators had come to view the lobbying effort as unjust. The school had made allowances. Beginning and Advanced Punjabi O-level exam classes were offered after school.[8] This policy was fair, I was told, for to bring Punjabi into the main timetable would "open the floodgates" to the demands of other language groups. (Jewish parents years ago had made a similar request that Hebrew be offered and had accepted the after-school compromise.)

The teachers sympathized with the parents' desire that their children learn Punjabi. Yet their efforts were violating a more fundamental social principle, the need to ensure equality of opportunity for *all* ethnic minorities. The Sikhs were perceived as wanting special privileges not available to other groups because of the way monies were allocated under policies such as Section 11. As the words of this senior administrator illustrate, conflicting views about the legitimacy of asserting collective rights triggered deep misunderstandings between faculty and parents.

I think the Sikhs in particular are very well organized and very farsighted, generally speaking, fine to deal with. But among any group you'll find those who I think are personally greedy, ah, want more than, you know, they ordinarily get out of the system, and they're ready to accuse you of racism as soon as they find that they're not going to get what they want. And that's very upsetting because, particularly in a school like this where we want to give equal opportunity to all ethnic groups. And I mean all. . . .

See, the West Indians have no reason, have they, to get money out of Section 11. They have no obvious individuality except for being black. They don't have a different religion, they don't have a different language—they do, but essentially it's the same thing. They don't have any culture that one recognizes as being specifically theirs. But they're different. I feel they do have a very serious predicament. But Sikhs can say, "Yes, we have a different culture, we have a different language, we have a different religion, we have a different dress, you know, we've got the lot."

Teachers and administrators judged the legitimacy of asserting collective rights from what could be characterized as an orthodox liberal position, a position that stands in direct opposition to the principles on which recognition politics are based (May 2000: 375–76). The parents' demands challenged a liberal sense of fairness and justice. Granting what they viewed as special rights to one group would undermine the strict impartiality that ensured fair play. The collective rights demanded by ethnic or religious groups in Britain were also "by definition, inimical to individual rights" (Kymlicka 1995: 35). Privileging what is good for the collective can, from a liberal perspective, deny individuals the freedom to pursue other social goods.

The positions taken by school faculty conflated a liberal concern for protecting individual rights with an educational concern with meeting academic needs. Sikh parents, they worried, did not have their children's academic needs in mind. Learning Punjabi in place of French or chemistry was not a wise academic choice: in the competition for jobs in Britain or Europe Punjabi would not be of much value. To become successful, Sikh students "needed" to assimilate, to learn to speak and write "standard" English and, perhaps, French or German.

The words of another school administrator clearly express this liberal view:

If any pupils in this school find that their timetable is being totally mismanaged in order to accommodate Punjabi, they will have a legitimate complaint. And that is one of the things I am worried about. I'm also worried about excessive privilege to one group, or two groups. I'm also concerned about the individual who gets pressurized into doing something by his parents which is *not really in his interest, because there is a fine chance that Punjabi is not really the best thing for them*, you know, in the time available.[9]

Sikh parents at Grange Hill High largely supported the effort to have Punjabi introduced into the school's mainstream curriculum regardless of whether they wanted their children to study Punjabi at school. Their opinions concerning the educational value of these classes tended to correspond to their class aspirations. Parents who thought strategically about education as a vehicle for achieving professional success or social mobility, while they wanted their children to know Punjabi, questioned the value of taking these classes during school hours. They wanted their children to acquire the knowledge and skills—including the languages—that universities or employers would recognize as useful. In the words of one father,

I think reading and writing are not very important ... we mostly speak Punjabi in the house. So they can converse, have conversation in Punjabi, no problem. Not very deep, but.... And they know a few words and they can start writing and reading, I think that could be beneficial.... You know the people in the meeting when the question was put, do you want them to not learn the other language, French perhaps, they do not want them to learn the language, you know, that's just nonsense. We've got to, we don't want to be just in Punjab, we want to be in the world theatre. Not only one small little state. So we want our kids to have that kind of education. I don't want my kids just, of course I want them to know that they are Punjabis, they are Indians, but I don't want them to just compete in Punjab. I want to see them in the whole in the countries and in the whole world.

Some of the parents who were more devoted to the Sikh faith or who identified with Sikh ethnicity viewed their children's educational needs differently. The purpose of education was not simply tied to future work trajectories. Being "successful" also meant becoming a "proper Sikh." If children were to understand and appreciate their faith and their traditions, they needed to know Punjabi, and they would learn Punjabi more effectively at school since they would take these classes seriously.

Sikh students at Grange Hill High expressed a range of reactions to the Punjabi classes. Some appreciated the opportunity to obtain an additional O-level grade, while those in the top college preparatory sets did not want to take Punjabi if it meant giving up exam courses they needed to get into university. Students not headed to university also questioned the value of studying Punjabi at school. They wondered how prospective employers would evaluate an O-level grade in Punjabi? One young man concluded, "The last thing that will impress an employer is a Punjabi O-level. If you have to give up a science for a Punjabi O-level that is really bad. And if they offer it all the parents will want their kids to take it. Bad news."

Some of the boys wondered how their peers would view their taking Punjabi. "Going to Indian class" was simply not cool. As Mohinder and

Gurdip explained, studying Punjabi after school, like all homework, took time away from important activities.

Mohinder: Most Sikhs don't go, 'cause you've got schooling in English, and that's. . . .
Gurdip: Homework and all.
Mohinder: Yeah, you've got your homework and everything. And then you want time, if you've got your girlfriend, you want time with 'er, and time to do the social things, like you go to clubs and things like that. You won't have much time if you go to Indian class 'cause you won't get off till about seven. So. . . .
Gurdip: Like some people prefer to watch television, they didn't wanna go down and learn some Punjabi.

Then there were other young Sikhs at Grange Hill High for whom the value of learning Punjabi had nothing to do with exam grades, conflicting academic interests, or the demands of keeping up a particular social image. These young people found learning Punjabi—at home, at the temple, and at school—a deeply meaningful experience. These youth—often but not exclusively girls—spoke of learning to read the sacred texts as profoundly moving, for it brought them closer to their parents and to a religion that was important to them. Still others chose to study Punjabi at school or at the temple more out of respect for their parents, because it was important to their families that they do so.

Still, most of the Sikh students I spoke with expressed some ambivalence about learning Punjabi at school. The idea of studying Punjabi in an otherwise English-dominated environment was still new and strange. Until recently, aspects of their lives lived through Punjabi had been completely segregated from the worlds they inhabited through English. The ambiance of Punjabi sounds and expressions infused the emotional tone of domestic intimacy, particularly with their mothers, who, if they had come from villages in Punjab, often spoke little English. It was the channel for communicating with loved ones in lands far away. Punjabi is the language of religion, providing the sounds that accompany the rhythms of ritual and the words that tell fantastic stories of the mystical adventures of the Sikh Gurus who embody the spirit of Sikhism. Many young Sikhs, religious and nonreligious alike, cherish these Punjabi-colored spaces, even if their understanding of Sikh religious and folk traditions is as partial as their knowledge of the language itself. Sukhvinder, age fifteen, spoke with great reverence of her relationship to Punjabi.

Sukhvinder: My dad's got lots of religious books, he wraps them all up and he's got them locked away, and you know, 'cause once my mom says, "You should try reading it," you know. 'Cause we've got a *Janam-sakhis*, it's kind of like the birth and the life of Guru Nanak Sahib and everything he said, you know, because he wrote it himself. Right up to when he died. So everything he ever did, all the miracles and everything, it's all written down. She said, "It'd be really good for you, you'd be able to know all the history of Sikhs." I read it a couple of times and sort of, I don't know what happened, and I just stopped reading it. And I said that I'd pick it up, but now I've got lots of homework and I don't really. And my dad didn't realize that I could read it. He thought it would be a bit too hard for me. So one Sunday he said, "Okay, I want to know, just read it to me." And he was fairly impressed.

KH: Where'd you learn to read Punjabi?

Sukhvinder: Well, I went to the temple for about one and a half years and picked it up from there, right, and. . . .

KH: How old were you?

Sukhvinder: Well I was, um, in the second year [thirteen years old], but when I came here I stopped. But I go after school now as well.

KH: After school here?

Sukhvinder: Yeah, 'cause, at first we didn't really want to do it. But, you know, my dad. . . .

Her friend: She wanted to do netball.

Sukhvinder: Yeah [laughter], but my dad said, that well, you know, "Why don't you do it?" And I said, "Okay then." I didn't want to. I did it, and now I think that, you know, it's okay 'cause it's pretty good. I'll finish an extra O-level and I think I'll easily get that, oh, now I'm bragging [laughs]. I think I'll get that but, it's definitely important that I can *speak the religion*, I mean speak the language, but I'm not, I don't think it's so important that I can be writing letters and reading books and everything. Because most of my relatives that are Sikh are in England, and I speak Indian with the parents, but English with the kids, the older ones. 'Cause it's not like I go to India very often. We're planning to go this December, but it's going to be after years, so many years.

Young Sikhs appreciate their parents' sense of loss in coming to Britain and their fear that future generations will not have a way of relating to a religion and traditions they feel a part of intimately. They will no longer be able to "speak the religion." Some feel a responsibility to learn the language to protect their culture's future in Britain. Yet, as this discussion with three Sikh boys depicts, even when they feel the need to learn Punjabi to protect their culture, other educational needs, such as job training, take priority during school time.

KH: So are you guys taking Punjabi before school or after school?

Ajit: No.

Harpal: I will only be doing it once a week because on Thursday mornings. . . .

Gurdip: Yeah, we have to go to college [job-training classes at a college of further education].

Harpal: We have to go to college so we can't make it on Thursday mornings.

Gurdip: Yeah, I'll only do it once a week as well.

Harpal: So I'll go on Tuesdays and that's it.

KH: Yeah. Are you taking it?

Sat: Yeah, but I might pack it in. 'Cause I learn at Sikh temple. Bit too, you know, much.

Gurdip: You know, on Thursdays, well, it's not really important for me to come Thursdays because I've been at the Sikh temple for three years and, you know, I've been revising it there and, you know, I'm past the stage where I have to revise every day, kind of.

KH: So you're going to do an O-level though?

Gurdip: Yeah. . . .

KH: Is it important to you?

Harpal: I think it is important. It's our mother culture and that. If no one here learns it, right, our Sikh community's going to fade away. It won't be there, it won't exist anymore. So I think, if you learn it right, it will be passed on to generation to generation, so it will still be there. And that's what I think. Keep it there, and that's it.

British Sikh teenagers use Punjabi in a variety of ways in everyday life. Punjabi mediates their relationship to their family, their religion, their community, and the homeland of their parents. Yet, they learn to use and value Punjabi situationally. At school, speaking Punjabi may mark them as inferior and can prompt teasing from English friends. But, as these same boys explained, Punjabi provides a useful weapon in fighting back.

KH: Do you ever speak Punjabi with your brothers and sisters?

Harpal: Sometimes yeah.

KH: Do you ever speak Punjabi with your friends?

Ajit: Never.

Gurdip: No. If we ever do it in front of our own friends, right, they kind of humiliate us, they feel we sound like this to them, "bbbbb," and that we sound daft. But to us we can understand it. But they can't.

Ajit: We have an advantage because we can talk about them and they can't understand us.

Harpal: Secret weapon [laughter]. We'll use it. It's just that Jason West gets on our nerves sometimes and, ah, we speak in our language what we think about him.

Ajit: He gets mad and he starts swearing at us. . . .

KH: Do your friends ever want to learn Punjabi? Or do they mainly just ask you about swear words?

Gurdip: They just ask you about, you know, words that is good for them because they just go and say something to Gurnam [a Sikh boy known to be big and tough], you know, something bad. And, you know, they try to impress him that I can do this as well. You know what I mean, you know, they kind of, they don't get the, all the other words kind of like, so they don't get all the technical that we speak, you know. They just want him to stop pushing or, so they just. . . .

KH: So they just want swear words so they can swear at people?

Harpal: Yeah. . . .

Ajit: So we sort of start teaching um the wrong words then they start yelling chocolate 'round the streets. And they start shouting chocolate outside people's houses. And all the Indian people inside are laughing their heads off [laughs].

The use of Punjabi within inter-ethnic peer groups, what Rampton (1995) refers to as "language crossing," was not common in interactions I observed at Grange Hill High, contrary to what Rampton has found in his work with British adolescents in the Midlands. Yet Punjabi and other South Asian languages are the common currency of British Asian youth cultural forms, particularly British Asian music (Sharma, Hutnyk, and Sharma 1996) as well as Indian films (Gillespie 1995). The rise of the British Asian music scene has created a unique site for linguistic innovation, one in which languages from across the South Asian subcontinent are mixed with Afro-Caribbean, African American, and other dialects of English and American English to create new hybrid linguistic forms. Together with its mix of music rhythms and styles—from hip-hop to bhangra, Bollywood to reggae—British Asian music draws from a range of languages in lyrics that give expression to issues and to interests of Asian youth in Britain and throughout the diaspora. Indian music and film also express messages in and are consumed through Punjabi; for Punjabi can mediate the consumption of these media, as Sikh families watching Hindi or Punjabi films discuss what they see and hear in a mixture of Punjabi and English.

As they move through the social worlds that make up their everyday lives, Sikh teens actively construct linguistic practices that use a mixture of linguistic forms and styles in relation to influences, expectations, and interests that are situational and shifting. Sikh teens assess and reassess the value of Punjabi as they participate in different types of social interaction, media consumption, and cultural events.

Punjabi: A Modern Foreign Language

The campaign itself was largely unsuccessful. Punjabi in the short term continued to be taught at the margins of the regular school day. But in the years that followed, a national policy was put into effect that paved the way for Punjabi, along with other community languages, to be included in the curriculum of British secondary schools.

Shortly after the campaign ended, Parliament passed the 1988 Education Reform Act that have instituted a national curriculum in Britain. In the years that have followed, heated debates about the purposes and practices of language education have been waged. Assimilationist and pluralist positions have continued to frame new controversies over two aspects of the national curriculum in particular—the National English and Modern Foreign Languages Curricula.

The development of the National English Curriculum resulted in "the great grammar divide" in which battle lines were drawn between pro-grammar conservatives and linguists. Endless reports over the years have taken different stands on the value of teaching "standard" English as well as on which local dialects should qualify as "standard" (Cameron 1995).

Issues concerning community language teaching are now addressed under the auspices of the Modern Foreign Languages Curriculum. The Harris Report (DES 1990), which set the parameters for the National Curriculum on foreign language teaching, highlighted a national need for students to learn to use and understand a diverse range of languages. The report recommended that bilingual students, paradoxically, be given the opportunity to study their home languages as foreign languages. The report identified nineteen languages as eligible for inclusion in the National Curriculum. "Modern Foreign Languages in the National Curriculum," published in 1995, required that an official working language of the European Union be offered in schools. But schools could also choose to provide courses in any of the other nineteen languages for which GCE and A-level exams were offered, namely Arabic, Bengali, Chinese (Mandarin or Cantonese) Dutch, French, German, modern Greek, Gujerati, modern Hebrew, Italian, Japanese, Persian, Punjabi, Polish, Portuguese, Russian, Spanish, Turkish, and Urdu. A new version of the curriculum, "Modern Foreign Languages, the National Curriculum for England" produced in 1999, responded to pressure for the inclusion of additional languages—notably those spoken by more recent immigrants and refugees—by ending the practice of designating specific languages. The European language requirement, however, was maintained.

Punjabi, together with other community languages, seems to have a secure place in the National Curriculum of England—as a foreign language. Students at Grange Hill High can now take Punjabi as a modern foreign language along with French, German, Spanish, Urdu, and Italian—and the school's website boasts that students have taken GCSEs in Chinese. Punjabi has been recognized—as foreign. In multicultural Britain, linguistic diversity might be celebrated, but true multilingualism continues to exist only in an imagined future nation.[10]

4. "Becoming like Us"

Take, for example, an educational institution: the disposal of its space, the meticulous regulations which govern its internal life, the different activities which are organized there, the diverse persons who live there or meet one another there ... all these things constitute a block of capacity-communication power. The activity which ensures ... the acquisition of aptitudes or types of behavior is developed there by means of a whole ensemble of regulated communications (lessons, questions and answers, orders, exhortations, coded signs of obedience, differentiation marks of the "value" of each person and of the levels of knowledge) and by means of a whole series of power processes (enclosure, surveillance, reward and punishment, the pyramidal hierarchy).

—Foucault (1982: 787)

In the public sphere of democratic nations, education, as we have seen, is a critical site for imagining national futures and creating ideal citizens.[1] But while few would deny the importance of education to democracy and citizenship, scholars have actually presented quite divergent views of what it is, exactly, that schools accomplish.

Two classic paradigms have emerged over the years in scholarship concerned with the role of education in modern nations. On the one hand, theorists from Durkheim (1977) to Parsons (1959), emphasizing the value of consensus and equilibrium in society, have framed education's integrative function in a positive light, as contributing to the maintenance of social order through the socialization of the next generation. Marxist theorists, on the other hand, have tended to look behind dominant forms of consensus in capitalist societies to consider how domination, or hegemony, is won through an acceptance, as "common sense," of the values, beliefs, and interests of the groups who benefit from the way society is structured. Schools do pass on and therein valorize particular cultural values, tastes, perspectives, and attitudes that may provide a type of social glue. But the educational sanctioning of particular cultural traditions over others contributes to the reproduction of relations of inequality; it reinforces the dominant status quo supported by a "social order."

Marxist scholars have long been concerned with understanding the central role educational institutions play in reproducing forms of inequality in capitalist societies (Althusser 1971; see Giroux 1983). More recent work in this vein, however, has moved away from earlier models of either structural (Bowles and Gintis 1976) or cultural reproduction (Bourdieu and Passeron 1977; Bourdieu 1984), to consider the role of agency in processes of cultural production, or the ways young people resist or rework reproductive forces in schools, and through creative play produce new cultural forms and identifications (Willis 1977; Foley 1990; Levinson, Foley, and Holland 1996; Stambach 2000). In this chapter I draw on formulations of cultural production as well as the work of poststructuralist Michel Foucault in analyzing the making and marking of difference in everyday practice at Grange Hill High.

Schools are sites in which people come together from various social worlds to construct and enact the rituals and routines of schooling in everyday practice. These rituals and routines entail two distinctive but related educational processes: the intentional or overt pedagogical practices, or direct teaching and learning in classrooms, and what has been referred to as the "hidden curriculum," or the values, beliefs, and norms that are transmitted tacitly through the social relations, expectations, and routines enacted during day-to-day life in schools (Giroux 1983; McLaren 1994). These normative routines and rituals of schooling are central mechanisms in processes of subject formation.

Our understanding of the mechanisms of power in modern schools has been greatly enhanced by the work of Foucault. He has revolutionized the way we view the role of schooling in modern society as well as the relationship between knowledge and power more generally. Foucault's work diverges significantly from traditional Marxist or functionalist formulations that locate power within the state-economy-school nexus. For Foucault, power is not simply a matter of political, economic, or social influence, of forces that work through the functioning of oppressive economic, state, or patriarchal systems. Power is diffuse or "capillary," working throughout the social body. Its force is neither negative nor coercive but productive and regulative.

Educational institutions, argues Foucault, socialize students through the productive power of disciplinary practices. Schools produce modern subjects or "useful individuals." They exercise techniques of correct training and systems of gratification/punishment that divide, rank, and normalize individuals. Knowledge acquired through such techniques as surveillance and the examination, or what Foucault calls "the normalizing gaze," "makes it possible to qualify, to classify, and to punish. It establishes over individuals a visibility through which one differentiates them and judges them" (1995: 184).

The ordering of individuals within hierarchies of normalization involves techniques of discipline and regulation that penetrate into the smallest details of everyday life. This is the basis of power's "capillary" functioning. Power is exercised through numerous surveillance and ordering techniques, including the organization of space, the distribution of individuals within these architectural spaces, and the structuring of time.[2] Schools achieve order, not through repression or prohibition, but through "the means of correct training." Schools are, in Phil Corrigan's words, "productive—differentially productive—of subjectivities, or social identities" (1987: 31). Schools attempt to fix subjectivities, to regulate, normalize, stratify, punish, reward, and thereby marginalize possible forms of human diversity: "to make difference equal disadvantage."

In this chapter, I turn to the school and to an analysis of the multiple discourses of difference that normalize and organize social relations at Grange Hill High. I consider the dominant discourse about difference—the common sense or taken-for-granted "knowledge" that informs and legitimates classificatory systems and status hierarchies within which Sikh and other Asian students are identified and positioned. Within discourse about difference are inscribed moral values and sensibilities, aesthetic tastes and appreciations, collective aspirations and normative expectations that teachers and students bring with them from their white and middle-class worlds. These discourses, I will argue, position students in relation to a number of identity constructs and classificatory systems that define, order, and thereby produce subjectivity among those defined as "normal" or as "different"; moreover, they provide symbolic resources that students use in fashioning subcultural identities that either conform to or contest the dominant relations of power in the school.

Sikh students, together with other non-mainstream students at Grange Hill High, find themselves and their lives represented and classified in relation to a number of normalizing judgments and corresponding status hierarchies. Their place of residence, placement in the school's set structure, choices in clothing and appearance, and classroom communicative styles are all identified and evaluated by white middle-class students and teachers alike in relational terms, on the basis of how "they," the others, compare to "us." Sikh students are "disciplined" by these normalizing judgments; and those who wish "to succeed" in school are required to conform to these expectations, to assimilate or "become like us."

Social Integration at Grange Hill High

Grange Hill is a comprehensive high school. Comprehensive schools in Britain were first instituted during the late 1950s and early '60s to bring students together under one roof regardless of their ability. The 1944 Education Act had required for the first time that local authorities provide "secondary education for all." But when this act was passed, secondary education for all separated students on the basis of an intelligence test—the eleven plus exam—into three types of schools (grammar, secondary modern, and vocational schools).[3] While the 1944 Act had aimed to create greater educational opportunity for the working classes, it was evident that student scores on the eleven plus exam were more a reflection of environment or class background than of "innate intelligence." These findings lent support to what during the 1950s had been isolated educational experiments—the creation of comprehensive schools as a way to unify the secondary system.[4] At first, comprehensive schools were instituted alongside the existing tripartite system. But in 1965 the then Labour government decided it was time "to end selection at eleven plus and to eliminate separatism in secondary education." They called on local education authorities to submit plans "for reorganizing secondary education in their areas on comprehensive lines" (from Circular 10/65, quoted in Lawson and Silver 1973: 439).

Grange Hill High is a child of the 1960s. The school's architectural style attests to these beginnings. Standing back from the road, the red brick school is a configuration of rectangular tri-floored structures encompassing a central outdoor patio. Separate and more temporary looking structures dot the periphery of the schoolyard; some of these contain classrooms.

A larger two-story structure houses the sixth form offices, classrooms, student lounge, and study areas. The main building fills with light, as the inner and outer walls are lined with windows from floor to ceiling in certain first floor sections. Sitting in their classrooms or moving through the halls, students and staff look out to the courtyard or across the football (or soccer) fields, the netball courts, and the parking lots to the red brick, red roofed, semi-detached houses on the tree-lined streets of this middle-class neighborhood of Moortown. A vast sense of space, leafy and looming large without, light and airy within, gives this school a "suburban" middle-class feel.

Despite Grange Hill High's solidly middle-class location and its homogeneous all-white teaching and administrative staff, the students came from quite separate and segregated social worlds. For many of the white middle-class students, daily encounters at Grange Hill provided the first and only opportunity to interact with people from class and cultural backgrounds different from their own. Their time outside school is spent quite sequestered in a very white and (Yorkshire) English middle-class world. Their "knowledge" about people from different cultures and classes is derived from what could be characterized as middle-class "folk legends" and from stereotypic media images and "moral panics."

Grange Hill High has always been mixed ethnically. During the 1970s, 30 to 40 percent of the staff and student body were Jewish and the school regularly closed for the Jewish holidays. Since then, the number of Jewish staff and students has decreased considerably. At the time I carried out my research, Jewish students made up only 11 percent of the student body. Asians had become the largest ethnic minority group in the school, approximately 18 percent of the student population. Afro-Caribbeans constituted about 5 percent of the student body, and another 5 percent were from European ethnic backgrounds, primarily Polish or Greek. There were, however, no persons of Asian or Afro-Caribbean origin on staff (with the exception of the two Sikh men who taught Punjabi language classes after school).

Students in this multiracial school not only come from different class, religious, and cultural backgrounds, they live in what are perceived to be quite distinctive areas of Leeds as well. The school's catchment area contains this middle-class area of Moortown, a neighborhood directly to the south called Chapel Allerton, and an infamous inner city area called Chapeltown. These neighborhoods have served as stepping stones in the path of successive waves of residential mobility. Following the mobility patterns of Jewish families, a substantial number of Sikh families had moved "up" and north from Chapeltown to Moortown, followed by fewer economically successful Afro-Caribbean families. These ethnic success stories have been played out in the halls of Grange Hill High—first by Jews, who had by then moved out to the upper-middle-class suburbs on the fringes of Leeds, and more recently by Asians, particularly Sikhs. Many Sikh families in fact moved into houses vacated by Jewish families. Yet in spite of these demographic changes Moortown is today, as it was in the late 1980s, predominantly white and middle class.

In striking contrast to middle-class Moortown, Chapeltown is considered the quintessential inner city area. Students who come to Grange Hill High from Chapeltown tend to be lower class and "black" (Afro-Caribbean and Asian). Most of these students find themselves placed in the middle to lower ability sets and tend to leave school after their O-level/CSE exams at sixteen. The upper ability sets are primarily the domain, of middle-class students: the majority white, the minority Asian, together with one or two Afro-Caribbean students. Students in the upper sets tend to stay on after sixteen in the sixth form in order to study for their A-level exams at eighteen before moving on to pursue some form of higher education.

To members of the white middle class in Leeds, Chapeltown is known as a no-go area, one through which Moortown residents travel by car or bus to reach the shopping arcades in the city center. White middle-class residents of Moortown experience Chapeltown only through glimpses caught through the windows of moving vehicles. Their knowledge about Chapeltown and its residents consists largely of media representations and local stereotypes. Few whom I spoke with had ever set foot in Chapeltown. Even fewer knew, beyond mere acquaintance, anyone who actually lived there. Yet, in spite of their lack of personal knowledge, most assumed they knew what Chapeltown was really like. What I came to see as the dominant taken-for-granted view of this area was communicated to me by James, a white sixth former, as he mapped his social life for me geographically.[5]

James: I pass Chapeltown on the way to town, 'cause you know the way to go, if you're driving in you have to go drive that way. It's not because of the people. It's because the actual area is just so depressed and it's just such a, there's no motivation, there's just no enthusiasm for anything. You know what I mean? But there's just no sort of get up and go. It's not like they've all given up, but it's just they've got nothing to go for. Nobody gives a toss, so why should we sort it.

KH: So do any of your friends ever go down to Chapeltown?

James: Ah, I wouldn't of thought so. When you said go down what do you mean, socialize?

KH: Just sort of walk around and. . . .

James: Oh, no, no.

KH: Go to Foxes [a club] or. . . .

James: Oh, yeah, though Foxes in a way isn't ethnically mixed really. It's a place that happens to be on the edge. It is on the edge 'cause it's more sort of Chapel Allerton, sort of, it is on the edge and it's not very mixed, and yes we do go to Foxes. It's only 'cause it's near the Regent [a pub], which is near the police station.

James's comments reflect some of the concerns many middle-class white people have about the area. They perceive it and its residents as being depressed, economically and spiritually, without hope, lacking in motivation. It is a sad and depressing situation. But nobody in Chapeltown seems to "give a toss," so why should outsiders try to do anything about it, particularly when it isn't safe for them to be there?

Memories of the urban protests (or "riots" as they are known by outsiders) in Leeds in 1981 and 1985 continue to color the feelings many middle-class white people have about Chapeltown. This can be seen in the way Lizzy, a middle-class sixth former, describes her reaction to Chapeltown and to the low-income neighborhood of Harehills next to it.

Well I tend not to like going down to Chapeltown or Harehills because of all the riots we had. . . . Big riots, petrol bombs and things like that. And I always think of them as the areas where the shops get boarded up and it's more violent than other areas. And I wouldn't wander around any of them on my own. Mind, I wouldn't wander around Roundhay [an ethnically mixed neighborhood next to Moortown] on my own at night. But I think more so Harehills and Chapeltown.

James, Lizzy, and their friends tend not to cross the socio-spatial borderlands marked by race, class, and cultural differences. In fact, they seldom recognize the workings of race or class inequality in their everyday lives. As James informed me when I asked him why there were so few Afro-Caribbean students (two girls and one boy) in the sixth form, "A lot of people don't think about it. There's no need to unless someone like yourself comes along." Racial inequality, to them, was largely an abstract issue, a problem to be tackled in classroom discussions or in answering essay exams.

Well the thing is, you see, because of, in the poorer areas it tends to be an issue all the time—race, color—because there's nothing else for them to argue about, as it were. And you've got to channel your aggression somewhere, it's a *natural* way to live. Where in a sixth form or comprehensive school, where you've all got one interest, getting your A-levels, you just tend to forget about it totally. The thing is, people tend to, like in general studies lessons, bring up the argument for the sake of it, so you've got to know it and expect to write essays on it, 'cause I've got to write basic essays on race, and race and class, and race in society, etcetera. So that's the only time you really think about it, and even then it's from a superficial point of view of what you know. So it's, unless I went out and talked to people in lesson and said, "Hey what do you really think about this," I wouldn't know, I'd just talk about what I think. So you tend to get a bigoted view anyway, I suppose.

Tracey, a middle-class resident of Moortown, was one of the three Afro-Caribbean students in the sixth form. In discussing her fellow sixth formers, she characterized their attitudes toward inequality as apathetic, shallow, and uninformed, reflecting the distanced and detached perspective that privilege provides.

And they're too boring as well. They're really dead [laughs]. They do, it's like we are having this conversation now, things that are happening in the world, outside of Grange Hill, don't concern them. They all run around trying to be grown up about everything and they're not. They're really babyish. Everything is, "Well what will mummy and daddy say." And they pretend that they're all grown up and everything's nice and happy. Things like racism, "Racism? I don't know what you're talking about. You don't discuss things like that." And you know, they're really shallow. They don't think about things like that because it doesn't concern them.

However ill-informed or partial, white middle-class stereotypes of the lives of lower-class people of color are taken for granted at Grange Hill High. Knowledge informed by the lived experiences of those outside the margins of the mainstream for the most part remain publicly unspoken, silenced by the power and authority of middle-class white discourse.

After I had known Tracey for a few months, I ran into her in the hallway one day between classes. She was upset and needed to talk. She was still reeling from a particularly disturbing discussion in her general studies class about "the inner city." Tracey's account of this encounter portrays vividly the social distance and tensions that separated her from the teacher and from her fellow classmates. They demonstrate, yet again, how very difficult it is to communicate across racialized class divisions, historic differences, and the deep fears they can generate.

Tracey: Oh god, I've got to tell you about this. General studies lesson. It was awful. I mean, I've never been so upset, I mean I have to face racism every day anyway, 'cause that's, you know. I went into the lesson, there were about twenty-five of us. We were having a lesson about inner city areas and Chapeltown's an inner city area. And the teacher was going on, she started off, I thought, okay, I thought, she's trying to be neutral about the whole thing, she's not saying, "Wow, Chapeltown's really good," or "Wow, Chapeltown's really really bad." She started going on about her personal experiences, when she went down there she had to go with her friend 'cause she was so frightened, she thought someone was going to jump out and attack her. And I said, "Jump out and attack you, why?" 'Cause I mean if you go down to Chapeltown they will not interfere with you, especially if they haven't seen you before, they're not going to do anything, you know, mug you or anything. "What do you mean you had to go with your friend?"

"Well, I mean, you don't know what it's like down there, all those black people. You know, they're more or less savages."

KH: She said that?

Tracey: Yeah. And I said, "Look," and I was getting really really mad and I was trying to keep it cool, 'cause when I'm having an argument, I'd rather say, than, you know, lash out like, 'cause if anyone who lived in Chapeltown had been there, she would have been on the floor. I mean, that's happened at this school anyway. Girls have hit their teachers. And I thought, no, be calm Tracey, sit down and have a real "civilized" debate about it. And I was trying to talk to her and she wouldn't let me talk, so she stood up in front, and she said, "Would you stop hollering, Tracey." I said, "I'm not hollering, I'm trying to speak to you." And every time I put my hand up she wouldn't, she just went past like, oh yeah, she liked listening to all the guys who were saying how um, "Oh, NF, NF. White Britain. White Britain." And I was going, "Oh god, can you hear what the guys are saying in the back, can I say something please?"

And she said, "Don't get so touchy about these things. You're overreacting, you're being paranoid." I mean, you've heard them all before, they all came out. She was going on and on and on, and I was getting really upset about it and I said,

"Look can I say something please?" And then I just had to stand up and I just had to say what I had to say, and I said, "Do you mind?"

"Oh, Chapeltown's a red light area. It can't be helped. The poor people down there."

"If there are poor people down there it's because the government isn't doing anything for them." They're not destroying the houses, the um, the rubbish doesn't get cleared sometimes and the mice, it's a mess. All the houses have been there since the eighteenth century. You know the old Victorian houses, they've still got them, and after all it's disgusting, they should do something about it.

"Well, the local government are doing all they can. Well, we won't talk about that now. We'll change the subject."

And I thought, "Oh god, no!"

Tracey had come to talk to me about this event in confidence, which did not allow me to ask the teacher about what had happened. I must qualify, too, that during my time at Grange Hill High students reported only two cases of teachers expressing prejudicial views. Most of the teachers I grew to know there were deeply concerned about social issues and were dedicated to making a significant contribution in the lives of students of color. Many felt that teaching was a kind of mission, a way to give students the opportunities they believed education could provide. But in the silences more than in what was spoken, in the lack of precise knowledge about or shared experience in the worlds from which these students came, teachers, often unknowingly and unintentionally, reinscribed the cultural boundaries that made students of color sense their difference and realize that race did matter.

As Tracey continued to talk, to process her feelings about the encounter, she expressed ambivalent feelings about Chapeltown. Her family had moved to "the suburbs" surrounding the school. They were "successful" Afro-Caribbeans who had been ostracized by the Chapeltown black community for "selling out," for becoming "coconuts" (black on the outside, white on the inside). While socially distant from her white peers, Tracey also felt socially as well as geographically separated from the "black" lower-class world her family had left behind.

But the thing about Chapeltown, and it's weird, because, it's one of these places where, even if you're black, if you live there and then you leave there, you can't come back, it's like you're selling out, do you know what I mean? So I used to live in Chapeltown, but that was a long time ago, and then I moved and I started living in what is called a suburban residential area now, and if I went back to Chapeltown, it's, "You think you're white," you know, dirty looks, the lot, you know, and you think, grrr, get out, I mean it's really bad. . . . When I go down, right, I think, I go down there a lot 'cause I still have relatives and things, when I go down I think, I feel okay. It's you I feel sorry for because it's not, it's like they've been all boxed up together in quarters. The houses are in bad condition, the air is in bad condition, there's prostitution, drugs, and that sort of thing, and there's the violence with the police and everything, and the police here are pretty bad as well and they tend to stop and search and all this lot and when they don't need to. And they like to pick up black guys off the streets and things. It's nowhere as bad as Harlem, 'cause we haven't got guys injecting stuff or, that's what I see on TV, I don't know what it's like. That's the other thing about Chapeltown, it's got its disadvantages in bad housing and things, but when you go down, you know you'll feel okay. The music's good, everyone seems so happy, and everyone knows everyone. It's like a village.

Tracey's views of Chapeltown, like her teacher's, expressed compassion for the people trapped in such "bad conditions." But unlike her teacher, Tracey did not fear these conditions. Her words captured the nuanced vision and contradictory feelings of an outsider/insider who had personal ties to and had experienced everyday life in Chapeltown. She also, interestingly, realized the limits of her own knowledge about life in Harlem, a place she had only seen on television.

The teacher's construction of Chapeltown (from Tracey's account), similar to middle-class student discourse, was complicated not by direct experience but by issues of separation, ignorance, and fear. These folks "know" Chapeltown only through images and representations. They live their lives unaware of and uninvolved in the cultural worlds of the racial and class "others" attending Grange Hill High. Yet their discourse, their conceptions of otherness, the images of difference they imagined, when imposed, possess a power to define, order, and evaluate: to create subjectivities that marginalized and excluded those who are so defined. Gurnam, a Sikh who lives in Chapeltown, expressed anger at the thought that a body of "knowledge" had the power to name and prejudge, marginalize and silence his world and his experience. Knowledge grounded in ignorance, he argued, should not have more authority than knowledge gained from experience.

'Cause people have different opinions of Chapeltown, they say that every person what's from there is violent 'cause the riots and what happened there. . . . Yeah they always say, well don't go down Chapeltown, they're all drug pushers. Now, to get to say that, you must get to know the neighborhood in Chapeltown. Until you do that you cannot force an opinion upon anybody else. . . . I mean if you don't live there you can't really see what it's like. I mean, if you were still living in America now, you couldn't exactly say that the English are stubborn, stupid, or something, anything you want to think of them, unless you really get to know em.

Few white middle-class students at Grange Hill High ever did "really see" or "really get to know" what life is like in Chapeltown or Harehills, for they lived their lives secluded in segregated social worlds. Yet, Grange Hill High did provide a context in which individual students from different cultural, racial, and class backgrounds could meet and interact. At school, students got to know one another in their classes or while participating in extracurricular activities, and they continued to socialize at lunch and during break. Many white students, particularly the girls, had Asian friends at school, usually Asian students who were in the same set classes. Friendship groups that formed during lunch and at break times included some mixed groupings, most often groups of white girls that included a single Asian girl or Asian girls in a group joined by a single white girl. But at the events I attended after school hours with Asian or with white students, I found much greater segregation. With few exceptions, racial integration happened only at school.

My sense of the limits of school integration was confirmed by others I spoke with at Grange Hill High. Mr. Crompton, a quite thoughtful history teacher, was among those who reinforced this view. I spent many enjoyable hours talking to this insightful and good-humored teacher about topics ranging from cricket to California, classic rock to class mobility, working-class clubs to racial politics. As the resident long-haired, gray-bearded hippie, he took the lead in supervising the audio-visual side of performances and dances, and each year gathered around him a diverse group of students he referred to as his "road crew." During one of our conversations, the topic turned to prejudice and to the role integrated schools like Grange Hill High played in bridging racial divisions.

Mr. Crompton: Racism's been endemic in every society that's ever been. It's the fear of the unknown, it's the fear of the stranger. Ah, I mean, I can't actually ever see it, people will always be afraid of strangers. You know, I mean, perhaps you ought to say that should be the job of the educational system to stop, somehow to stop that. . . .

KH: Do you think this type of school environment helps to make "the stranger" seem less strange?

Mr. Crompton: Oh, oh, yeah. But I mean, I'm not so sure it continues afterwards, you know, in a way. I mean this is a very artificial environment, isn't it? Ah, I mean that road crew of mine are amazing, I mean the ethnic mix of that is incredible. I like to think that that's a small version of what goes on more or less in the school. But I doubt very much whether any of them will stay friendly outside.

When white students described their relationships with people from different backgrounds at school, many of the girls, in particular, mentioned having had "an Asian" or "a black" friend. When I asked Amanda, a sixth former, about her friends, she mentioned two girls who were not "British."

Amanda: I mean obviously I've got more white friends, because, well more British friends, it's so difficult, you know, 'cause everybody's British, okay white, we'll call them white, friends, because there are more white people. Okay there's Katie who's colored [her mother is white, father Afro-Caribbean] and last year a good friend who's left now was Asian, Indian. And so. . . .

KH: What is that friend doing now?

Amanda: She's at Parklane College doing a secretarial, a medical secretary course.

KH: She was Katie's friend too?

Amanda: Yeah. But I think she found that sometimes people would say, "Oh, why are you," some of her Asian friends, 'cause she sort of knocked around with us and they'd say, "Oh, why don't you stick around with us a bit?" But you don't usually find that at all, it's just certain silly people.

While cross-ethnic friendships do form at Grange Hill High, the response Amanda notes of the other Asian girls suggests that ethnic friendships cross but do not erase existing social boundaries. Students are always aware that they are "mixing," and such mixing is marked as a choice with implications for the collective identity of Asian students. Choosing not to "knock around" with "your own group" can be viewed as rejection, implying that being with "your own group" is still considered the norm.

The normative nature of ethnic-specific friendship groups is apparent as well in Amanda's comments about the friends she saw most often outside school. These friends were all members of the dominant "popular" middle-class group of sixth formers, who were almost exclusively white.

KH: Do you have a friend you usually go out with?

Amanda: Generally I go out with, if it's on a sort of one-to-one basis, I go out with Katie, or Julia or Mary or Sheila. But for parties, you know the lot who were at Jonathan Smith's party? Lizzy, Olivia, James, Simon, Ernie, that's their little group.

The students at Jonathan Smith's party, and at all the parties I attended, were white. There were only two exceptions—Katie, who is colored or mixed race, and Hardip, the solidly middle-class son of a wealthy Sikh businessman, who had gone to middle school as well with "this lot" of friends.

Members of this dominant group seldom socialized with other Asian or Afro-Caribbean students, even if they thought of these students as "school friends." James's description of one highly atypical racially integrated evening out, a celebration he and I attended for a Sikh boy leaving the sixth form to take a new job, provides further evidence of this.

James: That night we went out for Sat's leaving do, we went for a drink, I'd hardly
met any of that lot before, because they're just not the sort of people I mix
with at school and at night, you know, it was really good. 'Cause I've never
thought about them before, 'cause all the people I mix with tend to be white,
with the exception of a few, from the sixth form, from old schools who I know,
from football matches, squash clubs, and so on, who I know. But, I was really
surprised. I was surprised. Sitting in a pub like the Deerpark, which is non-
ethnically mixed as well, one, two white people over and yourself with like
seven Asian guys. It's a strange situation, but I really enjoyed it.

KH: Yeah, it was fun.

James: Strange.

For James, socializing in public with a group of Asians was "strange."
"Strange" was a term students frequently used when describing things that
they "were not brought up with," that were not normal and seemed "out
of the order." Students applied this characterization not only to events but
also to particular forms of difference, to the habits, lifestyles, and practices of others. Richard, also a sixth former, illustrates this in describing his
reaction to Sikh boys who wear turbans:

People tend to look at people with turbans differently for obvious reasons because
it's out of the order. And, you know, it's still something to look at again, you know,
as it were, whatever you say. You know, you're not brought up with it, I don't think,
not unless you lived in the poorer areas and you see it everyday. And, "Hey look!
There's a white kid." [laughs]. That's the other extreme, you know.

Men in turbans, sari-clad ladies speaking only in Punjabi, and Asian girls
with plaited hair wearing trousers under their skirts are images considered
"out of the order" or strangely out of place, out of context in the white
middle-class world in which these students were raised.

In religious education lessons (part of the high school curriculum in
British state-maintained schools), "strange" cultural practices—like wearing a turban—are removed from the flow of everyday life and presented
as objectified "facts" in lessons about world religions (see Nesbitt 1999).
A central aim of religious education has been to expose students to the
basic beliefs and practices as well as the ethical or moral bases of the
"world religions" (Christianity, Judaism, Sikhism, Hinduism, and Islam), so
that they may reflect on ethical and moral issues in their own lives. World
religions are typically presented to the students as objectified canons, discrete traditions including ritual practices and artifacts in terms of which the
individual religions are identified and distinguished. Religious education

has tended to provide students with "factual" information about other religions. Yet, as Richard, who is Jewish, concluded, as a method for encouraging students to understand and appreciate cultural differences, these learning experiences are "not very effective":

getting to know other people's religions and getting to know their sort of cultures is important, like in RE, religious education, lessons. I was explaining to the class parts of what I do, you know, it can be a good laugh. But some people listen and some people are interested. You know, try and promote that more. But what will that do, just learning about other cultures? It's not very effective, is it?

Discourses about racialized class, religious, and cultural differences enter the school from the middle-class worlds that surround it. They designate the "normal," position the "other," and reinforce the boundaries of belonging at Grange Hill High. Yet these boundaries do not exist as static or impenetrable divisions; students make sense of each other in relation to discourses and categories of difference that invoke a range of status criteria that inform complex and shifting patterns of social interaction across different school settings and over time. Students at Grange Hill High are positioned in multiple discourses about difference, which support and legitimate a number of status hierarchies. I turn now to consider discourse that gives meaning to two overlapping status hierarchies: the school's academic placement of students in ranked sets and the popularity status system the students create among themselves.

Swats and Divs

Grange Hill High traditionally has enjoyed a reputation for upholding high academic standards. The overarching emphasis in the school has been on preparing students to take (what were still at the time) the national O-level/CSE and A-level exams. The school's strong reputation is supported by the consistently high exam grades attained by its students (scores are published in the local newspaper and more recently on the school's own website, among other places). While the majority of Grange Hill High students do not achieve top scores and most do not even take A-levels, the school's scores overall are highly competitive relative to those of other schools in Leeds. Maintaining these standards is a top priority for the school, and teachers devote themselves to preparing the "able" students to achieve these high marks, a pattern that marginalizes students who are not so academically inclined.[6]

Students are assigned to academically ranked "sets." They are placed in particular sets for mathematics and English, in "mixed set" classes for religious education, history, art, and gym, and are also set to some degree for language classes. Students are not formally "streamed" or allocated to the same set level for all their subjects. A student in set 1 for English could find herself in set 2 or 3 for maths. Many students are in the "top sets" (1 or 2) for maths and English, but the majority of students are not in the same set for both. Although not formally streamed, students are regularly designated as belonging in one of three levels, levels that functioned informally as "streams." As this teacher's comments suggest, teachers assign students to these different streams based on assessments of their level of academic motivation and ability. Students allocated to these streams, then, are set off on distinctive educational and career paths.

If you take any maths and English sets, 1 and 2 are motivated towards, you know push push push, amongst themselves, their teachers and their parents. [Set] 3 is usually happy for the quiet life, you know, they realize their shortcomings, they don't want to do too much. But 4 and 5, there's nothing but a barren wasteland of CSE grade 4 [lower than an O-level grade] coming up at the end of the fifth form and then Youth Training Scheme rather than a job, and then nothing.

Students at Grange Hill High take for granted that a student's set placement is a reliable marker of innate ability or intelligence. Set ranking is a standard against which students assess themselves and one another. More significantly, perhaps, the distribution of students into sets serves to organize student movement in time and space. Set-based classes provide the primary opportunity for meeting friends. For those who share the school's academic values and standards, as well as for those who spend most of their time rebelling against them, the set structure organizes social relations, influences the formation of peer groups, and provides symbolic resources for the creation of subcultural styles.

Students who find themselves positioned at different levels of the set ranking system understandably view this structure quite differently. "Top students" who typically share to some degree the academic values of the school tend to characterize set placement in similar ways, making distinctions like these made by Karl, a fourth former who, as we shall see, was "hip" and, hence, proud to be identified with set 2.

Seems to me that if you got into the top, say for instance maths, if you got in the top three sets you were all right. But if you go in the lower sets you were with the lowest of the low type people—people that didn't want to learn, people that just can't make it. In fact a lot of Afro-Caribbeans were in the lower sets.

In the eyes of most students I spoke with, the top sets were "predominantly white" and, in the words of a white male student, "as you get lower down, you get more and more, it gets blacker and blacker." The academically successful students had very little contact with students in the lower sets. They seldom questioned the disproportionate assignment of students of color (particularly Afro-Caribbeans) as well as working-class students to the lower sets. They assumed that these students, for various reasons, deserved to be there. A boy in the top sets explained that "you find that people of the lower financial bracket tend to be of, you know, sort of less intellect—well not really less intellect [laughs], but because their parents haven't motivated and cultivated their intellects." According to another female student, these students were there "'cause they mess about."

The students designated as academically successful accepted as legitimate the system that validated their worth. Hence they viewed the school, in part, as divided between those like themselves, the "intelligent" students, and the others, the "remies" (remedial students) or "divs" (idiots), who were characterized as "less intelligent," "backward," or "thick."

Coexisting with the academic ranking system, however, was a student popularity or status system. Students engaged this discourse when assessing status differences among themselves, invoking criteria that determined popularity. The "trendiness quotient," as I call it, ranked students according to evaluations of personal style and image. The normalizing power of this status discourse, moreover, stretched beyond the realm of popularity alone and into assessments of academic status. This status discourse superimposed its own authoritative distinctions onto the academic rankings. A group of "hip" fourth formers, including, once again, Karl, told me how this works.

KH: Do all these sets really mean anything?
All: Definitely!!
Simon: I won't associate with anybody over set 5 [laughs]. . . .
Karl: If you're in a lower set you get the skit taken out of you.
KH: The skit?
Karl: I was going to say "the piss" but I'm not allowed to say that, am I?

KH: What's the skit? I don't know what that means?

Karl: Well it's the same as taking the piss out of you.

Simon: Taking the Michael.

Richard: Taking the Michael, the Mickey.

KH: It's not cool.

Richard: It's not cool, no.

KH: What if you're in set 2?

Karl: If you're in set 2, that's all right, 'cause you're not a swat you see. . . .

Jason: It's sort of hip to be in set 2. It's better to be in set 2 than in set 1. . . .

Karl: Yeah, because set 1 means you're a swat, but 2 means you're better than average, you see.

KH: But you don't try too hard?

Jason: No, you don't try too hard. . . .

Simon: I got set 2 English 'cause I don't do any work. I don't mind doing that, 'cause I've got as far as I am today and ah, I'm in all right sets and I haven't done any work in my life [laughs]. I haven't done a spot of homework since I was five years old.

Gareth and Alex were in the top set and could be categorized as "swats." Despite their different social status, they came to a similar conclusion: The "cool" people were in the middle or in middle to lower sets.

KH: So are there cool people in particular set groups or are they interspersed throughout?

Gareth: They usually tend to be sort of middle-ish.

Alex: Or middle to lower.

Gareth: They could do well and be in top sets but they choose not to. They choose to be sort of rebellious against the teachers and things like that.

Alex: Oh yeah, that's being cool. . . . Cheeking teachers is cool.

Gareth: Yeah, so that everybody else says, "Oh he's good. He can cheek the teachers off."

Students who gave priority to the style norms of the popularity status system were engaged in another form of signifying practice (Hebdige 1979). Their assertion of the status of style served to subvert, to a degree, the value placed on academic achievement. The discourse of style challenged the academic normative standards, practices such as working hard, doing (too) well, and getting along with teachers. The teacher's pets, the "blue-eyed boys and girls," were rearticulated as "swats," who were also "uncool." In this way the "hip" students successfully subverted the school's ranking system. They challenged the hegemony of teacher favor using the power of peer popularity.

Fitting in, Not Fitting in, and Not Being Noticed

While students in the top sets were differentiated according to conflict-ing criteria associated with social status and academic ranking, they were grouped together within another student discourse about difference. This discourse classified various peer groups in school, differentiating them according to the way they participated in life at school. According to Nigel, another sixth former and a star "swat" on his way to Oxford, the social order of the school was made up of those students who "fit in," those who did not "fit in," and those who "were invisible." This classificatory scheme crosscut both the academic ranking and the social status hierarchy. Each of the three categories included students from different set levels, but for the most part students with high social status would be among those who fit in or among those who did not. Having social status, by definition, meant one was not "invisible." On the other hand, as we shall see, many Asians, particularly Asian girls, were categorized as "invisible." As invisibility implied a lack of status, it was difficult for Asian girls to achieve popular-ity in the eyes of the dominant group.

The majority of students at Grange Hill High, however, were defined as "fitting in." They identified with, were identifiable in, and largely con-formed to mainstream life at school. This was certainly the case for the school-identified "swats." It was also true for those among the slightly rebellious "hip" students, since they never directly challenged authority but rather tested boundaries, most notably by "cheeking" teachers and smoking in the handball courts. In addition to these, there were the students who fit in and were visible in less distinctive ways. Nigel characterized these students as "Mr. and Miss Average."

Nigel: I mean a large proportion I would say in the school are people who are just basically Mr. Average or Miss Average, who just come to school and they have their friends and they eat a Mars Bar at break and they do their lessons and they get Cs and Bs and Ds and they go home and they do as little home-work as they can to get by. And then every Friday and Saturday night they do something, and that's it. And perhaps they do have a hobby, like playing the piano or going to Scouts or something, and that's about all they do. And I would say that people like that, white middle class, take up a large proportion of our school.

KH: What will they do? Will they go on to sixth form?

Nigel: Yeah, generally. A lot of them will. The more intelligent ones, the ones who get more Bs than Cs or Ds probably will do.

KH: What will the ones that get Cs or Ds do?

Nigel: Well they'll either go to sixth form or they'll try and get a job or they'll go to Parklane or something or do a secretarial course or catering or something menial [laughs]. But then you get people who you can actually talk to, intelligent people, who have opinions on things and who think occasionally and watch decent TV programs and read books.

Then there were the students who did not "fit in" and actually challenged the normative authority of "the mainstream" at Grange Hill High. They were of two general sorts, which Peter, another sixth former (who went on to study geography at the University of California at Berkeley), described to me in great detail. First, according to Peter, there were those like himself, the somewhat artistic or critical intellectual types, those who challenged the authority of the school because they "examine what it's like, think about what it's like actually being there." Others, particularly those in the lower sets, challenged the school's authority more directly, threatening to disrupt the "smooth running of the school." This subgroup represented what Nigel called "the yobbo element" or what Peter designated as "the hooligan types." As Nigel mused in his cynical "swattish" manner,

Further down in the school, yeah, there are the yobbo element and you have to just ignore them and hope they go away, which they do at the fifth form 'cause they fail everything and nobody will have them then, apart from the youth training scheme who have to massage their employment figures—anyway, that's politics.

Within this "yobbo element," Peter explained, there was a particular group of football hooligan wanna-bes who called themselves the "Red Room Firm." In the way they dressed, inhabited school spaces, and generally represented themselves to others, these boys were creating their own subcultural response to life at school.

Peter: There's one group in particular that model themselves on a certain style of football hooligan, you see. And, you know, they wear the, you know, the special designer clothes and things.... Some of them have their hair cut, it's really short around the ears and grown long in the back. And they wear training shoes usually, and they're all particular models of brands of training shoes, Nike and Adidas and so on. But they come and go out of vogue very quickly, different models of trainers, so most of them have amassed about eighteen different pairs by the end of the year.... And they call themselves, they model themselves after, see in Leeds there's a gang of football hooligans called the Leeds United Service Crew. And they call them the service crew 'cause they traditionally travel on service coaches to football matches. Now, it's like in ah, all these kinds of football hooligans have names, like in West Ham in London they call themselves the "intercity firm" because they travel on intercity trains. . . . And you can actually, if you go to London, you take a risk of your life, you can actually go to the certain pubs where they all drink and you can go see what they're like. It's like a youth culture where they all dress in certain ways and they all go to football matches and they all go out drinking together afterwards. . . . But this lot in our school like model themselves on one of these things and they call themselves the "Red Room Firm."

KH: Why that?

Peter: Firm, well firm, it's a cockney, you know from London, it's London slang for like a gang, a firm. A firm as in a company.

KH: Where's the red room?

Peter: Well this, I think, stems from the red art room corridor. They all used to sit on the benches in there and they all model themselves on this kind of thing. And there was an incident on the news, what brought this to mind was there was an incident on the news where, I think it was Newcastle United and Millwall, which is another one of the really rough football clubs in London, ah, they pulled up and by some mistake the two coaches traveling, one from Newcastle, one from Millwall, met at the same service station and someone was stabbed in the throat and died, you know, slashed in the throat with a stanley knife and they died. And they found cards at the scene of the fight saying "Congratulations. You just met Millwall." These football hooligans are organized enough where they got calling cards printed up. And this lot, the Red Room Firm, some weeks afterwards got cards printed up saying, "Congratulations. You just met the Red Room Firm."

Firm members were mainly white working-class boys from the housing estate behind the school.

Then there were "the people you didn't notice." As with the other school orientation categories, this one too crosscut the academic ranking, including students identified with each of the set levels. Regardless of their academic status, what characterized this group was their invisibility. Their school participation went unnoticed. They were visible neither as conformists nor as rebels.

Nigel and Peter each independently concluded that most Asian students fell into this category. Teacher reports painted a different picture, however. On numerous occasions teachers told me stories narrating the antics of a few infamous Asian boys and fewer Asian girls, students who were described as "disrespectful" and "difficult" and as belonging to "bad" families. These depictions positioned these students as part of "the yobbo element." Other Asian students, as I describe in the next section, were noted and notable for having become visible by achieving a certain degree of popularity and social status. But, according to Peter, in the eyes of white middle-class students most Asians hung together in groups of "people you didn't notice."

The Asian kids used to, there weren't, I can't think of any that were like the intellectual rebellious type, you know, who fit into that category. . . . Like in the middle, some of them were academic well-doers who kept to themselves, who were included in the people who you don't notice. And a lot of them, you know, hung around, you know, went about with Asians as well, you know, the Asian kids used to hang around together and they used to go around together. So they were a clique in themselves, you know. The Asians had their own group really.

The invisibility of Asian students resulted from the social distance that divided white and Asian social worlds. Asian students, particularly the girls, whom white students did not get to know, were reduced to a category; they are classified as "strange," out of the order, unknown, and unknowable. They remained invisible, free of any semblance of individuality. This tendency to categorically define Asian girls as indistinguishable in their otherness is evident in Nigel's remarks about the nature of what he saw as their invisibility.

Yeah, especially Asian girls. Tend to be very quiet, have long hair and all look the same. They all have a center part. When you look at them you think, who's that? The last time they told you their name it was something like, Kamlishnashvinder or something. I just think, I'm just not going to bother. "Hi. How are you?"

Category to Person

Middle-class English students like Nigel tended to view ethnic others through a normative gaze that imposed essentialized identities and cultural stereotypes on the students they considered "invisible" or "strange." Ethnic minorities were perceived categorically at first. They became visible only if they made themselves known as individuals. As Godfrey, a popular academically successful fifth former, explained to me and to Gurnam, whom we met above, the onus was on Asians to create themselves as individuals. Gurnam engaged in "hooligan" exploits to gain acceptance, to become known as an individual, Godfrey suggests. This too is what his Sikh friend Jaspal had achieved. Jaspal, who like Godfrey was among the academically successful, had attained his individuality, his status, and his popularity by acting extroverted and friendly.

Godfrey: Do you think people have accepted you then, well not accepted you, but got to know you I suppose.

Gurnam: Yeah, they've got to know me. . . .

Godfrey: 'Cause I think you were probably fighting for your independence, or fighting for recognition as yourself. I suppose one view I've got is that when Jaspal first came in I probably defined him as "a Sikh." He had a turban on. And the way that he made himself Jaspal, the individual, the person to me, he was very extroverted, you know, he's very lively [Gurnam: He is lively], and he says a lot. And in that way he created himself as a person to me and made us friends. Whereas at the beginning, it is so easy, like on first impressions, to generalize and say, "Oh, they belong to that group, and that group, and they look like this." So it takes, um, a lot of outward emotion and showing to make yourself individual, as I suppose you did by standing up for yourself [Gurnam: Yeah] and fighting, and becoming known for aggression. And in that way you put yourself apart from the rest and make your own identity, I suppose.

KH: So do you think the turban and the skin color and the cultural differences disappear once you know Jaspal?

Godfrey: Once you get to know someone. But it does influence your first impressions though. That's always the problem. 'Cause you have to spend time to get to know people. Whereas in situations in the future, like, say you're being interviewed, there isn't that time to get to know people. And it's that ingrown, you know, sort of superiority or, well, racism I suppose, that is difficult to overcome. Like, so I suppose Jaspal and you did it in characteristic ways. Then in this interview you've got to put over that you are not the stereotype. You are a good person, I suppose. Does that make sense?

Asian students who conform to the normative expectations associated with both the academic and social status hierarchies are more likely to "become individuals" or "become like us." They are assumed to be "like us" because they "act like us." They study the same subjects, are interested in the same girls, play the same sports, and frequent the same pubs. They are "trendy" in dress and in lifestyle. Becoming "trendy" is specifically defined as becoming more Western (and middle class) and less Asian for both Asian girls and Asian boys.

Raymond: Rashida Khan. And she used to, ah, girls used to have to wear a skirt to school. She came with a skirt and trousers underneath.

KH: Has she changed a lot though?

Raymond: Yeah, she's become sort of fairly trendy now. There's a lad in the upper sixth who I don't really know, but he suddenly took his turban off and cut his hair dead short and trendy. I don't know why, I don't really know him. But the difference in his face, and he looks something like trendy, as it were. And he was just so different, it's just unbelievable.

As I have noted, however, there was a gender disparity at work in these status evaluations. Asian girls consistently seemed more foreign or "backward" to white students, particularly to white boys. They seemed much less "like us" because they did not participate in the activities that bred familiarity, visibility, and a sense of sameness. Different rules were applied in Asian families for daughters and sons. Going to discos or to pubs was not acceptable for Asian boys or girls, but for boys more backs were turned and more freedom was forthcoming. Asian girls remained at home with their families, unable to socialize on English turf and terms and uninterested in doing so. Despite their set placement, then, Asian girls frequently stayed together in their own groups. They remained among those defined as the "people we don't notice."

The most significant way Asians crossed the 'cultural-racial' barrier to become "like" the middle-class "us" was through academic achievement—by displaying middle-class skills and orientations in their academic work. Mrs. Pound, an English teacher, characterized academically successful Asian students as those whose culture did not come into it—those who no longer seemed Asian:

this is the other thing, isn't it, that the kids who are in the top set are largely middle-class Asian kids and they've taken on so much of our culture that they think like the rest of the class. And in poetry discussions particularly now, I give them the poem, like today, I give them the poem and I put them in groups and I say, I want you to talk about it. . . . And the Asian kid there, in the top sets, is exactly like the middle-class English kids, it is class rather than ah, culture. And in the top set that I have, well certainly two, Ravinder and Kamaljit, *I don't think their culture comes into it. I don't feel that they're in any way Indian kids. They're just kids like everybody else.*

"Achievement," as Mrs. Pound describes it, was marked by how "un-Asian" Asian children seemed (or how "un-working-class" working-class children seemed). The power of these assessments, moreover, was founded in part on a taken-for-granted assumption that it is a student's "natural ability" or "intelligence" that determines the student's ability to assimilate and therein to "achieve." As Mrs. Pound explained, for example, Ravinder blended in with the middle-class students because her essential "ability" or "intelligence" enabled her to transcend her "Asianness" in order to seem middle class and "become like us." However, as the following statement illustrates, for children who cannot or choose not to shed their culture, there is little room for academic success. Holding on to one's culture, if it is not

English and middle class, inhibits a person from seeming "truly middle class" and could make one seem "less able."

Mrs. Pound: ... they [Afro-Caribbean pupils] don't want to succeed in the same way. There's the pull to stay at the bottom end. And there's some sort of culture clash which is difficult to put your finger on. Ah, when they are in the top set, on the whole they're not as, not quite as much in tune with you as these Asian kids. I mean it's the same thing, well, let's say Polish child, or a child of European nationality, they're like the Afro-Caribbean children, no matter how middle class, they're still following their own culture, literature, for example.

KH: Are Polish children more like the West Indians?

Mrs Pound: They're more like the West Indians insofar as, ah, they're oriented to the Polish literature and the Polish culture, I find, where the Asian children usually seem to be on the same wavelength, and as though, like today we've been looking at Ted Hughes's poetry and like I say there was absolutely no difference. They all came to it with the same sort of assumptions, the same sort of open minds. And they discussed what they thought and they were all discussing the pictures they could see, what the poem was about. There was no difference. Now the Polish kids, I usually find there are certain aspects of English literature that's closed book to them, "I can't understand this, it's not like ours." And they tend to think allegorically. They want hidden meanings, they want images. And that's in their own culture.

Academic achievement requires a certain degree of assimilation. "Holding onto one's culture" excludes a person from participating fully in English culture and from becoming properly middle class. Students marked as "different" have the opportunity to succeed, but success in this meritocracy often conflates the ability (or willingness) to assimilate with academic aptitude.

Among white students and faculty, it was assumed that Asians should assimilate to "British" culture at school. While many of the teachers embraced a "sari, steel band, and samosa" brand of multiculturalism and encouraged students to bring cultural artifacts to school to share in classroom discussions, few saw the need to reimagine British history or culture in truly multicultural terms or to directly challenge the roots of racism and inequality through antiracist programs. White students in particular consistently expressed profoundly assimilationist positions, invoking in their discourse the age-old adage, "When in Rome, do as the Romans do." "British culture," I heard white students argue again and again, should not have to become "Asianized," but instead Asians need to learn to "fit in," to "become like us." And this was what they assumed was happening to many of their Asian friends.

"When in Rome . . ."

On one of many damp and dreary English mornings, I was lingering (with my tape recorder) around a set of desks with a group of sixth form boys, who as always were seeking a diversion from revising (studying) for their upcoming A-level exams. The boys were friends, members of a group considered the most popular in the school. I had been at the school for several months at this point and had grown to know these boys quite well, having spent a good deal of time with them both inside and outside school. On this particular morning, our conversation turned to tensions surrounding multiculturalism, prompting a debate about whether people from a different culture, specifically Asians, have a right to bring "their culture" into school, or in fact even into Britain. "What is the problem, I asked, "with Asians wanting aspects of their heritage to be recognized in school?" The boys turned immediately to numbers, couching their arguments about "fairness" in a liberal majority/minority framework.

Raymond: [You] have to make special sacrifices. . . .
Raymond: Because they have a different culture, don't they?
William: [The majority] *have to sacrifice* . . . special assemblies and all the rest of it, special holidays. The Jewish people, they celebrate Yom Kippur and they also celebrate Christmas. We don't celebrate Yom Kippur day at school.
Raymond: [who is Jewish and slightly defensive] Would you want to fast for a day?
James: Like Middledale [a middle-class middle school located in a white neighborhood], it's in a conservative area. There were only seven or eight [Asian students]. When you have over 50 percent they have a swinging opinion and so *they'll want extra additional services laid on for them. Which you can argue is fair, but it's not fair on the 40 percent of white people.*
Raymond: West Indian people seem to *mix in* more easily.
James: I was always taught, *"When in Rome do as the Romans do." And that's not a racist remark.*
KH: [intentionally provoking them] But the English didn't do that when they went to India.
[They all respond to this, talking over each other.]
James: That's nothing to do with it.
Raymond: We're talking about now, not the 1930s.
Jonathan: What I said was both communities will suffer for the minority, and Hardip [a Sikh boy] agreed with me on that aspect. . . .
Jonathan: . . . that the minority will be at a disadvantage . . . and Hardip agreed that they would. . . .
KH: Why would they be disadvantaged, what would disadvantage them?

Jonathan: Well if you get all the Asians they're going to want all those sort of things about Asia to be taught aren't they?

Raymond: They want Punjabi too, they can't all speak English but yet they want to speak Punjabi.

Jonathan: They were going to teach whatever it was and they weren't going to attempt to learn English. What's the point of that?

James: So you can understand *them,* Jonathan! I'm joking. It's rubbish, it's just absolutely ridiculous. It really makes me ill. Nauseating. Things like that, having to, when we have to, *it's okay their fitting into our way of life, and we don't mind letting them have their way of life, but when we have to fit into their way of life, then it's going too far.*

Jonathan: I mean some of them don't even attempt to learn English, and that's just not on. *They come into our country and we expect them to obey our laws and go by our standards....*

KH: But what about the Asian kids that you know at this school?

James: Well that's okay. We're not talking about them....

Raymond: 'Cause *they mix with us in a mixed society.*

James: They go to pubs with us, they go to parties, they go to school.

Michael: They sort of drop their trousers with us.

KH: They're okay as long as they live like you?

Jonathan: That's right, yeah. As long as they *live like us* and go by our rules and our standards. When they start doing their own....

William: You can't expect them to change their religion....

James: We're not asking them to change their religion.

Jonathan: They have to fit into our society.

William: But very often their religion goes in and out of a lot of their culture, 'cause like religion for us is like, okay it's Christmas so we'll have our knees up. That's as far as religion goes for us, it's an excuse to have parties all the time. But religion for them is like their food, dress, way of life, customs, and everything.

James: We're not asking them to change that.

Raymond: We're not discussing their culture.

William: But that's half their way of life, isn't it.

KH: He's right.

James: But we're not discussing their way of life, we're discussing the way that we have to fit into their way of life. We don't mind....

KH: How are they asking you to fit into their way of life though?

[They all talk at the same time.]

James: Teaching Punjabi and teaching this and should be allowed to do this.

David: It's the elderly people who can't speak English. When our generation grows up there will be a lot less hassle. 'Cause I mean I really hate, just really, really hate these big Asian ladies who go around ... dressed up in their fancy dress, and they can't speak a word of English, and they go into the supermarket ... they're picking up boxes of butter and walking around, they're doing a week's

shopping for eighty-four families at home. I hate that, it's really foul. It gets in your wig, *the way they can't talk English and, they have so much bloody money.* That's basically what it is. Having said that I hate them, *I've never actually met any of them.* I've never actually met them to talk, but I'm sure they're very nice. It's just kind of an image to me which I don't like.
Raymond: Yeah, *the image.*

The views expressed by these young men illustrate the disturbingly widespread reaction of the members of the dominant society to the presence of increasingly politically and economically successful British Asians. Their statements express a deep ambivalence, a tension between cultural aversion on the one hand and envy and desire on the other (see Rattansi 1994: 68). David's words, in particular, express this tension. The Asian woman was troubling to him because of the contradictory characteristics she embodied. She was foreign but near, new to this country but financially successful. David felt aversion to her foreignness while he envied her wealth. This juxtaposition was disordering and elicited a powerful visceral reaction. "I really hate, just really really hate," he says.

Politically assertive Asians were perceived as "not mixing," and instead as "making demands" that required "the British" to fit into "the Asian" way of life. The boys viewed this situation as a power struggle over who should decide what British national culture should be. Asians, they argued, were asking for "extra," for more than what was fair. It was unfair that they should even ask; the Jews, they argued, had not made such demands. Immigrants should not have the right to change "British culture": "When in Rome, do as the Romans do." Asians, like West Indians, should mix in culturally, fit in, and not threaten the "timeless continuity" of British traditions.

Their views invoke a particular conception of culture as a set of traditions and practices—like religion, but more—which identifiable groups are assumed to share. Distinctive "cultures" are incompatible and should "naturally" remain separate. Yet their sense of "fair play" leads them to reject a call for total assimilation. Ethnic groups should not have to "give up their culture," language, or religion, but neither should minority groups expect the British to change "their culture" for them. Theirs is a liberal model of integration, like Honeyford's, that accepts the presence of cultural pluralism but expects those defined as different to keep their culture to themselves and practice it safely in private, outside the public realm.

In conversations with white middle-class male students, sentiments of moral indignation and outrage flowed forth when policies like multiculturalism or antiracism were mentioned. These policies and programs were perceived to challenge the basis of British national identity and the foundations of family and tradition. Any suggestion that Britain might benefit from becoming multicultural was met with great emotion, as expressed by William, who otherwise was a polite and shy middle class boy, also in the sixth form.

William: We have some friends in Saudi and they've gone over there with the attitude that, well we're living in their society, therefore we adopt their rules and regulations. But the people who are coming over here don't seem to want to do that. And they're all very quick to stomp on you for prejudice if you say anything against that. That does annoy me and it does worry me to some extent.

KH: What in particular becomes annoying?

William: Well when they start saying that you have to have *halal* meat at your schools, I think that's wrong. If they want to send their children to our schools then they should either send them packed lunches or something, or eat what we eat. That's a, I think a bombastic attitude, but it's, I think it's what I think, I think so.

KH: How about teaching other languages in schools, Punjabi in schools?

William: That doesn't worry me too much because it doesn't affect me, it doesn't affect how we're going to live, and I think however many languages you have it's not enough.... The imposition of their culture on us, if they try to impose it on us then that annoys me. It's irritating to the English culture and I don't want to lose that English culture of, well the Yorkshire culture anyway, sort of having Yorkshire pudding and roast beef on a Sunday. It's introducing something else and I don't want that introduced. I wouldn't want it ... it's a conservative attitude.

"Asian culture" (it is assumed that there is *one*) is perceived to be a threat; it is visible, different, inferior, exclusionary, and it refuses to conform, to disappear. It is threatening, moreover, because Asians refuse to accept their "proper place." Asian cultural differences are alien, out of order, inherently disordering, and, hence, concluded William, evoke fear.

I think we're afraid of it basically because it's new to us. And anything that's new to us and we don't know of, we're afraid of and we don't want. And perhaps that's why I'm so opposed to this change, really, because it's new to us.... If you just take this halal meat—the way they kill the animals, for instance, is a very inhumane way.

I don't think that should be allowed. Well I don't think it should be allowed in Britain anyway. Many of their cultures aren't acceptable, um, to our way of life, I think. There was some incident some years ago where an Islami or something hung a dead sheep on the lamppost outside his enemy's house or something. Ah, it had something to do with the killing of animals in the street. Um, I don't think that's right and I don't think that's acceptable and I don't think it should be allowed.

As is evident in the first discussion above, the boys differentiated between the "threatening and undesirable" first generation and many among the second who in fact seemed less foreign. Their Asian friends, typically boys, were in the process of "becoming like us." Robin, a sixth form boy who was known for his right-wing views, predicted that when the first generation "died off" race relations would improve and the challenge to British culture would subside.

Robin: I don't necessarily believe in repatriation, because ah, ah, all the blacks that came over in the fifties, they didn't come over, they were invited over to do the more menial jobs, so ah, they were brought to this country by us, so it's not necessarily their fault that they're here. And the Asians, most of them who come over, it was part of the Commonwealth so it is one of their rights to be able to come and live here. But the main thing I don't like is like, I'd say 99 percent of Britain's population, they don't mind them if they'd integrate themselves more. But you see all these women going around in saris, talk in groups, they don't know any English at all, and, I mean, it just doesn't seem right to me. Like if you go to Saudi Arabia and you start drinking alcohol, and you get what, 50 lashes, something like that, if you're breaking the laws of the land. So, ah, as in, "When in Rome do as the Romans do," is sort of what I believe. . . . In Bradford they're building all of these Muslim schools and all that. Well that's there for the Indians themselves are segregating themselves away from everyone else by, you know, letting them have special meals and things like that. I mean, yeah, you should keep your culture, but you shouldn't sort of express it all the way around. Like ah, say if you're a Muslim, your employer's not going to be very happy if you're praying to Mecca five times daily, if it's sort of interrupting your work and that. And he's not going to be pleased. So although technically they've got to keep it up, it ah, it does disrupt the British way of life.

KH: So what do you think the solution is? If they can't maintain their culture and fit in?

Robin: Well when the first generation, they die off, then, you know, we'll be much better then because these kids have been brought up to be in English schools, they wear Westernized clothes and things like that, they have Westernized tastes, so it's not as noticeable now. If you hear somebody's voice, a lot of them, they're losing their Indian accents. That's all going away.

Nigel expressed similar hostility toward "racial minorities" who "impose" their culture and their practices on "us"—a phenomenon he characterized as Britain's becoming "Asianized." Asian cultural styles and practices were not valued, he contended. So, if Asians wanted to be accepted, *they* would have to change. Asians could not expect to stick a bit of Bombay in Chapeltown because it's simply "not fair."

Nigel: I mean, to be perfectly honest with you, I'm not particularly interested in becoming Asianized. If I were in India, perhaps I would be. But, you know, these people *are* in Britain, and the British culture isn't going to change before they do. So, they've got to make more effort ... *just be normal*. Because I don't think that a lot of people, I mean some people, yes, are racists. But, there's no problem with social acceptance, I think, with most white people, just because you're black. But most of the people I know feel very strongly about sort of like what's happening in South Africa and race discrimination in the job market and stuff....

You know, I mean, personally if I found, if I had a choice of two people coming to live next door to me and one was a white family with a culture the same as my own and the other was an Indian family who is going to paint the window frames turquoise and cook curry every night, I'd rather have the white people. Because people like the status quo, they like, one thing that people do like to have is to be left alone. And Indian culture, or Asian culture, in that respect can be very intrusive. Because, when Asians get together, when they sort of, um, take a lot of the houses on a street, the kids will tend to run about and it's all very, there's a sense of community, but they don't want the white people in their community, and the white people don't want to be in it, so the white people are left unhappy. And it's not really their fault. And it's not really the Asians' fault either, but I think people have to make an effort to fit into the society they're in. You can't expect to transport a little bit of Bombay and stick it in Chapeltown, because Chapeltown's in England. And you shouldn't try and do that, it's not fair. I wouldn't expect to try and pick up part of Leeds and stick it in Bombay.

KH: But the English people did.

Nigel: Yeah. But I wouldn't. That's why I don't, with people who say we should send Indians back to India and Pakistanis back to Pakistan is wrong because the British companies in India exploited the Indian people and they have to have some recourse, that's fine. Um, but uh, I don't think what the British did in India was right, but it doesn't mean to say trying to do the same thing in Britain is right either. Two wrongs don't make a right as my mother always used to tell me when I was small.

As a self-defined "liberal-minded person," Nigel was quick to assert that the basis for his sentiments was not racism. After all, he too abhorred the oppressive racism of apartheid that then still divided South Africa. People simply want to live among "their own kind." This was not racism; to him it seemed a natural response. Cultural differences breed social incompatibility. This transcended racism, he insisted, for Asians reacted the same way, "they don't want white people in their community." Cultural pluralism, he concluded, inevitably leads to ethnic segregation.

Cultural Racism and British National Purity

Nigel's words express assumptions associated with the "new cultural racism." This form of cultural racism is a normalizing discourse that represents differences in ethnically absolutist terms as natural, incommensurate, and unbridgeable. As a normalizing discourse, however, cultural racism not only classifies designated groups in seemingly objective terms, it also regulates these differences through the imposition of normalizing judgments. Asian cultural practices are not only different, they are "not normal," out of the ordinary, and therefore a source of fear and aversion. As such, Asians become targets of normalization, recipients of the call to assimilation.

Throughout the modern period, forms of nationalism have supported efforts to normalize difference. The British state has embarked on a number of projects of normalization or "civilizing missions."[7] These have usually taken the form of education, health, crime, and poverty initiatives directed toward "improving" the conditions of diverse segments of the "national community." Often referred to as "enemies within," "delinquent youth," "dirty and undeserving poor," or "alien and uncompromising Pakis," all have been perceived as needing to be "integrated" into the normative national moral "order." In Disraeli's day, it made sense to allude to "two nations" divided by class. More recently fascists have chanted, "There ain't no black in the Union Jack," symbolizing the way devalued populations have been imagined as existing beyond the borders of the national body.

But why are certain forms of difference and not others perceived as "disorderly" or disruptive or threatening to the purity of the national culture or to harmony in the social order? Why has nationalism been used—in relation first to class divisions and now to racial differences—as the central trope for distinguishing "us" from "them"? And why is the "other" so frequently stigmatized, so consistently characterized as immoral, dirty, and diseased (see Williams 1989: 429; Foster 1991: 240)?

Race and class inequality in Britain has long been legitimated in terms of bourgeois morality or norms of respectability. Dominant images of difference—characterizing the nineteenth-century London poor, Scottish Highlanders or ex-colonial peoples of color—have invoked moral values and established moral boundaries between those who belong and the "enemies within." Moral sensibilities have given categories of difference their profound affective power, legitimating the relations of inequality they support. As the boys' statements suggest, aversions to perceived differences and calls for assimilation continue to be expressed in a moral rhetoric that invokes social justice and fair play to legitimate prejudicial views and discriminatory practices.

State policies and public moral panics focus on protecting the boundaries of the national body from forces feared to create disorder from within. The health of the nation is tied to preserving the status quo and maintaining social order. As David Theo Goldberg argues, the classification of difference, of distinctions between peoples, provides a technique for determining and regulating "order."

Corporeal properties have also furnished the metaphorical media for distinguishing the pure from the impure, the diseased from the clean and acceptable, the included from the excluded. Classification of differences determines order. Hierarchy is established on the basis of a value of purity—whether interpreted biologically (in terms of blood or genes), hygienically (in terms, for instance, of body odor), culturally (for example, language as signifying the evolution of thought patterns and rational capacity), or even environmentally (virtuous character, like nose shape and size, determined by climate). Impurity, dirt, disease, and pollution are expressed as functions of the transgression of classificatory categories, expressed, that is, in terms of laws, as also are danger and the breakdown of order. (Goldberg 1993: 54)

What Zygmunt Bauman calls "the task of order" is "among the multitude of impossible tasks that modernity set itself and that made modernity into what it is" (1991:4). The process of nation-building is a primary modern vehicle for imposing order onto the potential chaos of human existence. Nation-building requires the creation of an identifiable national community and the construction of a collective identity. In the process of nation-building, the construction of a pure national identity typically involves the invention of an impure "other" from a particular point of reference: that of the unmarked "we" who have the capacity to name and to define difference. It is the imagined identity of the naming subject that is the "pure" essence of the valued national identity. In other words, attributions of identity and difference always entail relations of power, namely the power to name, classify, and therein define the bases of similarity and difference.

The modern proclivity to impose order by exercising control over the boundaries of social collectivities and nations has resulted historically in the production of what Simmel refers to as "the stranger" (see Ålund 1996). The modern world, Simmel argues, is ordered above all else in terms of friends and enemies. Friends are situated inside one's collective boundaries; enemies are those safely "out there," beyond the boundaries of belonging. They do not disrupt the order of things because they remain outside, in their place. Simmel's stranger, however, "is the man who comes today and stays tomorrow" (Simmel 1971: 143). He is neither enemy nor friend, but brings the unfamiliar, unclassifiable, or undecidable into the realm of the familiar. As Simmel explains, "the appearance of this mobility within a bounded group occasions that synthesis of nearness and remoteness which constitutes the formal positions of the stranger" (1971: 145). Levine (1985: 75) has pointed out that the stranger is not the "marginal man," nor is he the newly-arrived immigrant who aspires to assimilate, the friend-in-training as it were. His power lies in his disinterest in assimilating, which makes his relations with the host community indeterminate and equivocal. Because of his proximity, explains Bauman,

The stranger undermines the spatial ordering of the world—the fought-after coordination between moral and topographical closeness, the staying together of friends and the remoteness of enemies. The stranger disturbs the resonance between physical and psychical distance: he is physically close while remaining spiritually remote. He brings into the inner circle of proximity the kind of difference and otherness that are anticipated and tolerated only at a distance—where they can be either dismissed as irrelevant or repelled as hostile. The stranger represents an incongruous and hence resented "synthesis of nearness and remoteness" (Simmel 1971: 145). His presence is a challenge to the reliability of orthodox landmarks and the universal tools of order-making. His proximity . . . suggests a moral relationship, while his remoteness . . . permits solely a contractual one: another important opposition compromised. . . .

The stranger's unredeemable sin is, therefore, the incompatibility between his presence and other presences, fundamental to the world order; his simultaneous assault on several crucial oppositions instrumental in the incessant effort of ordering. . . . The stranger is, for this reason, the bane of modernity. He may well serve as the archetypal example of Sartre's *le visquex* or Mary Douglas's the slimy—an entity ineradicably ambivalent, sitting astride an embattled barricade . . . blurring a boundary line vital to the construction of a particular social order or a particular life-world. (1991: 60–61; see Douglas 1966)

The cultural racism underlying British nationalism has its genesis in the "stranger" phenomenon, set in motion here by the movement of ex-colonial peoples of color from their secure positions in the colonies into the British homeland. This process of exodus and estrangement has disrupted the memory of centuries of colonial rule, a remembered order of oppositions between "us" and "them," white and black, ruler and ruled, on which modern British national identity has long rested. The presence of the ex-colonial, the new stranger within, is particularly threatening at this historic juncture, I have argued, because the boundaries of the British nation-state and British cultural identity are being challenged on several fronts. The fear of the ambiguous stranger is but one component of the current crisis of hegemony in Britain.

Ernesto Laclau has stated that "hegemony is a process of rearticulation, of the internalization through new articulations of something that was external" (1988: 252). Cultural racism is a product of this process of articulation. Its rise in Britain, and possibly throughout Europe, reflects an attempt to order ambiguity. The contemporary ideology of British nationalism inscribes the boundaries of difference between "natives" and "others" in absolute terms, terms that ascribe "purity" to a putatively distinctive cultural tradition (Williams 1989). And so, in the cause of social order regained, or an imagined nation rendered safe for its citizenry, the stranger as transgressor is made into the "enemy within."

The meritocratic ideology enshrined in liberal democratic education is a central individualizing force that directly contradicts modern essentializing forms of cultural racism. When the stranger enters the school she encounters the "liberal call to assimilate." She is invited to claim her right to embrace the modern principles of equality of opportunity, freedom of self-constitution, and individual achievement—to transform herself through education by removing her difference. This is the central contradiction of modernity. The "liberal message of cultural assimilation sounds a death knell . . . to the ascriptive nature of inferiority" (Bauman 1991: 69). At the same time, however, it reinscribes the superiority of the dominant culture in the act of calling strangers and internal enemies to assimilate to it. These contradictory pressures and possibilities, among others, provide opportunities for individuals to negotiate the politics of difference in their own lives. It is in these ambiguous spaces that black ex-colonial citizens will, through their struggles, continue to challenge the boundaries of belonging.

Boundaries that separate strangers from friends, that demarcate the national barriers of belonging, are inherently historical and cultural. There is a great deal of variation in how national identity and belonging are defined and addressed in the public spheres of different nation-states and across historic periods within a single nation. Within a nation at a particular point in time, there can be a range of views about what the nation is as well as imaginings about what it should or could be. While forms of nationalism and the national identities they support often assume a homogenous unified sense of peoplehood (whether based on religious, cultural, or racial commonalities), these national ideologies mask what are typically multiple and contradictory notions about the nature and basis of social order in that society. "The nation" is given distinctive meaning and form in the context of debates about the basis of unity and the nature of difference, or the ways in which a national "community" comes to be imagined. In this sense, then, the potential for "social integration" or "assimilation" or "recognition" of difference varies among and within nations across time in relation to the ways national unity and social order are imagined.

The promises and possibilities inherent in the ideology of meritocracy allow "able" individuals to rise "above" their origins, to break out of the stigmas and stereotypes that bind to re-create themselves as members of the middle class. These individual accomplishments contradict ascribed racial differences. But acts that contradict do not transform the categories of difference or the structures of inequality in which these categories are embedded. Quite the opposite is true. For in their attempts to achieve, to assimilate to the dominant standards and values of English middle-class society, individuals valorize and legitimate the dominance of these very same standards.

For Asian students at Grange Hill—as for all persons struggling against the forces of imposed identifications of inferiority—to assimilate, in this context to become "trendy," "brainy," or "middle-class," is to distance oneself from signs of otherness. Distancing oneself, however, unwittingly and unavoidably reaffirms the undesirability of these categories, the undesirability, in this case, of things "Asian."

Schools produce modern subjects, including middle-class subjects. British Sikhs who want to be "successful," to achieve academically—to become individuals and belong among the middle-class "us"—have to negotiate among a range of contradictory positionings. They have to allow themselves to be remade in school, to be produced by the disciplinary practices and normative judgments that regulate life in school. Assimilation is required; but what do Asians gain in the process? To become "like us" is to become accepted as no longer "strange." Yet will being "like" ever lead to becoming the same as "us," to the erasure of the racialized boundaries of national belonging?

This question is a critical one for British Asian citizens who are struggling to achieve what the liberal ideology of meritocracy promises to provide. They are achieving the exam grades, the university placements, the occupational positions, and the trappings of a proper middle-class style of life; but still they feel excluded, marked, and marginalized by race. Yet by fashioning new lifestyles and identities as members of the British middle class, this generation will continue to challenge these boundaries of belonging. The class mobility of British Sikhs in the end, however, has contradictory social consequences. Social mobility through academic achievement inevitably provides evidence of the permeability of the class structure, evidence that can be used to "blame the victim" or to explain inequality in individual rather than social or political terms. Yet the success of British Sikhs also contributes, however slowly, to the "declining significance of race" in Britain, at least in relation to determining life chances (Wilson 1980).

5. Mediated Traditions

There is a classic human problem that will not disappear however much global cultural processes might change their dynamics, and this is the problem today typically discussed under the rubric of reproduction (and traditionally referred to in terms of the transmission of culture). In either case, the question is, how do small groups, especially families, the classical loci of socialization, deal with these new global realities as they seek to reproduce themselves and, in so doing, by accident reproduce cultural forms themselves? In traditional anthropological terms, this could be phrased as the problem of enculturation in a period of rapid cultural change. So the problem is hardly novel. But it does take on some novel dimensions under ... global conditions.

—Appadurai (1996: 43)

Sunday in Leeds, England. On this Sunday, like almost every Sunday, Harjit crawls out of bed, too early for his taste, to go with his family to the gurdwara. Upstairs from the weekly religious service, he meets his high school mates, has a laugh, and sometimes listens as the teacher tells stories from the Sikh religious tradition. Later, in the privacy of his bedroom, Harjit lies back, wired to the sounds of his favorite CD. He tunes into a world created by the words of Sikh pop musician Apache Indian, an artist who mixes Caribbean reggae rhythms and Punjabi bhangra beats with verbal riffs about aspects of British Asian identity. Through commentary and metaphor, the songs frame and configure aspects of the diaspora experience, from arranged marriages to hybrid "black" style to travel (via magic carpet) across the places that symbolically map the South Asian diaspora's spatial imaginary. Sunday ends with the near nightly ritual: the family collectively turn their gaze to television's window on the world. Pre-packaged programs call them to participate in distinctive and contrasting constructions of British social life. On an evening they can venture from the remarkably white and culturally homogeneous everyday settings of soaps and sit-coms to the formulaically crafted multicultural streets of "East Enders" to the isolated and alien "ethnic minority" communities represented in documentaries about "the faiths next door."

For Harjit and other British Asian teenagers, growing up in England involves engaging with a wide variety of contradictory cultural influences, global as well as local. As they move among the social worlds that make up their everyday lives—family, school, gurdwara, and leisure activities—Sikh teenagers encounter and negotiate very different constructions of and normative expectations for being British and Sikh.

Children of transnational migrants may encounter unique forms of cultural complexity in their lives, but cultural acquisition in this era of globalization has become more complex for all young people. As Hannerz has suggested, as culture has become more complex, so too have processes of cultural acquisition. A young person, in our globalized world,

can take various paths through social life ... and so she can be constructed and reconstructed, eventually perhaps finished, in different ways as she goes along. Let us just enumerate, not entirely systematically, some of the things that may happen to her in the world we now inhabit. She will be fitted into a division of labor which makes her specialize in some particular kind of knowledge, and which assigns her to a particular kind of life situation, and life experience. The state may have its ways of making a citizen of her, which entails knowing and doing certain things, and in the market-place there are a great many agents, large and small, who will not only cater to her choices such as they are but will indeed try to develop and bend her tastes to match particular commodities. Bodily, at any one time, she will be in one place, and in this setting she may learn things through face-to-face contacts and observations, just as does the inhabitant of that anthropological classic, the little community. But over time, it may be that she moves between places, so that new things can be learned, and so that some old things may even have to be—to a degree at least—unlearned. Furthermore, this contemporary unfinished animal need not always have others physically present to pick up a thing or two from them. She may read a book, look at a picture, listen to a record, watch television.... As she changes jobs, moves between places, and makes her choices in cultural consumption, one human being may turn out to construct a cultural repertoire which in its entirety is like nobody else's. (1996: 37–39)

Globalization—more precisely, increased mobility and the expansion of media and communication technology—has revolutionized the way culture is experienced, produced, circulated, and consumed. It has also created more complex processes of cultural acquisition, of "education" defined broadly as socialization. The complexity, Hannerz argues, is not simply a matter of "varied confluences at the level of collectivities" but has powerful consequences in the lives of individuals.

The media play a significant role in processes of socialization in the lives of second generation British Sikhs. What I want to explore more closely in this chapter is how various types of media shape the particular forms of Sikh culture and tradition that are in fact produced and represented. The mass media in late capitalism are playing an increasingly significant role in processes of identity formation, particularly in the lives of teenagers (Morley 1980; Buckingham 1993). The mass media, along with the youth commodity industry more generally, are a critical source of what Angela McRobbie (1994) has called "identity formation materials" or Arjun Appadurai refers to as "imaginative resources," signs and symbols that young people use in crafting collective and self-identities and imagining possible lives (1991: 196). But mass media discourses play a far more complex role in processes of identity formation than simply positioning subjects, making multiple subjectivities, or generally providing the symbolic stuff identities are made of. While these are important aspects of the way mass media discourses mediate identity formation, mass mediation entails additional semiotic processes.

First, media discourses, like other forms of discourse, assert, index, and thus "mediate" the social construction of imagined communities (Briggs 1996; Irvine 1997; Spitulnik 1997). Technologies of communication, such as print and electronic capitalism, provide the opportunity for groups of people separated across space (and time) "to imagine their communion" (Anderson 1983; Briggs and Bauman 1992; Lee 1993; Appadurai 1996). Through their consumption of these media, people come to share in collective experiences that enable them to develop a feeling of belonging to imagined communities that extend beyond the immediacies of face-to-face interaction.[1]

Second, as my depiction of Harjit's Sunday suggests, communities are imagined in a range of ways across media discourses. Contrasting and contradictory concepts of culture and identity inform the ways communities are represented. Harjit's consumption of media discourse positions him in relation to distinctive types of "community": from the timeless and monolithic construct of "the Sikh tradition" in Sikh religious education texts to the "ethnic minority" resisting assimilation in British television documentaries to the hybrid and fluid notion of British Sikh identity in Apache Indian's lyrics.[2]

Finally, as British Sikhs engage different media and find themselves identified in relation to distinctive representations of Sikh/Asian identity, the contrast between these discursively imagined communities creates the possibility for the emergence of consciousness about and reflection on culture, identity, and difference (Hannerz 1996: 50–52). Media discourse becomes material for dialogue and reflection.[3] These "metacultural" dialogues about culture and difference are aspects of cultural acquisition that are central to ongoing processes of identity formation, informing how people defined as "other" interpret and respond to contradictory cultural influences, expectations, and opportunities in everyday life.[4]

Different media objectify Sikh identity, culture, and tradition in distinctive ways that use contrasting metaphors of and assumptions about the nature of culture and identity. This in turn creates a paradox: on the one hand media rigidify forms of culture and identity through processes of objectification, and on the other the circulation of reified images of Sikh tradition and identity allows for reflexivity, for reflection on and dialogue about difference. Objectification, in other words, both rigidifies and enables reflexivity.

Entextualizing Tradition

Sikhs in Britain—and in the diaspora generally—represent and transmit versions of "their tradition" through a range of printed texts: newspapers, magazines, web-page documents, pamphlets, and books. Discursive representations of "tradition" vary widely according to genre, presumed audience, and proposed purpose. I consider two types of texts: religious education materials circulated across the diaspora in the form of booklets published by the Sikh Missionary Society in the UK and information available on the Sikh.net website.

The Sikh religious tradition intertextually represented in these distinctive media reflects a process that has been ongoing within Sikhism since the nineteenth century, a process of producing "a highly systematized discourse of what it means to be a Sikh," to create a "monolithic, codified and closed culture" (Oberoi 1994: 25).[5] A uniform modern Sikh (Khalsa) identity was articulated within two types of texts in particular, the *rahit-namas*, manuals specifying the Sikh *rahit* (dharma or code of conduct); and the *gur-bilas*, narratives telling stories of the lives of the ten Sikh Gurus (hagiographic literature emphasizing the heroism of the Gurus). These works have entextualized selected aspects and particular versions of Sikh religious history, practice, and belief, decontextualizing tradition to give it a despatialized and detemporalized meaning. Entextualization in this instance serves as a mechanism through which an authentic and authoritative version of Sikh religious tradition has been scripted, asserted, and transmitted.[6]

The entextualization of Sikh religious principles, history, customs, and practices in the Sikh Missionary Society pamphlets and the Sikh.net materials considered here gives a reader the sense that there is a single version of "the Sikh tradition." Pamphlet titles, such as "The Sikh Symbols" (the five symbols of the faith worn by baptized Sikhs) or "The Sikhs and Their Way of Life," index rhetorically a homogeneous ethnoreligious group for whom belonging involves keeping the symbols of the faith and practicing the traditional religiously sanctioned "way of life." Quotations and symbols displayed on booklet covers communicate the significance of this unity of identity and of preserving "the tradition" across time and space. "So long as the Khalsa [the "brotherhood" of Sikhs] maintains his identity," a quote from the tenth Guru, Guru Gobind Singh, proclaims, "he shall remain imbued with my vitality." Printed below this statement, circling underneath the Sikh emblem of a wheel, a dagger, and two crossed swords, are words written in both Punjabi and English, "Worthy descendants narrate stories of their great grand ancestors." Through these stories pamphlets entextualize a discourse of tradition representing a single historical narrative illustrating the fierce resistance and the ultimate martyrdom of Sikh ancestors (specifically the ten Sikh Gurus).

Many Sikh Missionary Society booklets discuss the religious rituals and institutions, principles and practices considered central to the Sikh faith. These titles include "The Marriage Ceremony," "The Soldier-Saint," "The Sikh Woman" (which explains the position of women as set down in the teachings of the Gurus and provides portraits of the lives of "some prominent Sikh women"), and "The Gurdwara." Other pamphlets, such as "The Supreme Sacrifice of Guru Tegh Bahadur," contain narratives of the heroic acts and teachings of the ten Sikh Gurus. The hagiographic literature on the lives of the Sikh Gurus, the *gur-bilas*, dates back to the late eighteenth and early nineteenth centuries. This tradition of heroism is also represented in paintings depicting the martyrdom, acts of violence, and torture many of the Sikh Gurus and their followers endured.[7] Reproductions of these paintings are frequently displayed in the gurdwara together with classic portraits of the first and final Sikh Gurus, Guru Nanak and Guru Gobind Singh.

Similar to many constructions of tradition, these representations of "the Sikh tradition" gain authority and legitimacy by forging a sense of historical continuity. The invocation of the past gives tradition an apparent naturalness or primordiality (Eller 1999: 83; Hobsbawm and Ranger 1983). The historicizing of tradition is evident in a booklet entitled, "A Spur to the Sikh Youth." The booklet begins with a letter from a son living in America to his father in Singapore. The letter documents the son's struggle with the question, "What is Sikhism and why was I a Sikh?" "Where," he asks, "should I go in search of more facts about the history and heritage of the Sikhs in this foreign land?" He finds the answer in the card catalog of his local library: the textual representations of Sikh history and tradition. The essay that follows this introductory letter also begins with a question: "My Sikh brethren, have you ever considered why you are so brave and martial? The whole world resounds with your acts of heroism. Who can forget your brave deeds displayed during the World Wars?" The writer provides a reverse chronology of the victories of the Sikhs in battles stretching back to the year 1738, when Nadir Shah invaded India. Then, he stops to ask,

Friend, that is one out of the so many incidents of *your* chivalry and patriotism, two hundred years ago. Have you ever considered what was the secret behind it and *where you stand now*? My friend! Do you know why you are so undaunted and fearless even in the face of death? ... *You* were bricked alive, you were seated in boiling cauldrons, you were flayed, you were sawn alive, your flesh was pinched with pincers, you were hacked to pieces by being tied to wheels, you were cut to piecemeal, your skull was chopped off, your babies were cut into mincemeat to be necklaced for you, you were burnt alive, you faced the rifle bullets, unflinchingly, you were hanged, you were beaten to death—you suffered all these without ever slinking away or shirking death. (Sikh Missionary Society 1972/1985: 9; emphasis mine)

These graphic images powerfully evoke the heroism of the Sikh Gurus in the face of centuries of horrific persecution and martyrdom. Rhetorically, however, the stories make an additional semiotic move. As illustrated in the passage above, the shift to the pronoun "you" indexes a timeless connection, joining the readers with *their* Gurus and *their* persecuted ancestors. This discursive construction expresses a central tenet in Sikh religious ideology, the timeless spiritual oneness of the Sikhs. What the Guru suffered, all "Singhs" have suffered. The spiritual strengths and qualities the Guru possesses are also integral to the bodies and souls of those who have "become integrally one with him." Through the taking of *amrit* (nectar), Sikhs become Singhs; they are converted from lamb to lion (the literal meaning of "Singh"). They are imbibed with the spirit of the Guru and adapt themselves to his living and his form.[8] A visual marker of the oneness of the Sikh heritage, at least for Sikh men, is the turban. Therefore, the author concludes, "Keep your turban intact, my friend."

This image of the transcendent Sikh spiritual community is reflected in materials transmitted by one source of Sikh religious education, the internationally focused website, Sikh.net. Similar to other Sikh websites, this one includes a page that aims "to educate our young and to increase their awareness to the Sikh Religion." Sikh young people are instructed about key aspects of the faith, finding answers to such questions as "Why do We say this in Sikhism? What does this mean? When did this happen?"[9]

The representation of a Sikh community unified spiritually across time and space has been entextualized in classic form in the Sikh ritual prayer, the *Ardas*. On a page dedicated to explaining the *Ardas* to the next generation, a two-page text describes its content, history, and meaning. The word *ardas*, they write, "seems to have been derived from Persian '*arz-dasht*,' meaning a petition, a memorial, or an address to superior authority." It is recited in the morning or evening or whenever a religious service is held. The text continues to explain how this prayer when spoken creates a spiritual atmosphere that unifies the supplicants within a timeless spiritual community.

Broadly, the *ardas* consists of three parts. As the audience rise for ardas, the officiant leading the prayer usually begins by reciting *pauri* or stanza from the *Sukhmani: tu thakuru tum pahi ardasi....* Thou art the Lord-Master; to Thee our ardas (supplication) is addressed.... Then will follow recitation *verbatim* of the prelude to Guru Gobind Singh's composition *Var Sri Bhagauti Ji ki*. This 41-stanza invokes the Timeless One and the first Nine Gurus. The first addition that the Panth made was to extend this invocation to include the name of Guru Gobind Singh himself and the Guru Granth Sahib. The second part is a recital of Sikhs' deeds of dedication and sacrifice. The *ardas* thus encapsulates Sikh history, but transcending the time-and-space setting. The third part comprises words improvised to suit any given occasion. After the initial invocation, ardas goes on to recount and reflect upon memorable acts of the community's martyrs and heroes—men of unswerving resolution and unrelenting fortitude, who upheld faith with their sacred hair unto their last breath. In this respect, history has been continually contributing to ardas with the result that, along with the martyrs of the Guru period and of the periods of persecution following, it recalls those of the Gurdwara reform movement of the 1920's and those who laid down their lives for the sake of their faith at the time of the partition of the country in 1947. *Ardas* is, thus, the epitome of Sikh history and enshrines in its text the community's aspirations at various periods of its history and enables the devotees to unite in a brotherhood of faith over the centuries, transcending time. These aspirations are couched in expressions coined by minds saturated in faith. After recounting the deeds of faith and sacrifice over the expanse of time, the congregation recounts Sikh places of worship over the expanse of space. Thereafter, prayer is made for and on behalf of the whole community, seeking the Lord's protection and grace for the entire Khalsa, ending with a supplication for universal weal. Then it asks for the specific boons of holy discipleship, a life of restraint, discrimination and faith and a firm and confident attitude of mind inspired by the holy Name.[10]

In reciting the *Ardas*, Sikhs themselves recount a unified history of Sikh heroism, sacrifice, and faith. As they listen to the prayer, view Sikh iconography, and read religious educational materials, young Sikhs are introduced to powerful images that connect them to ancestors, brave martyrs who have been fighting for centuries against persecution. These images in turn provide a highly gendered interpretive lens through which Sikh boys in particular often view their own struggles against British racism. Their connection to the martial tradition of the Sikh "soldier-saint" gives boys who choose to keep the symbols of the faith a sense of collective courage—a vision of strength they may draw on in dealing with adversity in their own lives. The power of this identification is evident in this discussion I had with three thirteen-year-old Sikh boys (who wore the turban) about racism at Grange Hill High.

Harpal: Well my brother was here [at Grange Hill High] and he told me there was a kind of racialism against Sikhs.

Rajinder: There were two gangs. And they started causing trouble on us. They had this hockey stick and hit it over this Indian kid's head. But he had the turban on so there wasn't that much damage. But when we found out that they did this, right, we went over, right, and we said, if you're going to act violent, right, you're going to cause trouble, right, we'll defend ourselves. But they just started causing violence so we just stood up for our rights. . . .

Harpal: They're scared of us now. They're scared of us . . . because we wore turbans, 'cause they know that Indian people are strong. We're one of the strongest.

Surinder: That we assassinated the Prime Minister.

Harpal: Yeah, and our RE [religious education] teacher said, "The toughest people
   I know are the Indian Sikhs' cause they'll stick by themselves and they'll . . .
   stick together and they'll fight together in any need," and all this. . . .
Rajinder: And die together.
Harpal: And he goes, "I think they're the strongest people."

The imagined spiritual community of "the Sikhs" represented in the entextualized tradition of Sikh religion, martyrdom, and martial strength incorporates a construction of culture as monolithic, timeless, and traditional. The martial image, in particular, is a powerful potential source of identification for young Sikhs—particularly for boys, due to its masculine construction.

As becomes evident in the analysis that follows, however, this construction of Sikh identity and tradition is one of many that young Sikhs encounter in Britain, and one that they interpret and relate to in varying ways. To some, identification with the Sikh religious tradition and belonging to the religious community is profoundly meaningful and provides a significant source of strength. Young people who gravitate to more "modern" Sikh or cosmopolitan "Asian" identifications and lifestyles sometimes feel that "being traditional" or "religious" is personally limiting or socially constraining. Religious tradition, interestingly, depending on a young person's perspective, can have contradictory meanings. Some youth view religion as a restrictive and socially limiting force, while others consider it to be the ultimate path for self-expansion and personal growth.

Representing Ethnicity

In the homes of most Sikh families I visited, the television played continually, sometimes as a source of entertainment and other times simply as background noise. When families watch the screen together, they encounter a wide range of cultural orientations, normative standards, and representational perspectives. They watch as British society is portrayed "realistically" and they are not present in the picture. They watch as progressive producers and savvy advertisers include black people in their constructions of a multiracial Britain, depicting "representative" groupings in artificial social settings. And they watch shows and films produced by and for Asians that are broadcast on satellite and cable channels, often segregated from the realm of mainstream viewing.

But what do Sikhs learn from the images they see and the words they hear? And how do they respond to the messages they receive? The relationship between what is projected on a screen and how viewers interpret these images is complex. Viewer "decoding" is never a transparent process. Viewers consume media images in relation to contextually defined interpretive frameworks. As forms of subjectivity, interpretive frameworks are multiple and often contradictory, as is illustrated vividly in the remarks made by Sukhvinder, age fifteen, about the very different feelings she has while watching intimate scenes in Indian movies and on British television:

Sukhvinder: I used to watch a lot of Indian films. They're the only films that used to make me cry because ... they'd bring moral issues and principles of our culture into it, you know love marriages and you know, one love, whether it be arranged or not, you know, there'd be only one love. And if you touched a girl before marriage it was really bad, she'd commit suicide. It was that shameful. Respect, honor, families, and stuff.

KH: Were these Punjabi or Hindi?

Sukhvinder: Both, um, Indian films. They'd always enforce that sort of thing. Now, there'd be one or two things ... you know ... really bad things in the sense that, they'd never show anyone kissing. Ah, that was morally, on moral grounds. But nowadays they do.

KH: How do you feel about that?

Sukhvinder: I feel funny, in the sense that every time I watch it I start getting funny, you know, to *see* it on an Indian film seems to be rude. And also, when I was younger they never used to show, ah, a woman's body. The arms and just about to there on the chest [points to area above bra line] would be shown. But nowadays the Indian girls wear bikinis and stuff. And there was one film where you even saw bits of her body, you know, her top half and even her back. Which to me, it looked really disgusting. You know, for an Indian film, I felt like it was X-rated.

KH: But does kissing on American TV have that effect on you?

Sukhvinder: No, no, because it's sort of, you've grown up with it. American and English films and other films, it's just a way of life. If you turn on the TV and an English film's on and there's kissing, you'd expect that. But in Indian films, if you, everyone was brought up, until now, to believe on Indian films you don't show that sort of thing.... They're just becoming more and more Westernized. You know, but to me it's a shame really.

Viewers bring varying degrees of critical vision to the viewing experience. They can "see through" the way a film situates them, as "a Sikh" for example, and respond critically to a particular form of representation. Or they can identify with the message they receive and appropriate the image or information in ways that are significant to them personally.

Watching television engages viewers in public discourse about issues given popular currency by the media. In Britain, "ethnic minority" issues are frequently given such currency. As Sikh families watch television together, they are brought into a national discourse about aspects of "their culture." Finding themselves the topic of programs they did not themselves produce teaches them a great deal about the views and assumptions the dominant society holds concerning "them" and "their culture."

The media also mediate processes of intergenerational socialization in families.[11] Television documentaries and dramatizations of "real life" scenerios abstract aspects of cultural practice from contexts of everyday social relations. Watching these programs allows British Sikh families to discuss sensitive issues in relation to a distanced and removed social context—the story and the people introduced by television.[12] A prime-time television drama entitled *Love Match*, for example, addresses the issue of arranged marriages in a story about an eighteen-year-old Sikh girl. The girl's parents, against her will, put an end to her educational pursuits when they arrange for her to marry a boy who, it is later discovered, is deaf. She, however, has fallen in love with her high school teacher, who is English. The two of them run off to London to avoid the arranged marriage and protect their "love match." But the love match ends badly, leaving the girl alone and far from home. Her father, meanwhile, has come to London in search of her. They are reunited, and she agrees to return home and go through with the arranged marriage.

The day after the broadcast, the program was a hot topic of conversation among Sikh girls at Grange Hill High. Most of them had watched the show with their families. In a group interview that day, Manjit explained how watching the program had enabled her to direct her father's attention to problems that arise in Britain when marriages are arranged without consulting the future couple.[13]

KH: Did you see that program last night? What did you think?

Manjit: Yeah, the *Love Match*. Yeah, 'cause I watched it and I made my dad watch it as well. At first I thought, 'cause I find it a bit awkward talking about these things in front of my parents, so I walked out of the room, cleared the dishes away, I went into the front room to watch it, and suddenly it got to the bit where she didn't want to get an arranged marriage, so I said, I'm watching this, I'm going to see how my dad reacts [laughter]. So I sat down, put the volume up and I says, "Are you watching this dad, it's really good, you should really watch this. You'll learn a lot from this program."

Media representations of "real life" create a public space where viewers in the privacy of their homes are brought into a zone of "time-space compression." In this space a fiction is created that seduces audiences into believing they can know other realities by simply encountering them in the decontextualized media world. The knowledge gained from television (and other media forms purporting to report "the facts") can give audiences a sense that they understand people and situations they are separated from in daily living (Said 1981).

But dramas like *Love Match*, as well as news coverage and documentary programs, produce selective and partial views and interpretations of the complex cultural worlds they represent. Programs focusing on "ethnic minority" issues discursively constitute "ethnic minorities" by objectifying these groups, their cultural practices, and their traditions. The images they project, frequently though not exclusively, rely on certain constructs of ethnicity, more specifically, on a vision of ethnic groups as homogeneous collectivities separated from the dominant British society by boundaries that are largely unbridgeable. Representations of the lives of Britain's ethnic citizens of color are frequently couched in terms of alien customs— differences assumed to create deep divisions between the host society and the ethnic groups as well as between generations within the groups themselves.

Representations such as these have permeated the coverage of issues associated with Asian citizens in Britain, from arranged marriages to the Rushdie affair. One event in particular directed the attention of the media specifically to the Sikhs. On June 5, 1984 the Indian government invaded the Golden Temple, the historic sacred seat of the Sikh religion in Amritsar. Operation Bluestar left the Akal Takhat (the throne of the Immortal God), the most sacred section of the Temple complex, utterly destroyed. The Sikh library housing handwritten volumes of Sikh scriptures went up in flames. Sant Jarnail Singh Bhindranwale, one of the thousands who were killed, became the most recent in a long line of Sikh martyrs. Following the invasion, Prime Minister Indira Gandhi, who had ordered the storming of the temple, was assassinated by two of her Sikh bodyguards, Beant and Satwant Singh, who were acting out of their own sense of duty to their faith. Beant Singh was killed on the scene by other members of the Prime Minister's squad. Satwant Singh was tried, convicted, and hanged for the assassination. In the aftermath of the assassination, Sikhs in Delhi—particularly *amrit-dhari* Sikhs—became the target of violent attacks; four to six thousand Sikhs were killed. Thousands were left homeless and were settled in refugee camps.[14]

News coverage of these events circulated images of Sikhs brandishing swords amid stockpiles of ammunition, together with commentary describing them as "militants" and "terrorists." For a British public largely uninformed about Sikhs and the situation in Punjab, representations of Sikhs as violent militant extremists raised fears about Sikh neighbors next door.

Members of the Sikh community in Leeds frequently asked me how the crisis in Punjab had been represented in the American press. Had the media in the States portrayed the Sikhs as militant extremists and terrorists? Or had coverage depicted the suffering and tragedy the Sikhs as a people had endured? Others—supporters of the fight for a Sikh homeland, Khalistan—asked me whether Americans understood the weight of justice behind the Sikh struggle for nationhood and political sovereignty. The crisis in the Punjab had been captured within a global mediascape, to borrow Appadurai's (1996) term. Media coverage of these events was worldwide and was producing, transmitting, and perpetuating representations of Sikh identity and history that the Sikhs themselves could neither influence nor control.

In the days following the invasion, first generation Sikhs were dependent on news coverage for information about events in the land they had left behind. The images transmitted to their television screens—and recorded by their parents for repeated viewing—provided the young with powerful new impressions of a world and a people in Punjab they more imagined than directly knew. For the eldest among the second generation—those born in India—these images evoked distant memories of the landscape of early childhood. But many of the younger Sikhs—those born in Britain or East Africa—had never been to Punjab. If they had visited their parents' villages they had felt more like British tourists than natives.

The invasion and desecration of the Golden Temple was experienced by all Sikhs as a deeply painful insult to their honor as a people and to the sanctity of their faith. In the lives of many young British Sikhs, the phenomenon was both powerful and transformative. Having grown up as targets of racism, young people found in these media representations a new source of pride. Media images depicted majestic saffron-turbaned men and boys brandishing swords and protest banners, streets covered with crowds of Sikhs demonstrating against social injustice, and passionate spokespersons on news broadcasts calling Sikhs a courageous people. The collective solidarity sparked by this event gave many young Sikhs a sense of belonging to a movement with global significance, a cause more tangible and less ambiguous than their understanding of British racism. A Sikh boy, in a speech at a youth conference sponsored by the International Sikh Youth Federation in Bradford, spoke of this connection in these words:

I would like to tell you why I am a Sikh. I am a Sikh because of the poetry I draw upon quite strongly in the way of mind and soul put together. I like meditation because of the spiritual strength and power over the mind. *And I know I'm going to stay a Sikh because my brothers and sisters in India are discriminated against by the Indian government.*

In Britain the event became a focal point of public debate about how British the Sikhs had actually become. The celebratory response of some British Sikhs to the assassination of Mrs. Gandhi reinforced concerns that British Sikhs remained more closely tied to India than to their new place of citizenship. One documentary in particular, with the telling title "Where Do I Belong?" captures this tension clearly. This program was one among many in a genre of 1980s television documentaries addressing a national obsession with the "cultural conflicts" faced by second generation British Asians.[15] Barely masking their overriding concern with whether the children of ex-colonial immigrants were assimilating, these programs provided more insight into British fears than into the cultural experiences of second generation British Asians. Nevertheless, this discourse reflected and informed dialogues and debates about the status of Asian ethnic minorities in Britain. They also provided for British Asians a window on dominant British assumptions about cultural difference.

This segment from "Where Do I Belong?" opens with a Sikh family sharing with the interviewer a picture of the family taken in front of the Golden Temple during their holiday. The narrator provides the audience with a brief history of what led up to and followed the invasion of the Temple, then turns immediately to question family members about their reactions to Mrs. Gandhi's assassination.

Son: I think in any religion it's the right of every person to defend it to the last. In Sikhism we have that sort of spirit and we're defending it.

Interviewer: But you can't get away from the fact that it was Sikhs who assassinated Mrs. Gandhi.

Son: I think that's a natural reaction to, ah, because she did invade our Holy Temple, she did destroy our Parliament which is the Akal Takhat. If, ah, any person would, ah, destroy Parliament, we would naturally react in that way.

Interviewer: How did you react when you heard she had been killed?

Son: [Pause] I knew that it would come eventually, because it's happened before. People have invaded the Holy Temple, and it has happened before. The person who did invade it, they had been killed.

Father: She was the person responsible to authorize the attack on the Golden Temple.

Interviewer: So how did you react when she was killed?

Father: Well, I certainly was shocked. But, ah, I have no sympathy for those people who encourage violence. For example, if somebody wants to attack the Vatican, if somebody's going to attack Mecca, if somebody's going to send an army to attack a Hindu temple, it doesn't matter which holy places they are, they have got certain sentiment of the people. So if somebody is going to attack the holy places, doesn't matter what reason, they are certainly, they will certainly encourage a kind of, ah, violence. They will certainly provoke violence, which a sensible person should not do.

Interviewer: How did you feel when Mrs. Gandhi was killed?

Daughter: To an extent we were sorry because she had been the prime minister of our country for so long, and she'd pulled India through quite a few crises. So we were sad that she had died. But when she did die, before she died, our Saint had died, Sant Bhindranwale had died. Well we knew that, when he died, my mom and dad and all our relatives were really upset, and we were expecting her to die, everybody knew that she was going to die, 'cause it was just a form of revenge for those Sikhs.

Interviewer: Because in Southall [outside London] they came out in the streets and cheered, the Sikhs in this country [her voice registers abhorrence].

Daughter: They did it in quite a few towns, because we were in Wolverhampton [near Birmingham] at the time. . . . And they did it there too. In the temples they were celebrating and giving out food and drinks and people who had shops, they were kind of like, there was free champagne. Everybody was really celebrating. But I suppose that is, that is wrong, after somebody's died you don't celebrate. But one thing that people get confused with, 'cause Guru Gobind Singh, he's one of our Gurus, he was a fighter, and because he was a fighter, Sikhs also have to be fighters and follow in their footsteps, and therefore agree with violence and everything. But that's not necessarily true, because he fought for a different reason, you see, he fought to keep our religion alive.

On one level, programs like this introduce the audience to "real people" responding to crises—people viewers might not otherwise come to "know." The public watch as interviewees struggle to explain their experiential reality in terms they hope will translate across divided cultural perspectives. The father and son create an abstract connection, a rhetorical frame that merges the Sikh desire for revenge with other "natural" human responses—

a Catholic's response to an attack on the Vatican or a secular humanist's to the invasion of Parliament, as the Golden Temple is the Sikh's religious and political center. The daughter openly acknowledges her ambivalent feelings about collectively celebrating someone's death, but reminds the interviewer that the act was provoked and, given the nature of the provocation, was an act that should have been expected. The overarching message, however, from the perspective of the British public, is that these second generation Sikhs—despite their East London accents—remain "un-British" in their sympathies toward "fundamentalist" beliefs and violence enacted in the name of religion. These young people became two more examples of "the enemies within"—British citizens expressing loyalties to an alien (and inferior) country and culture. They had not assimilated and might never properly fit within British society.

The imagined Sikh community, the ethnic minority, discursively constructed in British documentaries such as this, differs in subtle yet significant ways from the Sikh community represented in Sikh religious education texts. On one level, each of these discourses about tradition positions those defined as "Sikh" in relation to a unitary, homogeneous, clearly bounded, and enduring culture, representing Sikh identity in essentialist terms. But the two essentialist conceptions of Sikh community are defined in terms of entirely distinctive historical trajectories, relational social fields, and geographic imaginaries. The construction of the Sikh religious community represented in Sikh Missionary Society texts conceives of Sikh identity and tradition as outside time and space. This is precisely what makes it possible to imagine an unchanging tradition joining Sikhs across historic time and a vast space reaching from Amritsar in Punjab across the migratory paths of the Sikh diaspora. Identifying Sikhs as an ethnic minority, on the other hand, locates an imagined Sikh community within the boundaries of Britain. Sikh ethnic culture is that which endures in Britain and refuses to be lost through assimilation to the dominant British culture. This construct represents community as the shared cultural customs and orientations that mark Sikhs as alien and as "other," as a minority group within the postwar British nation.

In the final section, I consider a third type of media discourse that defines identity in terms of cultural hybridity. British Asian youth culture self-consciously celebrates the hybridization of identity, cultural forms, and style in Britain, in the South Asian diaspora, and across the "black" postcolonial imaginary.

Fashioning Hybridity

July 13, 1991: Bhangra Festival/Town and Country Club, London. Unlike the other late night club events sponsored by Capital Radio and Coca Cola in London that week, the Bhangra Festival was scheduled for 3 P.M. on a Saturday afternoon to accommodate the Asian girls whose parents kept them home in the evening. That week's *Time Out* (one of London's weekly entertainment guides) had advertised that "some of the foremost exponents of Indian disco music including the young turk, Apache Indian—whose latest single 'Movie Over India' fuses reggae and bhangra"—were to perform. I arrived at 4 o'clock to find the event had not yet begun.

I entered a pre-show ambiance created by engineers testing flashing colored lights, bhangra blasting from the sound system, and a television crew setting up to film the event for a future broadcast. Black turbaned teenage boys lined the walls. Girls in shalwar kameez and saris dotted the dance floor, moving together to the recorded rhythms. In stark contrast to these youth were the "rappers" or the "hip-hop" contingent. Decked out in baggy trousers, suspenders, and high-top trainers, boys with baseball caps (or turbans) and girls with "big hair" strutted through the auditorium, asserting their freedom and their attitudes. Others still were dressed in "club wear," the boys sporting oversized suits with silky shirts unbuttoned to display a requisite gold chain and with a gold earring in one ear. Fewer girls were glamored up in dresses and high-heeled shoes—shades of Saturday Night Fever. The evening's host, a radio DJ, made his entrance in vintage John Travolta-form—white suit, red shirt, black turban—with the accessory-lady on his arm, a gorgeous long-haired, long-legged creature encased in a black bare-backed mini-dress, striding in atop her black spiked heels.

After making my rounds, I found an empty seat facing the dance floor and, taking out my notebook and pen, settled into my ethnographer mode while I waited for the show to begin. My presence immediately incited the curiosity of my neighbors, three boys smartly dressed in suit jackets, who looked to be in their late teens. The leader of the group asked me what I was writing. "Notes for a research study," I replied. Intrigued, they decided to help me get it right. Moving their chairs in closer, they settled into their roles as my interpreters for the evening.

The Bhangra Festival eventually got underway. The event brought together bands and performers that, I was later to learn, had emerged at different stages in the development of bhangra in Britain. Bhangra is associated with what is referred to as the "new Asian dance music" (Sharma 1996; Huq 1996), a genre that encompasses a broad range of music styles: from early "traditional" bhangra, to the more recent "post-bhangra" rap or jungle, to Bally Sagoo's "Bollywood" remix of Bombay movie soundtracks with British dance beats and heavy bass lines, to Apache Indian's "Bhangramuffin" fusion of ragga and bhangra. These hybrid musical forms each bring together different combinations of musical, cultural, and, in some cases political influences.

My interpreters were avid fans of what have become known as the older "traditional" or original bhangra bands. These young men, who were Punjabis (one Muslim, two Sikh), saw themselves as defenders of the "pure" bhangra sound, a form free of the influence of rap or reggae. As they recounted the history of the bhangra trend, they expressed nostalgia for the height of bhangra fever—a period from about 1986 to 1989 when daytimers (afternoon bhangra parties at clubs such as the Hippodrome) were packed with Asian students skipping school. Bhangra dance music in Britain has evolved over the past two decades into various forms. Basically, however, it fuses the traditional rhythms and sounds of rural Punjabi dance music with the sounds, instrumentation, expressive styles, and production techniques of disco, pop, hip-hop, house, rave, and reggae. In Punjab, bhangra has long been a prominent form of celebratory folk music and dance, typically performed by men, in counterpart to women's songs called giddha, during the harvest and New Year festival of Baisakhi. Bhangra is performed throughout the Indian-Pakistan borderlands by Sikh, Hindu, Muslim, Jain, and Christian Punjabis, and it has been taken abroad by Punjabis to communities across the diaspora. As new hybrid forms are created, the rhythmic beat of the Punjabi drums (the dholak in particular) gives the music its distinctive character as "bhangra." This early form of bhangra continues to be popular with a broad range of Punjabis. Bhangra has become a popular feature at Punjabi wedding celebrations in Britain. I was also told that bhangra bands, like Alaap, have been hired to play at gurdwaras as entertainment for the elderly. Bhangra is one cultural form whose popularity crosses class, gender, and generational boundaries.

But bhangra has had its share of critics. The mainstream media in the 1980s and early '90s were not at all kind to this music genre. Articles characterized the early bhangra musicians as "tacky, lame-suited bhangra groups" and the bhangra scene itself as foreign, unhip, and quite marginal to what mattered in the British music world. Newspaper reports and documentaries on the daytimer phenomenon rehearsed the typical cultural stereotypes in their stories of oppressed daughters of tyrannical Asian parents having to sneak out of school for a fleeting moment of teenage fun (Banerji and Baumann 1990: 14).

The 1990s saw the development of alternative forms of Asian dance music and performance venues alongside the more traditional forms of British Asian music. The particular event I attended was typical of performances during the early 1990s. This period represented a second phase in the history of British Asian music. In addition to the regular daytime events at particular venues, large-scale highly promoted bhangra special events were held for Asian youth in clubs rented during late afternoons and early evenings. Next came the era of the "club scene." In 1994, *Time* magazine featured an article on Bally Sagoo, a "fixture of the 'New Asian Kool'—the name for the hip Anglo-Asian club scene" (Huq 1996: 75). These clubs—or Asian music nights held at trendy London clubs—were set up as fashionable alternative dance scenes for "style conscious Asian youth." They aimed to be "almost elitist establishments, making an explicit effort to distance and indeed disassociate themselves from the 'naff' Bhangra nights that had taken place before them." One such club, Outcaste, opened in June 1995 and had its own record label. A British paper reported that Outcaste "hopes to give Asian bright young things the kind of profile currently reserved for Black music culture" (quoted in Huq 1996: 75).

The mid-1990s saw the emergence of a variety of "post-bhangra" or "beyond bhangra" styles. Some of these innovations, such as the work of Bally Sagoo, continue to draw heavily from South Asian musical resources. Albums such as "Bollywood Flashback" use sampling and remixing technology to create a hybrid Asian sound that interweaves favorite Hindi film songs with trendy techno beats. Although still not in great numbers, Asian women are also more visible in the music scene, from the Voodoo Queens (an all girl punk band), to London DJ Radical Sista (Ranjit Kaur) (Huq 1996; Housee and Dar 1996).

Other genres of Asian dance music create a fusion of different black music styles adopted from Afro-Caribbean, Afro-American, and Hispanic American sources. These music forms—such as Asian hip-hop, rap or jungle, bhangra-ragga, and the post-bhangra electro scene—have been linked to forms of expressive youth culture, such as fashion, and, among some British Asian youth, an identification with Asian "gangs." In a 1989 edition of the British music magazine *I-D*, Veeno Dewan explained that in London

A new scene based around pirate radio, 14-year-old DJs, bootleg tapes and Troop tracksuits is replacing the Bhangra scene of daytime discos and middle-aged men in sequined suits. Welcome to the birth of the Asian Zulu Nation.... [W]hen Bhangra was at its peak Asian Hip-hop crews were setting up their own pirate radio stations. In the early days of Afrika Bambaata, Asian b-boys identified, not with the black rappers and dance crews of the U.S., but with radical Hispanic crews like the Breaker Crew, the Bronx Warlords and, of course, the most famous of them all, the Rock Steady Crew. Many Asians regarded themselves (and still do) as the UK equivalent of America's Latinos—both are made up of different ethnic groups and both are a marriage of two cultures. (1989: 20–21)

British Asian hip-hop is tied to a trans-Atlantic market driven by a complex youth status culture with an expansive and flexible consumer orientation. These performers are creatively fashioning a British Asian identity through signs and symbols appropriated from trans-Atlantic black "street culture." By adopting the status markers of a trendy global youth cultural form—one also associated with black youth musical protest—British Asian hip-hop-ers are challenging derogatory racist stereotypes of Asian culture and are demonstrating that British Asians can also be stylistically aggressive and "cool." A depiction of El Torino, "an 18-year-old, West London-born-and-bred Punjabi rapper" in *I-D*, the self-proclaimed "trendiest fashion organ on earth," illustrates the success of these stylistic innovations.

Wearing a 20-year-old American baseball top ("I got it in a thrift store on holiday in Los Angeles last year!"), Troop tracksuit bottoms and the black turban of his religion, he represents Asian Hip-hop's new generation. He speaks four languages fluently (English, Punjabi, Hindi, Urdu), goes to the temple to pray three times a week, tells me he's under vows never to cut his hair like some of his mates—but eats McDonald's hamburgers (beef is forbidden under religious law to most Asians). El Torino is the product of two cultures. "Look yar (friend) we are talking the best of East and West." (Dewan 1989: 21)

These music styles and commodities circulate across the South Asian diaspora through a wide variety of media, from magazines to a massive network of websites. While many scholars have noted bhangra's role in the "engendering of diaspora" (Gopinath 1995), Kaur and Kalra argue that the global connections the new Asian dance music creates cannot be adequately captured by a term like diaspora that emphasizes a single origin and hence does not account for the multiple parts of the world that have become focal points in these various styles. They propose using the term "Transl-Asia" to refer to global connections joining a complex constellation of spaces in

Europe, South Asia, North America, the Caribbean, East Africa, Australia, and the Far East in continually changing configurations (1996: 223). The concept of Transl-Asia may be a better term for the imaginary space forged by the multiple and complex patterns through which Asian expressive culture flows. Still to be addressed, however, are the multiple ways of imagining community that different Asian dance styles assert and permit.

Across the genres of Asian dance music are distinctive ways of imagining community and signifying "Asian" identity. Traditional forms of bhangra as well as Sagoo's "Bollywood" remixes combine "traditional" South Asian musical genres to produce a "modern" South Asian hybrid style. Each is a "diaspora" style, one that creates new cultural forms from symbolic resources associated with shared South Asian traditions and Indian "roots." Contrastively, hip-hop/rap and bhangra-ragga envision Asian identity through postcolonial lenses, emphasizing communion based in a collective "black" consciousness. These popular cultural forms connect Asian experiences to "black" ex-colonial histories. Musicians such as Apache Indian forge a sense of community between Afro-Caribbeans and Asians by mixing Asian and Caribbean rhythms, referencing a shared postcolonial imaginary, and "code-switching" among a range of linguistic styles. The politicized lyrics and fashion choices of many Asian rap musicians express a trans-Atlantic solidarity among black people in the struggle against racism and class oppression.

Asian musicians, however, engage in different styles of cultural politics. For some, politics remains primarily a matter of style, while others, like Apache Indian, give serious attention to social issues. His songs stylistically index an Asian/Afro-Caribbean communion, but his words speak to the issues and concerns of British Asians, from arranged marriage to alcoholism to the need for "Indians" to "fix up" if they want to be accepted in Britain. In his song "Fix Up" he writes,

Well you no [sic] when the Indian come the, Indian come with the bran new kind of talk
    Originate from Down Town cross the side walk. And we trust no shadow after dark,
    Excuse me, will you fix up yourself up—fix up. Your shoes pants fix up your belt. Excuse me there the Indian talk—fix up your shoes and fix up your walk
    Excuse me, yes me talking to you—better fix up Yourself if you want to get through.

Among politicized Asian musicians, black music is seen as a medium for transmitting, not only new rhythms and sounds, but the politics and principles of anti-racism. Some Asian rap musicians, such as Hustlers HC, use their music as a vehicle for addressing the politics of culture and identity in Britain and within Asian communities themselves. In this song, "Big Trouble in Little Asia," Hustlers HC confronts the rise of Asian ethnoreligious gangs.

Religion breaking up the community
Asian man the storm coming and we need unity
The Hindu, the Muslim and the Sikh
United we stand, divided we are weak
Weakened the most by the coconut
The sell out to the white the coward in the fight
But the Judas must learn together we will burn
Every dog has his day and he will have his turn
Big trouble come I wish I never see the day
I challenge the BNP to march on Southall Broadway
Big trouble comes and by any means
The Blood will stain it and it ain't easy to clean
I know I'm telling you this story
And it may not phase ya
But it causes Big Trouble down in Little Asia.

Other Asian musicians direct their political commentary to global forms of racial injustice. They draw from the history of African American struggles for civil rights, black power, and black pride, from the Rastafari ideology and the independence movements in the various nations of Africa. The images and ideas encoded in these musical styles circulate social critique and commentary as well as positive identifications and resources for the empowerment of blacks throughout the diaspora. In "President Propaganda," we see how the group Fun^Da^Mental finds inspiration from the political perspective of the Nation of Islam.

1995, Elijah is alive
Louis Farrakhan, the Nation of Islam
That's where I got my degree from
So watch out now I'm comin' at ya! . . .
Back in the days of slave ships
You had us whipped, raped and lynched
Took away the Quran, you gave us the bible

Now we're livin' a nightmare
Where black is bad and white is supreme
Fuck that shit, I'm comin' at ya!

Asian expressive youth cultural forms affirm while they protest, generating positive identifications for British Asian youth. The art of these musicians, in bell hooks's words, "remains the site of imaginative possibility" (1990: 18). Asian dance music in particular has created channels for multiple levels of dialogue. Four are most obvious. First, in its most "traditional" form, the performance of bhangra at weddings and celebrations has provided a cultural bridge between first and second generation Punjabis. On the dance floor, parents, grandparents, and children can suspend their differences as they collectively (in gender-segregated groups), share in the pleasure of moving to the bhangra beat. Second, among the second generation these forms of cultural production have articulated new sources of identity as well as a space for dialogue about being British and Asian. Third, "conversations" and cross-fertilizations between the blacks and Asians in the British post-colonies have provided a space of empowerment, a channel for transmitting powerful signs and symbols created in the struggles of black people against race, gender, and class inequality (Gilroy 1987). Finally, when these music forms enter the mainstream—when they are given air time by radio DJs, played in mixed-race clubs, or marketed by major recording companies—the images and messages they express become part of the "conversations" that circulate in mixed-race crowds throughout the world.

The Politics of Representation

Media, as Gilroy argues, provide a means of distribution "capable of dissolving distance and creating new and unpredictable forms of identification and cultural affinity between groups that dwell far apart." The circulation of media brings about what Gilroy has described as the "transformation of space and the subordination of distance," contributing to changes in the significance of appeals to tradition, time, history, and culture (1993: 194). What I have explored here are the various models of culture, tradition, and identity that are appealed to or produced within media discourse as well as the forms of reflection and dialogue that become possible in the borderlands between these distinctive imagined communities.

The media discourse about "culture," "tradition," and "identity" depicted in this chapter engages British Sikhs in various cross-cultural dialogues about difference. Each of the types of media mediation I have described circulates constructs of imagined communities configured differentially in space and time. Entextualization abstracts religious tradition from a location in any particular space or time, creating a continuity with the past that frames a sense of peoplehood in the present, one that extends across the Sikh diaspora. Television documentaries frame Sikh life in terms of ethnic traditions and conflicting cultures, locating Sikh identity firmly on British soil in a particular moment in the history of British race relations. Finally, British Asian popular cultural forms provide resources for creating hybrid identities and imagining ties to multiple communities simultaneously across space. These media create and reinforce communal ties and forms of identification between Asians, other people of color, and increasingly whites through transnational networks of style.

Media mediation plays a unique role in the politics of difference in class-stratified, culturally plural nations. Television documentaries and films as well as literature and other aesthetic productions circulate discourse about difference within which people find themselves positioned. Media discourse provides material for dialogue and reflection. While engaging in these dialogues, people marked as different develop a consciousness of what it means to be ethnic and a minority in the nations in which they reside. Media discourse, in other words, mediates processes of identity formation.

Representations and identifications in the media and popular culture also provide symbolic material for what Butler (1990) refers to as "subversive play" (or, for that matter, nonsubversive play).[16] Alternative identifications allow young people to "disrupt the categories" or come to understand that the essentialist racial stereotypes ascribed to them are neither natural nor absolute. These symbolic struggles associated with the politics of representation may eventually result in transformations in the dominant ideology or in new ways of conceptualizing social difference.[17]

6. "You Can't Be Religious and Be Westernized"

In my conversations, particularly with young girls, the discussion would often turn, as it would with most teens, to the subject of generational conflicts, to tensions with parents over issues such as "going out," talking to boys, dress, and the Sikh religion. In one such discussion, Amrit shared these words and feelings about growing up in Britain.

It's hard for kids at my age, or kids at any age to be brought up in a place totally different from their parents. I go to school and get Westernized ideas pushed into my brain day and day out. When I get home, I only get it when my mom and dad shout at me or when there's a lecture given to us all when you go to the gurdwara (temple).... I mean, you get pulled between two ways of life, I mean the thing that really bugs me is you can't be religious and be Westernized. You have to be religious or be Westernized. You can't have both of two worlds. And if you do, then it's hard. I mean, I try. I think I've got both of two worlds, and I've done it quite well, in the sense that, you know, I've got friends which are boys.

Amrit expresses a feeling shared by many young Sikhs, a sense that they are being pulled between two ways of life—between "two worlds" that are separate and mutually exclusive, and that it is hard to "have both of two worlds." They express their cultural dilemmas in dichotomous terms, but in practice they engage a broad range of cultural influences interwoven in the taken-for-granted fabric of their daily lives. Their tastes in clothing, food, television programs, and styles in decorating their homes all reflect cultural mixing. Why, if their worlds are infused with such a wide range of cultural influences, do they make sense of their lives in dichotomous terms? Why do they feel "caught between *two* worlds"?

On the surface, it might seem obvious that Amrit's dichotomous world-view corresponds to what innumerable ethnicity studies have called "culture conflict." I propose, however, that these contradictions—and oppositions such as Indian/English, traditional/modern, black/white that teens apply in making sense of their dilemmas—each exist at the level of ideology as objectified forms of culture abstracted from the more fluid, ambiguous, and plural processes of cultural production that occur in daily life.

Young Sikhs encounter two contrasting ideologies—the ideology of family honor and the ideology of British nationalism or British cultural purity. These ideologies support two dominant status hierarchies that are distinct but mutually interrelated—the relations of class and racial inequality in British society and the rankings of prestige and honor in the Sikh caste communities. These ideological formations, in turn, support a dynamic process of reciprocal cultural exclusion. This dynamic has been fueled in part by a "cultural racism" specific to Europe in the era of decolonization, one that has arisen in response to the postcolonial reversal of migratory movements in which ex-colonial peoples from the old colonies have settled in the old metropoles. Articulated within notions of nationalism or national purity, the dominant theme of this form of racism "is not biological heredity but the insurmountability of cultural differences" and "the incompatibility of life-styles and traditions" (Balibar 1991a: 21). This construction of social difference in terms of incommensurable racialized cultural essences informs ongoing processes of cultural reification and corresponding acts of social exclusion that continue to divide the dominant white population from Britain's newest citizens of color.[1]

These two ideological formations each reify a particular cultural order, a set of hierarchical and idealized values and standards. Each reflects a shared desire for social wholeness, a desire to impose order in a world of cultural flow and flux, to protect boundaries perceived to be under threat. As conservative forces—as versions of "invented traditions"—they attempt to halt the forward march of social and cultural change. To maintain the status quo is to maintain the relations of authority and the distinctions of sameness and difference (or social inequality) by means of which a dominant group strives to control social power. The conflicting demands in these young people's lives, then, do not result in any simple sense from conflicts between two distinctive bounded cultures. They derive from contradictory expectations associated with two status systems that, as ideological formations, exist as partial expressions of the broader and more complex heterogeneous cultural orientations in Sikh communities and in British society.

At school British Sikhs confront the contradictions between the promises of the liberal ideology of meritocracy and the limiting boundaries of race and class differences. In addition to the contradictory forces they encounter at school, these young people also face conflicting sets of demands in their families and communities, those related to the ideology of family honor and to the status system this ideology supports. I turn now to an analysis of cultural production in Sikh communities.

Fields of Capital

The politics of difference and of status reckoning in Britain involve individuals in overlapping systems of classification and relations of inequality. Categories of social inequality are never absolute, natural, or in any simple way deterministic, but certainly individuals who are defined by racial or even gendered categories are not free to "play" with identities in an unconstrained manner. Contradictions within and between classificatory systems, however, allow spaces for the negotiation, contestation, and reinterpretation of difference. These contradictions are worked out in situated practice. The status positions of particular individuals or groups take on situational meanings as social actors negotiate what are often conflicting status markers and claims based on divergent sets of evaluative criteria. At the national level, groups become integrated into a hierarchical social order as a result of the ongoing dialectical process of attribution and self-assertion. At the level of local or community politics, the claims and counterclaims of status and prestige take their meaning from the perspective of particular groups or individuals.

Social differences are constructed in relation to both ascribed and achieved criteria that become salient in and take on different meanings across particular fields of power. In defining these fields, I draw on Bourdieu's construct to emphasize the relational basis of these types of power dynamics. A field is

a network, or configuration, of objective relations between positions. These positions are objectively defined, in the existence and in the determinations they impose upon their occupants, agents or institutions, by their present and potential situation in the structure of the distribution of species of power (or capital) whose possession commands access to the specific profits that are at stake in the field, as well as by their objective relation to other positions (domination, subordination, homology, etc.). (Bourdieu and Wacquant 1992: 97)

British Asians participate in multiple fields of power in which groups who define themselves in opposition to one another negotiate status inequalities, planes that become enacted at different levels of social scale. Social fields emerge at the points where, as a result of ongoing historical processes, distinctions among British Asians become meaningful sources of difference or conflict, or potential sources of collective identification and solidarity. Significant markers of difference (of collective identification as well as status position) have been associated with the migration histories of East African and South Asian migrants (and those who came at separate times from South Asia); distinctive language group populations in Britain (Punjabi, Gujerati, Bengali, Urdu, and Hindi primarily); religious traditions (Hindu, Sikh, Muslim, Christian, and Jain); caste membership; class position; generation; gender; family status (*izzat*); and place of residence in Britain and in a particular city, such as Leeds. Potential collective identifications cross-cut one another. For example, the East African Asian community includes people who originated from Gujerat (Hindus and Muslims) and from Punjab (Sikhs, Hindus, and Muslims); among Punjabi speakers there are East African Asians (Hindus, Muslims, and Sikhs), Pakistani Muslims, Hindus from India, and Sikhs from India. The relational dynamics in certain social contexts at particular moments in time determine which of these potential identities is significant. For example, during the mid-1980s, following the assault on the Golden Temple, a deep emotional, ideological, and political barrier separated Sikhs from Hindus on a global scale. At the microlevel of situated social interactions, being a speaker of Punjabi takes on different meanings for young British Sikhs depending on whether they are speaking to their parents at home, to their Punjabi Sikh, Muslim, or Hindu friends at school (when they will often use the Hindi they learn from Indian films instead), or in town surrounded by white English people who may react with disapproval to the sound of a foreign language in public. Speaking Punjabi in these instances indexes different contextual affiliations and divisions.

A number of events over the years have galvanized British Sikhs to come together as a people. Particular issues and concerns have been shared by all Sikhs and have spontaneously triggered mass demonstrations of collective support for shared "interests." The legal controversies over wearing a turban and the outrage over the storming of the Golden Temple each awakened a spirit of collective solidarity in the British Sikh population as a whole. The recognition of differences among those who identify as Sikh, however, has also led to the development of factions.

The Sikh population in Britain has become increasingly differentiated in social class terms, or in relation to possession of what Bourdieu (1997) refers to as distinctive forms of capital—economic, cultural, and social. The distribution of these forms of capital, among others, provides the basis for the structuring of relations of class and status inequalities in modern capitalist societies. As Bourdieu explains,

> The social world can be conceived as a multidimensional space that can be constructed empirically by discovering the main factors of differentiation which account for the differences observed in a given social universe, or, in other words, by discovering the powers of forms of capital which are or can become efficient, like aces in a game of cards, in this particular universe, that is, in the struggle (or competition) for the appropriation of scarce goods of which this universe is the site. It follows that the structure of this space is given by the distribution of the various forms of capital, that is, by the distribution of the properties which are active within the universe under study—those properties capable of conferring strength, power and consequently profit on their holder.... These fundamental social powers are, according to my empirical investigations, firstly *economic* capital, in various kinds; secondly *cultural* capital or better, informational capital, again in its different kinds; and thirdly two forms of capital that are very strongly correlated, *social* capital, which consists of resources based on connections and group membership, and *symbolic* capital, which is the form the different types of capital take once they are perceived and recognized as legitimate. (1987: 3–4)

As members of the British Sikh population acquire different levels of economic, cultural, and social capital through their occupational, academic, and social accomplishments, they have become further diversified in terms of the life chances they enjoy and the lifestyles they are creating.[2]

The distribution of types of capital and the structuring of class and status relations among British Sikhs has shifted over time in relation to transformations in the British (and the global) economy. Because early postwar immigrants were largely unskilled and working-class laborers, the arrival of East African Asians possessing higher levels of economic and cultural capital created the first obvious class divisions. Since then, the economic and educational success enjoyed by segments of the first and now the second generation has widened the gap separating the lower and upper classes.

British Asian class distinctions, based on the possession of cultural, economic, and social capital, correspond to five class positions. First is the cosmopolitan South Asian elite—artists, intellectuals, and the independently wealthy. The status of the cosmopolitan elite derives from their cultural and social capital, their sense of style and taste, and their cultural knowledge and social connections. Second, the upper middle class, designated as such by their economic or educational achievements, includes a growing number of successful Asian businessmen as well as professionals, particularly doctors, dentists, solicitors, and accountants. Third, a British Asian middle class comprises businessmen with mid-sized companies (small warehouses, travel agencies, car dealerships/repair shops) and well-educated service industry employees such as teachers, chemists, nurses, and government employees. Fourth, owners of corner shops, market stalls, or other small businesses are considered lower middle class, having much less economic, cultural/educational, or social capital. Finally, the working class can be divided into three segments—managers and laborers in industry, independent laborers, and, finally, workers without work.

The British Asian working class was originally made up of people with little in the way of economic, cultural, or social capital, primarily men employed in factories, particularly textile manufacturing among those in Yorkshire. Many lost their jobs in the late 1970s and '80s when, with deindustrialization, employment opportunities moved from heavy industry and manufacturing to service industries.

Sukhvinder, age fourteen, is from what could be considered a working-class family. Her parents' work history is similar to that of other Jat farmers who migrated from a village in Punjab to a home in Chapeltown. They created working-class family lives, the rhythms and routines of which are structured by the time/discipline of factory work and school schedules. Sikh women like Sukhvinder's mother often bring in extra money by sewing clothing for British Asian retail manufacturers, at home or in small factories.[3]

KH: What do your mom and dad do?
Sukhvinder: Well, my dad works at [a wool mill in Bradford] and he's a foreman . . . and my mum, she sews. . . . My mom was watching some sort of television program about, you know, most people, like parents they go to work, they leave the children at nursery and the children don't really get to have a good relationship with the parents. And my mom started yakking my dad, she said, "They're never with their father," and everything. "Get a day job," right,

"so that you can stay with them at night." So he worked at Ford, but then only for a couple of weeks, because he said that we were getting on his nerves, because, you know, we were living with my dad's parents, you see. And there was me, my brother, and sister. We were only small and we always cried, and my dad said he never got enough sleep. So he went back to [firm name] [laughs]. So he's worked there for ages and he's been, you know, promoted and all now, so he's got his own part now, so he's like the boss there.... But there's a lot of people who are quite jealous of him now because, um, you know, there's English people who work there. And, you know, it's not like they're exactly racist. It's just that they think, you know, how come we've been working here for ages, we don't get pay raises and he's just getting them like this. But my dad says, well, you know, it's just like you've got to really put your back into it, work hard and, you know, be reliable.

KH: And what does your mom do?

Sukhvinder: My mom sews for [a Sikh firm] ... ladies' and children's wear. She works at the factory, but ... she prefers to be at home with us. So during the, specially the summer holidays, 'cause if it's just mid-term break then she'll still work at the factory. If it's like long summer holidays, she'll work at home. So she's a pretty good sewer. She brings it home and works.

When factories closed, working-class families often opted to pool their capital and invest in market stalls and corner shops as a way of securing employment security and independence.[4] Surinder's family bought a shop in Leeds. They live in Bradford about twenty minutes by car from their shop, but the shop is close to Grange Hill High, where at thirteen, Surinder is completing her first year. I asked Surinder and her friend Parminder, whose family also own a shop, what it was like to own a shop.

KH: Do you like owning a shop?

Surinder: Apart from the fact that I can eat all the sweets, yeah [laughs]. No, it's all right.

KH: Is it hard work?

Surinder: Um hm. Especially newsagents, you have to wake up really early in the morning. It opens at six.

Parminder: Yeah. My dad gets up at four o'clock in the morning.

Surinder: I don't. I wake up at the last minute. 'Cause you see, I usually get ready at the shop, for school and that. I brush my teeth there and all that. Because then at home I can just wait till the last minute, you know, you hear the car going outside and you go, oh no, and you have to hurry up....

KH: What time do you have to be at the shop?

Surinder: We open at six.... When we get there, my brother and me dad will stay in the morning and me and me mom go upstairs to sleep. And then at half past I get up and get ready to go. And then I go downstairs and my brother comes up. And then my dad will drop us off. And then the rest of the day me mum, she has to do all the hard, well it's only really serving and putting things on the shelf. Usually they'll leave that until I come.

KH: So you have to get up in Bradford and go over at six and then you go back to bed over there?

Surinder: Yeah, I've got used to it. I didn't at first, I was yawning and everything, but now I've got used to it.

Many Sikh immigrants from Punjab have followed this migration path from villages to working-class jobs and more recently to owning a shop or a market stall. A smaller number of Punjabi men have created profitable businesses in one generation. Some of these men have maintained solid if small businesses, while others have established highly successful factories. Fewer still have amassed great amounts of money in international export businesses. These men typically have little formal education. They have acquired a good deal of economic capital but little in the way of cultural capital. Their children, however, have grown up middle class in middle-class neighborhoods and schools.

Many East African Asians arrived in Britain with both academic degrees and a comfortable amount of economic capital (at least those from Kenya, as Ugandan Asians were usually forced to leave their possessions behind). While they too have encountered barriers along their occupational paths, the benefits of cultural capital—an English education and a middle-class lifestyle—eventually opened doors to middle- or lower-middle-class careers—in government, industry, or service industries, primarily.

A quite different path has been paved for a smaller number of immigrants who arrived from India or East Africa with money as well as cultural and educational capital. The Puthohari community in London is one such group. Hari, a graduate of Leeds University and a member of this group, describes the community and his family:

My parents are Sikhs. They come originally from a region called Pindi, which is right in the north of ah, it's actually now in southern Afghanistan. And they're known as, as a grouping they call themselves Puthohari, which is a regional grouping. Traditionally, of course, they're seen as a caste apart in the Sikh communities and the simple reason for that is that ah, they were a group of people who the British in the last days of the Empire sort of cultivated as administrators, etcetera, as business people, so they had all those facilities of education, of travel, etcetera. Now what happened is that after Partition, when they moved down and came across into India, because they had been equipped with those sorts of skills, of course they became the wealthy business people, yeah? So they were treated with some relative sense of suspicion and kind of resentment, which is quite correct, you know.

In Britain, they've of course formed themselves into what they call the Putho-hari Association. It started really in the late sixties when they started coming into Britain. Okay, in the late sixties of course there was a very very wide grouping of people from all social classes, ah, now, ah in the nineties, it's really only very wealthy people who are in the Puthohari Association. . . . What has started happening is that there have been subgroups forming, yeah? . . . You have the sort of group who'll be doctors and lawyers, and . . . then you've got the business people who are different again. And neither of them really get along with each other, that's the other point, socially they don't. They don't have much to kind of exchange with each other. . . . It's quite funny, there's a lot of comedy in all of it. There's a film . . . I've forgotten the film, but it's actually quite a significant film, it was made in the six-ties. . . . There's this wedding scene, this Jewish wedding scene in America, and . . . it's really come into my mind because I went to this wedding very recently, it was a Puthohari wedding and I could have sworn that the characters were exactly the same as in the film. . . . The conversations were exactly the same. This treatment of consumerism was exactly the same. . . . This cousin of mine had just come out of Balliol, Oxford. And he just got this wiz degree, etcetera. And there was a party for him. And ah, do you know the Dustin Hoffman film, "The Graduate," yeah? . . . There is this scene in the Hoffman film where somebody comes over to him and puts his arm around his shoulder and he says, "Look, there's only one thing I want to say to you," and Hoffman looks up at him. And after a few moments he says, "Plastics." And exactly the same experience happened, and I saw him, this guy came and put his arm over him and instead of plastics he said, oh I don't know what he said, but it was right down to a tee.

Those among this status elite possess and express their combined portfolios of educational, cultural, and economic capital through exclusive patterns of interaction and expensive styles of consumption. Elites who arrived with money and educational capital have been joined by others who have acquired these status markers through their educational accomplishments and their pursuit of professional careers in fields such as medicine, accounting, and law. They and their children are Asian cosmopolitan elites. Yet, while elite, they remain Asian, and being Asian, their position in British society more generally continues to be marked to some degree by race. Among Asians who have acquired these levels of cultural, economic, and social capital, however, there is, in William Julius Wilson's words, a "declining significance of race" (1980). Race matters, but for upper-class Asians it plays a less significant role in determining life chances.

A central division among the Sikh population in Leeds arose from the distinctive migration histories that separate Sikhs from India and those from East Africa.[5] At the most mundane level, the decorating styles of East African and Indian Sikhs each evoke influences from their respective "homelands"—East African families display African elephants carved in wood, in contrast to the stuffed and sequin-covered Indian elephants in the homes of families from Punjab. East African Sikhs organize local gurdwara-sponsored hockey teams (though hockey is popular in India as well), while those from India prefer cricket or kabaddi (a Punjabi sport that involves wrestling).[6] But there are also Welsh East African Sikhs in Cardiff who are mad about rugby—a point that draws me safely away from this momentary lapse into ethnic athletic essentialism.

East African and Indian migrants, however, did come to Britain from very different social worlds. East Africans had lived in what were largely racially segregated Asian communities in the urban centers of Uganda, Kenya, and Tanzania. They had benefited from the availability of British education and had occupied administrative and professional posts as the "middlemen" in the British colonial infrastructure. East African Sikhs, particularly those from the Ramgarhia caste, had also created a more "conservative" approach to Sikhism. They had instituted caste associations and had succeeded in tailoring religious practices to life in an urban middle-class context. One man from Kenya, for example, explained that Ramgarhia Sikhs had introduced the practice of wearing neatly pressed white turbans to create a style that would "look smart with evening wear." East African Sikhs, then, had arrived in Britain already urbane and middle class.

The East African-Indian divide has been further complicated by caste. The majority of East African Sikhs are Ramgarhia, members of the artisan castes, which include Tarkhan (carpenters), Lohar (blacksmiths), and Raj (bricklayers). A majority of the migrants from Punjab are Jat, members of the landowning/farming caste. While there are Jat East Africans as well as Ramgarhias from India, the central tension in Leeds has been between Jats from Punjab and Ramgarhias from East Africa. There are also a few Sikh families from other castes whose status, traditionally, has been lower than either Jat or Ramgarhia; among these are Bhatras (peddlers), Jhirs (watercarriers), Nais (barbers), Chamars (leatherworkers), and Chuyhyas (sweepers).

In Britain a classificatory inversion has created a contradictory status relationship between the two major caste groups, the East African Ramgarhias and the Indian Jats. Considered the highest of the Sikh caste groups (with the exception of Sikh Brahmins, who are few in number) and numerically dominant in Punjab, Indian Jats in Britain have generally been of a lower class position than middle-class East African Ramgarhias, at least among first generation immigrants.

In Leeds, this inverted status relationship has fueled competition between these groups. At first there had been a single gurdwara to which members of all castes belonged. In the late 1970s the Ramgarhias established their own separate religious institution, the Ramgarhia Board. Since then other caste and sectarian groups have followed suit. Today there are three gurdwaras on Chapeltown Road: the original Sikh Temple (first located in a converted gothic-style Methodist church but recently moved to a new gurdwara built across the street); the Ramgarhia Board (housed in a huge two-story renovated post office with a large extension); and the Gurdwara Shri Kalgidhar Sahib Ji (held in a terraced house and attended by the Bhatras). There are two gurdwaras in South Leeds as well.

The splintering of gurdwara congregations has occurred in response to a range of historic, religious, social, and political factors. The "Sikhs" as a religious body is a constantly changing mosaic of sectarian divisions. It encompasses established sects (such as the Nirankaris, Radhasoamis, Namdharis, and Ramdasias—the last two with important links to particular caste groups), as well as newer sects that have grown up around charismatic teachers (for example Ramgarhia followers of Sant Puran Singh). These sects frequently disagree on issues ranging from the proper performance of rituals, the legitimacy and authority of Gurus who follow the original ten Gurus, and whether particular rituals are authentically "Sikh" or "Hindu."

Caste alliances have also played a significant role in local politics.[7] In the 1980s local authorities and the central government sponsored initiatives (such as the Urban Programme and Manpower Services) that made money available for ethnic minority programs and projects. Though the money was designated for "ethnic groups" in "inner city areas," Ramgarhia and Jat leaders applied separately for government funds to build their own community centers. Leaders from the two major caste groups each asserted that their group represented the true "Sikh community," and both succeeded in obtaining funds. There are now two Sikh community centers on Chapeltown Road less than a mile apart, one associated with the Ramgarhia Board and the other with the Sikh Temple.

Young Sikhs who have grown up in England seem to have a difficult time understanding the communal politics that divide members of their parents' generation. When members of the second generation go to the gurdwara they define themselves as "Sikh,"—or as "Indians" who are also Sikh. For them the critical distinctions are racial—"English" from "Indian"—and religious—Hindu, Muslim, and Sikh. They identify less with caste affiliation, if in fact they even know the caste to which they belong. When I asked, most young Sikhs associated caste with occupation, "We're Jat, we're farmers," but they often got it wrong. Caste divisions in their minds are contrary to Sikh teachings (as doctrinally they are). Caste, they believe, threatens the collective solidarity, the unity of the Sikhs as a religious/ethnic group.

I asked Manjit (a Jat) and her friend Satvinder (a Sikh Brahmin) what they though about caste. Their response illustrates the insignificance of caste and the relevance of ethnicity (in this instance, "Indianness") to their own lives in England.

Manjit: I don't really believe in it, I mean. . . .
Satvinder: I don't either.
Manjit: I don't care if they're Ramgarhia Sikh. . . .
Satvinder: [interrupting] I don't either, this is all I've heard from my mom and dad, you see. Like to me it's all considered if you're Indian you're Indian and I don't go into detail, you're Jat, you're Sikh, you're Ramgarhia, like I think it's stupid. . . .
Manjit: Yeah, I. . . .
Satvinder: . . . the way they've got two churches and they come to do one church higher than the other when churches should be the same, they should be just a holy place.
Manjit: Yeah, it should be a holy place; you shouldn't regard it as higher caste or lower caste.

Second generation British Sikhs vary considerably in their feelings about and relationship to the Sikh religion. But even those who do not practice the faith respect the anti-caste egalitarian principles on which the religion was founded. For some, contradictions between Sikhism's egalitarian principles and local group practices become a source of deep disillusionment. Rani, in her early twenties, is a Sikh feminist who is committed to her political work with local community organizations. Her family, though Ramgarhia, are from India. They choose not to attend the Ramgarhia Board but go to the "main" Sikh gurdwara instead. When I asked her what role caste has played in her life, her words painted a complex map of identifications. She speaks as a second generation Sikh, describing caste in terms of the class snobbery she hates. Yet she is also a Ramgarhia from India, whose family in class and ethnic terms identifies more with the Jats.

KH: Do you see any difference between Ramgarhia girls, Ramgarhia Sikh friends, and Jats?

Rani: Um, yeah.

KH: What sort of differences?

Rani: They look down, Ramgarhias look down. . . .

KH: On Jats?

Rani: They just look down on everyone. And they think the Ramgarhias are top. . . .

KH: You're Ramgarhia aren't you?

Rani: Yeah, and I'm ashamed, at times, to be called one. Because the friends I have, they're Ramgarhia, and they go to the Ramgarhia Board [gurdwara]. And they have, sometimes the opinion of what they have comes out in their conversation, comes out in what they say. And I act totally different to them, and I can't believe that I'm Ramgarhia. *To me, class has never meant anything.* Um, *someone's status in life hasn't meant anything to me.* I treat everyone equally. And I always get, when I first, I didn't know I was Ramgarhia until the Ramgarhia Board split up and my dad . . . explained it to me and then turned around to me and said, "We're Ramgarhia." And I was, I went, I was astonished and I said, "Dad what do you mean we're Ramgarhia." And he says, "We're one of them." And uh, my dad, the thing is, the Ramgarhia don't realize they're going totally against the principles of our religion. There should be no caste system.

KH: What do you think those divisions are based on? Why do they think they're better?

Rani: Status. Like these Ramgarhias were landowners. They weren't peasants. They had the money and everything.

KH: The Jats were the landowners though.

Rani: The Jats, they looked in the sense that Jats did the work and Ramgarhias are the people with the money. You see . . . Jats are working class, have ten, fifteen children, and that's it. It isn't, it isn't. I mean Jats are just, I mean some Ramgarhias are just exactly the same as Jats. You've got to point out, you've got to mention their name, and then say, well they must be a Ramgarhia [surnames other than "Singh" denote caste membership].

Well Ramgarhia people think they're well off, well educated, into everything . . . in the sense that they know everything. You know, you name it, they would probably know it. They're not stupid and thick. Whether you are or not, is a different matter. But they just think, you know, you're into the money, regardless of how much you have, they just think you're into money. And they look down at everyone. And they also, they're big-headed, totally big-headed. If you go to a Ramgarhia Board and just stop and look around, they don't have to say anything, you can just see it on their faces. I've been there once or twice and people just look at you. It's like a fashion show over there. Showing off what they have, in the sense of clothing and the sense of what they wear, how they talk.

Well once you go to Sikh temple, the main one, no one looks, in that sense, you're all equal there. Okay, you have the one or two women saying, well what kind of suit she's got on? Where did she get it from? But they don't say, well is she a Jat or is she that, or there's a Ramgarhia walk through the door or a Jat walk through the door. But seldom will a normal Sikh go in there unless he's a Ramgarhia or unless he's invited or anything. And if a Ramgarhia, if you know a Ramgarhia who goes to that place and comes to the main gurdwara, that's the only time you're going to get noticed. If you've never been there a lot.

KH: How about Bhatras? Do you know many Bhatras?

Rani: I don't know many. I don't associate with them.

KH: Why?

Rani: Because I don't know any of them. But their opinion is the same. They're just supposed to be working class. And I mean they have these working class/ upper class stuff and it's ridiculous, because we're not supposed to believe in that. And for it to exist, you know, and to have these two different temples and everything. My friends, right, they get a big kick outta saying they're Ramgarhia Board and everything. And I used to say to them, it's not even a temple, so why can you call it....

KH: Why is it not a temple?

Rani: I don't think it's a temple, in the sense that to me it doesn't hold the principles, the morals, the attitude. To me what a temple is it doesn't fulfill. The rules a temple holds and everything, the Ramgarhia Board doesn't, to me it's just a house with a Bible put in it and being called a temple. And just by a certain class of people allowed to go there. I mean in the sense that they give it Ramgarhia Board in the first place, means just for the Ramgarhia.

British Sikhs like Rani often confuse caste with differences in class background. They do not comprehend what caste means in their parents' lives, either as an ongoing cultural practice or even, as Rani's statements illustrate, as a set of historic relations. They have acquired a distinctively British classificatory discourse about social differences. They identify themselves in census category terms, identities designated by "objective" criteria such as class, religion, culture (or ethnicity), citizenship, race, age, gender, family, and area of residence.

But caste for the first generation has also taken on different meanings and new forms of expression in Britain. British caste divisions are not incorporated into a single systematic hierarchy of ranked occupational groups, if they ever were in India. Rather, caste operates in British Sikh society more like an endogamous status group, but one that denotes a sense of peoplehood.

In an interview, scholar and Leeds resident Dr. Sewa Singh Kalsi explained that among first generation Sikhs caste ties are similar to the primordial forms of solidarity that unify nations.[8]

The Jats are more pragmatic, you know.... Because they've been landholders, in the villages they've been landholders, right, the panchayat [village] leaders and everybody deciding everybody's fate. Right.... So Ramgarhias when they went to East Africa were very good at keeping their symbols and everything. And they organized the Sikh temples, and the Sikh temples were opened to anybody. Very few Jats were able to manipulate the control of the Sikh temples. It's a fascinating story. In Nairobi, I was told that they built one Sikh temple, the Jats took over the control. Then they built another Sikh temple, the Jats took over the control. They built another Sikh temple, Jats took over the control with the help of some of the Ramgarhias, right? And eventually the Ramgarhias said, "Bly me, what shall we do?"

Then they said, "Right. We'll establish a Ramgarhia Board." Don't call it a gurdwara, if you call it a gurdwara everybody will be allowed, you know, has a right to come and participate. So Ramgarhia Board, it means you can go to Ramgarhia Board, and it's exactly like Sikh temple. Ramgarhia Board Sikh Temple—Ramgarhia Board gurdwara, that's what they said. Then they started writing up constitutions. Hmm. You've got to be Ramgarhia that's number one. It's the *Quam*. Quam means, it's used as a nation, but they were not a nation, they were talking about the caste. Right. But caste is a bad name. Literally, Quam means a nation. It's a word from Urdu. But this is the word people use in the village. Our Quam, our nation—our community is what they mean.[9]

Members of the first generation repeatedly stressed that caste divisions are social and have nothing to do with the Sikh religion. Caste divisions continue alongside religious practices that centuries ago were begun in order to break down caste barriers (practices such as the *langar*, the communal meal served at every gurdwara to ensure that all people, regardless of caste, eat the same food communally). Caste divisions, I was told, are based on historic, social, and political divisions, very like national boundaries. A leader in the Ramgarhia Board temple supported this view.

The division has been there ever since the Sikhism. Even before that these were there, even though Guru Nanak had preached that ah, all human beings are alike. There should be no discrimination against color, creed, sex. He has been preaching that. But this division is not on the religious basis. It's on the social side, really, politically. In India, the Jats, they are dominating because they're more in number, and the Ramgarhias are in minority, and so they just wanted things their way. But the Ramgarhias felt that the biggest reason why these groups still sort of prayed separately is a social one, the marriages. The marriages don't take place between a Jat Sikh and a Ramgarhia Sikh, you see. They still tend to be within their own sect.

Marriage endogamy, he states, is the reason Sikhs pray together in their separate caste groups, and, as Dr. Kalsi explains, caste is perpetuated in Britain and elsewhere through restrictions on marriage.

The Sikh family. The Sikh family, that's it. That's my hypothesis. It's the family. And family is organized, developed through a very important institution that is marriage. Everything is associated with this institution. If you break this institution, you break the caste system. And purity, the notions of purity and pollution, are associated with marriage. If you marry outside, then you bring in the notion of purity and pollution. Otherwise, there's no such thing, as far as the Sikhs are concerned. That is caste dharma. That's the institution. That's how caste is going to survive.
   The Ramgarhias, for example, why are there Ramgarhias? Right. There's nothing special. How do they remain Ramgarhias? That's the most important thing. Not because they're thinking like Ramgarhias, you know, simply because Ramgarhias are born to Ramgarhia families to Ramgarhia mothers. Right. They still organize marriages on the principles of caste endogamy. That is the fundamental criteria, because that is how they know caste members. Right type of marriages produce right type of caste members.

First generation Sikhs define peoplehood in terms of caste membership. "Pure" members of these caste communities are produced through ensuring the "right" types of marriages between members of a caste group.[10] This sense of caste community is remarkably similar to the British notion of national identity, an identity based in primordial ties of kinship and cultural purity. Moreover, each of these identity constructions, these "imagined communities," bears a strong resemblance to what Weber defines as the most extreme form of a status community:

The status structure reaches such extreme consequences only where there are underlying differences which are held to be "ethnic." The "caste" is, indeed, the normal form in which ethnic communities usually live side by side in a "societalized" manner. These ethnic communities believe in blood relationship and exclude exogamous marriage and social intercourse. (1946: 189)

The imagined communities associated with caste are status communities in the sense that the basis of solidarity, of belonging, is assumed to flow through blood. Membership is ascribed by birth. Boundaries are preserved through proscriptions for group endogamy, and a privileged status is granted to those designated as belonging. In keeping with their status, members of caste status communities are expected to uphold a particular style of life linked to criteria of social honor. Again, in Weber's words:

In contrast to classes, status groups are normally communities. They are, however, often of an amorphous kind. In contrast to the purely economically determined "class situation," we wish to designate as "status situation" every typical component of the life fate of men that is determined by a specific, positive or negative, social estimation of honor. This honor may be connected with any quality shared by a plurality, and, of course, it can be knit to a class situation: class distinctions are linked in the most varied way with status distinctions.... In content, status honor is normally expressed by the fact that above all else a specific style of life can be expected from all those who wish to belong to the circle. Linked with this expectation are restrictions on "social" intercourse.... These restrictions may confine normal marriages to within the status circle and may lead to complete endogamous closure. (1946: 186–88)

Status communities in Weber's terms are status-bearing reference groups involving different audiences at specific levels of social scale. Societies, particularly culturally diverse social orders, are composed of many different status groups or communities. They vary according to their points of reference, their level of organization, and their degree of social encompassment; and they can take many forms, from occupational status groups to racially defined collectivities to an elite social class.

The caste status communities are the central reference groups for status negotiations among first generation Sikhs. These status negotiations are informed by what I call the ideology of Sikh family honor and are directed, at the most fundamental level, toward reproducing the various caste communities through prescribed forms of marriage. It is at this level, in the context of rituals of marriage-making, that the status negotiations of the first generation become meaningful in the lives of the second.

The Market for Marriages

The Sikh parents I grew to know were deeply concerned about the future well-being of their children. They considered education and a good marriage key to their future happiness and success. Working-class parents in particular hoped that by getting a good education and entering a profession their children could avoid the racism they had experienced.

In Sikh communities more broadly, educational qualifications are commodities in the market for marriages. Marriage advertisements on Internet websites, similar to these from the "Matrimonial" section of a Punjabi diaspora newspaper, illustrate this quite explicitly.

Sought a suitable match for a clean shaven Jat Sikh Doctor 28 yrs. of age, 5'8" tall with fair complexion. He graduated in MB CH.B from Britain and belongs to an educated and well settled family in U.K. The girl must be pretty and most preferably a Pharmacist or Lawyer or a person of that Calibre.

Educated Jat Sikh parents seek suitable match for their 22 yrs. old, 5'4" tall, British born daughter. She appreciates both Indian and Western cultures and has "O" levels, 9, a diploma in business studies . . . has taken a Secretarial Course, [and is] now working for the Civil Service. Boy should preferably be clean shaven and suitably qualified.

Suitable match required for a pretty Jat Sikh girl, Barrister, 5'7" aged 29, has a fine balance of modern and conservative views; very domesticated, kind, loving and faithful; from a very respected and educated family.

Internet services like IndianMarriages.com and IndianDating.com (two of many websites) have made the matchmaking process more systematic—for purposes of dating as well as finding potential marriage partners. Individuals or families who wish to use these services fill out a multiple-choice "search profile" online.[11] IndianDating.com, similar to other services, allows people to search for potential partners according to a series of criteria. Some of the information gathered for the database is standard for Internet personals sites, while other data seem to be uniquely significant to people of South Asian origin. The "advanced profile" asks prospective service users to characterize themselves and their desired date or mate in relation to the categories and qualities I have reproduced below. People across the globe who have Internet access can take advantage of services like these. IndianDating.com, however, includes information—in questions related to income and immigration/citizenship status in particular—that suggests that its primary users might be looking for partners in the United States and Canada.

Sex: Male or Female and Groom or Bride
Age: 0 to 100
Country (where your match resides): Any, Unspecified, India . . . (followed by a long list of countries beginning with Afghanistan)
Province/state (your match lives in): Lists provinces or states in India, the United States, and Canada.
Birth Country (where your match was born): Any, Unspecified, India, Afghanistan . . . (same list as for country of residence)
Will Travel (how far your match is willing to travel for someone): Any, City, State/Province, Country, Any distance
Caste (your match's caste): Cosmopolitan, Warrior, Catholic, Protestant, Muslim, Other . . . (a long list of recognizable caste names as well as other identifications)

Subcaste (the subcaste of your match): Any, African, American, Australian, British, Gujarati, Kannada, Maharastrian, Malayalee, Marathi, North Indian, Other, Punjabi, Sengunthar, South Indian, Tamil, Telugu (mix of language groups, regional and national identifications)

Cultural Values (your match's cultural values): Any, East & West Mix, Eastern, Western

Star Sign (the horoscope sign of your match): Any, Aries, Taurus, ...

Native Language (your match's primary language): Any, Bengali, English, ... (list includes Indian languages in addition to French, German, Japanese, and Chinese)

Other Language (your match's secondary language): Any, ... (same list as above)

Height and **Weight** (up to 300 lbs.)

Body Type: Any, Average, Athletic, Petite, Slim/Slender, Large, Few Extra Pounds

Religion: Any, Buddhist, Christian, ... (lists most world religions, including Atheist)

Religion Degree: Any, Very religious, Somewhat religious, Not very religious

Wears Turban (for Sikhs): Any, Yes, No

Occupation: Any, Administrative, Business, Clerk, Computers, Construction, Consulting, Dentistry, Education, Engineering, Executive, Journalism, Medicine, Other, Sales, Science, Self-Employed, Student, Supervision, Technician, Unemployed, Architect, Lawyer, Attorney, Homemaker

Education: Any, High School, Bachelor's, Master's, MBA, Ph.D., Engineering

Income: Any, <50K, 50-100K, 100-500K, 500K+

Has Children: Any, Yes, No **Wants Children:** Any, Yes, No

Marital History: Any, Unspecified, Never Married, Separated, Divorced, Widowed

Skin Color: Any, Dark, Tan, White, Black, Fair, Very Fair

Drinking Habits: Any, Don't drink, Drink occasionally, Drink often

Smoking Habits: Any, Don't smoke, Smoke occasionally, Smoker

Diet Habits: Any, Non-Vegetarian, Vegetarian

Passport: Any, Indian, UK/European, USA-Full, USA-Green Card, USA-H1, Canada, Other

Immigration (citizenship status): Any, Citizen, H1B, F1, Green Card, J1 (USA designations)

Living Situation: Any, Live alone, Live with friends, Live with family

Family Honor

Status discourse in Sikh communities in Britain stresses distinctions such as wealth, education, and occupation—markers of class position that resonate with class distinctions in British society more generally but have a decidedly Punjabi slant in terms of the professions viewed as desirable, notably medicine, pharmacy, law, accountancy, and, more recently, information technology. But in addition to these markers of individual achievement, Sikhs are concerned with family honor, or *izzat*.

Family honor is a quality possessed collectively; it is reinforced or ruined in social transactions, most significantly by the actions of unmarried daughters. Amrit quite eloquently explains her sense of the meaning of family respect and honor:

The thing is, English girls I know, respect and honor comes to them through earning it through the job they do, through whatever they do, they're not born with it. And if they respect their mom and dad, it's not ... because they give birth to them, [that] doesn't mean anything to them. It's just human beings and it just happens that you give birth to them. But with an Asian girl, because it's your mom and dad, you respect them, in the sense that from birth, your mom and dad are everything, honor and respect them. You don't turn around and say, "Mom, shut up." You can't say, "Mom and Dad, shut up, okay?" And there's a lot of people out there that don't understand that Asian girls have honor and respect given to them at birth. A guy is given it, but it's not shown. He can lose his respect and honor and nothing bothers him family-wise. No one will look at the family and say, "Well that boy does that." But if a girl does it, that's it, bad name for the family, whole life ruined.

For a Sikh woman, she as a person, is the pole of the family ... in the sense that, she holds it up. If the pole breaks, the whole thing breaks.... She has been given a gift from god, to bear children, which no man can touch. And the fact that they've been given the purity until they're married, that has a lot to do with respect and honor. You respect a woman who hasn't been touched by a man.... You know, it's sort of like, her virginity is like a gift given and if a woman can hold that, you know she's strong. And to give it to her husband, you know, is the utmost thing a woman can do, you know, in our religion. You know, and to break that, there's no point of a woman existing if she does that.

Family honor is critical for marrying children into good families. Marriage is a joining of families. Sikhs marry ideally within the same caste and generally with others of the Sikh faith, but caste membership can override religious divisions between Punjabi Hindus and Punjabi Sikhs. Interracial marriages, though they occur (and they do with increasing frequency), are generally not acceptable, particularly among Asians and Afro-Caribbeans or Africans. While East African Sikhs seem a bit more liberal in their views, Asians, on the whole, still show low rates of interracial marriage (see statistics in Chapter 1). It is the ties created through the institution of marriage that perpetuate boundaries of caste and class, race and religion within and between Sikh communities, as well as between Sikhs and other racial groups. In this way the ideology of family honor is deeply tied to the reproduction of the Sikh family, Sikh caste communities, and the racialized boundaries of belonging within these status groups.

The ideology of family honor finds its expression as it is embodied in restrictions and disciplinary judgments and actions focused toward controlling female sexuality—toward protecting the "gift" of female purity and virginity until it can be given away at marriage. The bodies of unmarried women are the sites on which the dynamic struggles of sociocultural reproduction within Sikh communities are fought.[12]

Before concluding this discussion, however, an important issue requires further attention and clarification. In any discussion of arranged marriages among South Asians in Britain, it is important to note and challenge the way this practice has been represented in discourse about South Asians. Arranged marriages, like wearing the veil (*hijab*) among Muslim South Asians, is associated in dominant discourse with the oppression of South Asian women. Noshin Ahmad, in an article describing why she, a well educated and "modern" British Asian woman, chooses to wear the *hijab*, argues that such criticisms conflate cultural principles with despicable individual practices.

Time and again the problem of forced marriage surfaces and girls are reported as having been duped to vacation in their parents' country of origin unaware that soon they will be married off for a huge dowry.... While no one doubts that these events occasionally take place and that their impact on the individuals involved is profound, the way in which incidents are represented denigrates women's relationship to Islam. There is rarely an attempt to contextualise media representations within an Islamic framework based on the *Qur'an* and *Sunnah* (the traditions and practices of Prophet Mohammad). Consequently, Islam comes to be judged by the actions of Muslims, rather than the judging of Muslims by Islam.... It is misleading to take cultural, political and social patriarchal practices of Muslim men and define these as "Islamic." In many cases the oppression of women is not a religious condition, but a political issue, because their rights and interests conflict with male advantages. (1999: 76)

The same slippage occurs when the institution of arranged marriages comes to be judged by the sexist or abusive acts of individual families. Many of the young women I grew to know were open to and even embraced the notion that their parents would assist them in finding a suitable marriage partner, while other young women rejected this practice altogether. The differences in their responses, however, had more to do with the connection these young women felt to the Sikh community and to the identities they were forming as British women, and did not reflect any sense that the arranged marriage practice in and of itself was sexist or oppressive.

Family and community relations are powerfully constitutive forces in the experiences of Sikhs growing up in Britain. These relations provide social support and solidarity just as they give birth to interpersonal conflicts. They are the source of various forms of capital that either enhance or constrain the life chances of Sikhs from different class and caste backgrounds. But family and community are two among the several different sites of power that constitute identities and social statuses in the lives of British Sikhs. These social worlds are situated within the wider cultural landscape young people cross in the practice of everyday life.

7. "There's a Time to Act English and a Time to Act Indian"

Mapping Identities

In crafting this alternative account of immigration, citizenship, and identity formation, I have focused so far on the shifting fields of power in the public sphere, the cultural politics at work in the domains of law, policy, education, the media, and Sikh families and caste communities. These discursive formations articulate regulatory schemas that define citizenship statuses and immigrant identities as they differentiate between racial and religious, gendered and generational, class and caste categories and classifications. I now shift from these broader contextual dynamics to the activities of everyday life. In this chapter I map the cultural landscape Sikh teens cross as they move among the social worlds that make up their everyday lives. I explore identity formation here from the perspective of the Sikh youth themselves, portraying the ways in which their sense of imagined or possible selves is shaped by normative rituals and routines enacted within different social settings.

In the routines of everyday life, Sikh teenagers move through a number of different social contexts—home, school, shopping arcade, temple—with specific kinds of people, networks of relations, and styles of interacting. These practices transform places or locations into spaces, in de Certeau's sense of a space as "a practiced place."[1] I refer to these socially inhabited spaces as "cultural fields."[2]

Cultural fields are "relatively autonomous social microcosms" in which social life is organized around different constellations of power and authority, cultural competencies and normative expectations that are "specific and irreducible to those that regulate other fields" (Bourdieu and Wacquant 1992: 97–98). The regularities of routine practices in a cultural field both reproduce and create cultural expectations for bodily gestures and dress, for appropriate manners and signs of respect between the generations and the sexes, and for the cultural knowledge people use to interpret social interactions.

British Sikhs enact distinctive sets of normatively regulated performances across the different communities of practice in which they participate. Regulatory schemas condition social practice over time through the reiteration of norms, or what Butler calls "performativity." Performativity is the process through which regulatory ideals—in Butler's work, those constituting the category "sex"—are "materialized," or norms are "assumed, appropriated, taken on" (1993: 3). Subjects are formed in performing these imposed cultural norms "by virtue of having gone through such a process of assuming" (3). Performativity, it must be stressed, is not a single or intentional act by which a person enacts an identity, in the usual sense of performance. Rather, performativity "must be understood ... as the reiterative power of discourse to produce the phenomena that it regulates and constrains" (2).

Sikh teens consistently portray their cultural dilemmas in ethnically absolutist terms, while they are also just as apt to acknowledge that they never feel completely "Indian" or completely "English." Rather, they move through their lives understanding that, as one young woman phrased it, there is "a time to act English and a time to act Indian." In their everyday lives, second generation Sikhs participate in a number of cultural fields in which they "act Indian" or "act English" or, more accurately, within the limits of normative constitutive constraints, perform identities that produce something in between. Together these cultural fields constitute a sort of cultural landscape inscribed in the consciousness of the young people who move within and between these cultural fields. Sikh teenagers imagine this cultural landscape—or the relation between the various cultural fields—in terms of their perception of restrictions or freedoms, the opportunities for different types of activities in each cultural field. Second generation Sikhs symbolically order or map this cultural landscape both geographically and bodily in accordance with the way cultural identities are signified and enacted in these fields. Regulatory practices are highly gendered, enforcing distinctive types of restrictions on women's bodies, women's movements, and the interactions between unmarried youths.

Not all youths move across exactly the same set of social situations, but an ideal typical cultural landscape, shared by Sikh girls and boys alike, would encompass four cultural fields. These fields (together with the forms of dress, activities, and gender relations associated with them) fall along a continuum from spaces where they feel most compelled to act "Indian" to contexts where they act more "English"—the Sikh gurdwara, home, the shopping arcade in the Leeds city center, and school.

Within these cultural fields, it is the signs and practices, transactions and interactions that constitute the field, not simply its location in a partic- ular place, such as the gurdwara. The relationship between a place and a cultural field is never natural or pre-existing; rather a place becomes a cul- tural space as it is "habituated or deeply inscribed in everyday routine," as lived in culture (Comaroff and Comaroff 1991: 25). A striking example of this relationship is how during wedding parties the cultural field most reg- ularly found at the gurdwara expands to fill the back room of a local pub or the reception hall of a social club. As a gurdwara community enters the pub, the regulatory ideals and interactional norms that structure social life at the temple come into play for the duration of the event—although, as the scotch continues to flow, policing at the borders, at least from the men, becomes a bit more lenient.

Within each of these cultural fields there is room for symbolic play.[3] The shifts in the relations of power and culture from one cultural field to the next also provide varying opportunities for second generation Sikhs to "play" with cultural identities and images. In each field, differing forms of cultural production are at work mediating the effects of the ideological forces of family honor and British cultural purity. Collective memory and personal fantasy provide imaginary spaces that also "play" into the way young people make sense of and respond to the contradictory pressures they face. As British Sikhs participate in these different cultural fields, they enact multiple situated identities and forms of subjectivity.

Acting "Indian"

The Sikh temple is the place where the teens feel they act most completely and "authentically" "Indian." Girls come to the gurdwara dressed in their "Indian suits," or *shalwar kameez*, wearing their hair uncut (or looking as uncut as possible) and tied back in a braid. They never wear makeup (or makeup that looks like makeup), and they never overtly talk to boys—who, in any case, are positioned safely far away due to the gender-segregated seating during religious ceremonies. The watchful gaze of cousins, aunts, and family friends polices the boundaries of proper gender relations in this cultural field. Any boundary transgression is immediately noted and entered into the stream of gossip that circulates across gurdwara community networks.

The gurdwara is the primary site for the formal transmission of religion and culture among Sikhs. The temple is the space in which young Sikhs are told the stories that convey a sense of Sikh peoplehood and learn the language that brings these stories to life. More informally, as teenage boys escape the service to hang in groups outside, girls press close to whisper secrets to their best Sikh friends, and small children run from lap to lap tracing the networks of the extended families, young Sikhs learn subtle lessons, lessons that instill a certain subjective sense—experiential, aesthetic, sensual—of being Sikh.

The temple is a world filled with the sounds, sights, and scents of their parents' homeland. Musicians, lecturers, and *granthis* (readers of the Guru Granth Sahib in charge of a gurdwara) bring India to Britain when they travel to perform and provide religious services for Sikhs across the diaspora. On Sundays, British-born Sikhs enter an atmosphere that has a sensory identification with "things Indian": the portraits of sainted Gurus; the close proximity of same-sexed bodies sitting long hours "Indian-style," heads covered and feet bare on the white-sheet-covered floor; the brightly colored garlands criss-crossing the hall; the air perfumed with incense and reverberating with the atonal wail of the harmonium and the thud of the tabla; the holy man with his long sword, standing behind the silk and satin shrouded holy book, beating the air reverently with a whisk of white horsehair. This is a world transplanted in England, but one that summons memories and a sensual awareness of "things Indian."

The Intimacy of Indianness

At home, Sikh youth reside in the routines of "acting Indian." Punjabi is their language of intimacy. Children speak a domestic form of Punjabi with their parents, almost always with their mothers, but English with one another. Their mothers, particularly those who came from India, frequently do not speak English. They seem to resist speaking it with their children, while they enjoy English-based American and British programs on television. More "traditional" families require their daughters to change into "Indian suits" when they come home from school. Most families expect their children to uphold what the children view as an "Indian" code of respect, the cherished tradition of honoring one's elders. Family gender roles, at least from the perspective of the girls, favor their "lazy" brothers. Girls, on approaching their teen years, are expected to help out in the kitchen and with other household duties. Homework takes priority, but a girl's life at home is largely structured by her gender-specific participation in domestic chores.

Sikh parents stimulate their children's imaginations by recounting memories that bring life to the past. Stories of lives in India or East Africa transmit a second-order nostalgia for a place the children hardly know. Family legends are formed, relatives' names become attached to personalities, and expectations for future travels are nourished.

The advent of video technology has played a key role in the making of family memory, for it has become a traditional practice to document rituals and festivities in great detail, particularly those surrounding weddings. When visitors arrive from other parts of Britain or India or the diaspora, women immediately begin preparing food for a communal meal as the most recent family wedding video is inserted into the VCR for collective consumption. I enjoyed watching as children, after viewing a video several times over, added amusing commentaries, poking fun at "unique" participants and family members. These jokes then become an integral part of the family viewing ritual.

Privacy for indulging fantasies and the play of imagination vary considerably among families and sometimes among children in the same family. Yet even teenagers who have little private space enjoy free rein of the television's remote control. Teens savor the soaps (*Dallas* and *Dynasty* were extremely popular in the late 1980s and early '90s). Families frequently watch them together as family events. When I asked Amrit why Sikh teenagers seem captivated by American soaps, she attributed it to

The fact that they're very unbelievable. The fact that you know it can't really, really happen. And the fact that it's something that you want to do, you know, you want to wear them fancy clothes. You want a life that's so exciting. And the way it's all worked out, you know, sort of very, very unbelievable. But then again, believable, like it could happen, maybe it does happen. And the way that they just, they don't have any principles or any moral issues. You, it's so, they don't care, you know, who they sleep with, how many and stuff.... There's nothing holding them back. There's no religious issue holding um back.... There's nothin' stopping them doin' what they want to do.... Because in our religion, because my culture is the fact that religion stops me from doing a lot of things, or my culture stops me from doing a lot of things. Or, it stops other people from doing a lot of things, maybe not me personally, but to a majority of people. And then to see something which doesn't let you do that—you just can do anything and you're okay. It's just because it's a total different way of life. That's what really excites me about it. Anyway, to get away from reality probably. You know, they just don't have any problems. The only problem they have is the problem with money, and not even that at times. That's probably why it interests me so much. That's why it fascinates me, or I enjoy it because it's away from reality.

Bedrooms become spaces for "getting away from reality," particularly through consuming forms of popular culture. In the privacy of their rooms, Sikh teenagers, wired to the sounds of their favorite tapes or CDs, can tune into cultural worlds created by British pop or Asian musicians, where the lyrics and rhythms provide symbolic resources for imagining possible identifications and futures, Sikh, Asian, and British. While Sikh boys paper their bedroom walls with traditional symbols of British masculinity, posters of football or cricket heroes and favored teams, or movie posters from the latest action flick, girls transform their rooms into shrines to their favorite male pop stars. Their image-covered walls become windows to possible worlds of fantasy and desire. McRobbie and Garber argue that the fantasy relationships represented in "teeny bopper" commodities articulate narratives of imagined futures that reproduce "traditional" gender roles.

There seems little doubt that the fantasy relationships depend for their very existence on the subordinate, adoring female in awe of the male on the pedestal. The culture also tends to anticipate the form of future "real" relationships, and in so far as these are articulated in the magazine articles and stories, directs the girls hopefully towards romance and eventually an idealised version of marriage. (McRobbie and Garber 1976: 221)

Asian girls adore the commodified images of white English, American, and Indian movie stars. But Western fairy-tale and Indian epic narratives that articulate dreams of falling in love, exciting and exceedingly romantic as they may be, conflict with traditional Asian marriage practices. Fantasy loves with Western teenage idols, as well as with "Bollywood" film stars from India, open up an imaginary space for Asian girls, a private life where the only limit to resolving life's conflicts is their own creative capacity.

For girls, fashion provides another symbolic space for fantasy and imaginative play. Sikh girls feel free to express their creativity at home and at the gurdwara by playing with possibilities for "Westernizing" the Indian outfits they make to wear to events at the gurdwara and especially to weddings. The eyes of young girls would light up as they described to me their latest design ideas or their desire to make a *shalwar kameez* especially for me—given the time I was spending at the gurdwara, they concluded, I should have my own Indian suit. I spent many hours fabric shopping, discussing the relative aesthetic qualities of the different styles women were wearing in England and India (as noted in films), or the "look" of the long skirts their moms were *finally* letting them wear to school.

Fashion shows are particularly popular events for Asian girls. During my initial year in the field, two such events were held, one at the Sikh temple and another at Grange Hill High. The fashion show at the school was particularly notable in light of the number of Asian girls who participated. This was the only after school event that was attended by a substantial number of Asian girls. Other events, such as sports activities or dances, consistently drew only one or two.

During an interview with an older Sikh girl named Jaspir, who at the time was nineteen and attending a further-education college while living at home, I asked why Asian girls seemed so drawn to fashion and to fashion shows.

The thing is, you've got to ask many Asian girls what do they do on an evening. And, they don't do anything, they watch TV, do a bit of cooking and that's it. And the next best thing they can do is go to temple or make clothes. And the latest thing, well it's been for a long time, is to get really really fashionable, in the sense of your Indian wear. Make a sort of simple, tight fitting dress, V-neck, you know short-sleeved, two massive splits at the sides ... let's get a bit more Westernized, let's have different styles, you know, the back wing, you know, the low-cut, the back that splits at different places, little buttons here, a bit of flowers here, a bit of bows here and there and change. Change your colors. Don't have all a one-piece suit in the sense of all one color. Change a bit. Or buy a dress and then put a different color pajama on top. Change, that's what it is really. Just make sure your body is covered.

Sikh family life establishes an environment of interacting, a cultural field that shifts with families as they enter and domesticize other spaces.

Public places become private family spaces when local sports centers reserve a pool for Sikh women. On Sunday evenings, I was invited to share this private space with girls and their mothers, aunts, and close female friends. We swam or enjoyed one another's company while wading in the water and lounging in the sauna. The ladies chatted animatedly while the girls, individually wired to Walkman radios but all tuned to the same channel, shared running commentaries on the week's "top of the pops."

The British tradition of "the holiday" structures time for Sikh families to travel together. Summer is the season for weddings, and families spend these months traveling up and down the motorways in cars and specially chartered coaches coming and going from weddings. When school reconvened after the summer months, the white middle-class students returned with tans and tales of beach adventures in the south of France or the Caribbean. Sikh students told me of the fun they had at weddings. They shared stories about particularly good bhangra groups and about cousin-sisters, siblings, or friends who had been romantically transformed into beautiful brides.

Visiting relatives locally and across Britain engages British Sikh families in travel throughout the year. I enjoyed many such visits, time spent sharing food, laughter, videos, and wedding pictures, shopping with the women, and simply spending time gathered together in the same domestic space. Sikhs travel to India or East Africa as families with less regularity than do Pakistani families, but most young people I interviewed had been to India (and possibly to California or Canada) at least once or twice during their childhood and adolescence. Family and village friends frequently visit from India, bringing a new vibrancy to the collective memories families share.

As the second generation grow older and the third come into being, family relations are changing. An expanding "yuppie" class of young married second generation professionals is thriving economically, and patterns of living and of traveling are shifting accordingly. Hari, who moved back to London after finishing his degree at Leeds University, described to me his sense of the growing influence of class divisions within the Sikh population:

It's like another grouping of people. And they're sort of taking part in what would normally have been considered sort of normal things for white kids, things like holidays abroad, you know, and the holiday back to the subcontinent has been replaced by the holiday to Disneyworld, you know, to Europe. Asians are doing that more and more.

[Class differences among British Asians are] very visible now. It's quite visible in dress, in where people live, choices of places to live in, speech, you know, accents, etcetera.... The bourgeoisie live in the sort of salubrious areas of places like Osterley, which are surrounding Southall. Osterley, also Wembley, yeah? It's only the very rich who have moved heavily into Central London, into areas like Chelsea, and so on. But amongst, you know, the accountants and the lawyers and the teachers, etcetera, they certainly don't live in Southall. They would move out into the yuppie flats, ahm, you know, houses with green around them near parks, and things like that.

While their newly acquired domestic spaces range from expensive flats in London to houses in posh areas of Leeds, their domestic relations renew deep commitments to their families. As young people from lower-class families achieve social mobility, they continue to intersperse family visitations with honeymoons to Greece or Turkey and bicycling holidays in France.

As they marry and create families of their own, however, the second generation face a difficult decision: should their parents be incorporated into the newly formed family units? The three-generation family has been the norm, if grandparents reside in Britain. But this has been changing. For the first time, the care of the elderly is becoming a problem in Asian communities as more and more second generation couples choose to live in nuclear families. Young women raised in Britain often have difficulty adjusting to living under the authority of their mothers-in-law, as tradition dictates. Well-educated middle-class women question the cultural prescription against their own parents residing with them after marriage, viewing this as unfair and perhaps sexist. However, the emotional and communal pressures to respect one's elders, protect family honor, and submit to what is best for the family as a whole continue to keep families together, for the most part, as solid supportive social units.

Public Englishness

The cultural fields of family and temple community are worlds deemed private, in contrast to public domains where British culture is dominant. The rhythms of their daily activities take British Sikhs into a number of public domains where life is orchestrated largely according to British social standards and sensibilities. During daylight hours, many Sikh girls and most boys are allowed to go into the Leeds city center by bus with a same-sex friend to shop. The shops in the maze of the market arcades offer teenagers as many possibilities for "fashioning identities" as their purses will allow them to consume.

Safe within the temples of consumer capitalism, British Sikhs feel they have the freedom to "act English," but not without caution. In town they encounter aunts and uncles, Asian taxi drivers and market-stall keepers, all, they assume, on the watch for young and unmarried boundary transgressors. Therefore, to act "too English" or to subvert, in town, family and community restrictions, entails the risk of being seen and found out. So, while girls go to town in English dress, their outfits remain modest—typically jeans and "jumpers"—the makeup light, and the meetings with boy-friends, if they occur, are tentative, extremely secretive, and therefore all the more exciting. The city center is where British Sikhs also most often encounter overt forms of racism. As Mohinder and Gurdip explained to me, the city center is a popular hangout for teenage supporters of the National Front. In this space where they can "act English," they face the most direct challenges to their "Englishness."

Mohinder: When you're going downtown you see quite a lot of NF people and punks.
Gurdip: Yeah, near Boots [a drugstore]. They're all hanging out there, all the NFs and everything.
Mohinder: And the thing is, if you're by yourself and there's a big group of them, the first thing they're gonna to do is try and knock your turban off and things like that.
Gurdip: We got chased in there 'round Boots. We went to town and got chased.
Mohinder: [loudly] Like if they're by their-self they won't say anything, but when it's all in a group they'll just do or say something.

Leeds city center has a number of clubs that young people frequent after the sun goes down. Yet "English nightlife" is a world Sikh high school girls hear a lot about but do not experience firsthand. Sikh girls in most cases are not allowed out at night—they do not attend social functions at school nor do they go out on their own, unaccompanied by family members, to parties or pubs as do white English girls (the drinking age for cider is sixteen, for all other alcoholic beverages eighteen). For the girls who do enter this very English field—with or without parental permission—if they are "seen," the consequences are serious, both for them and for their family's name and honor. Jaspir described to me her experiences of "going out" as well as her parents' reaction.

The issue with my parents is what people think of me if they see me. To my mum, if I'm in a nightclub she'll say, "Look, if you're out in an evening at a nightclub and some Indian person sees you what are they going to think? They're going to think "bad," straight away. Or if you walk into a pub, regardless of whether you drink coke or not, as soon as you walk into a pub, it's got a little image of itself for being a pub—you could have been sweet and innocent, you could have stayed there two seconds, it doesn't matter. Once you walk in you're labeled. It does bother my mum a lot, in the sense that she'll say, "Look, everybody will probably know about you walking out. How am I going to marry you? They'll say, 'Look she walks around. She's been around all parts of Leeds and everything. She hasn't lived a sheltered life.'" And another issue is, if you haven't lived a sheltered life about going out, then they think immediately with boys. They'll think you've associated, somewhere along the line, with boys. And, just one thing leads to another thing, you know.

British Sikh girls often have highly ambivalent feelings about the possibility of "going out" to a nightclub or a pub. As their brothers and English girl friends share their experiences, Sikh girls try to imagine the excitement and romance they too might enjoy. But as Baljit, who was seventeen, described, the fear of hurting her family kept her from acting on romantic desires.

Sometimes when you see some, you know, some boys—I haven't even said this to my sister!! [She giggles, then lowers her voice.] But sometimes, you know, you know that they like you. They start talking to you and everything, but you just can't, and you know what they're after, well they're not really after, they're really nice people and they're not the kind that just want, not one thing, but just want to go out with you, they really do care. But, you know, you just like sort of freeze up. And I know that, I know that I feel guilty. That's what I feel straight away. I think that, I mean, let's not get into this thing.

You know Jaspal [her cousin]? He goes to parties and he drinks and he smokes. But my mum doesn't know this. And I think he can talk to me because he knows I won't tell anybody or anything like this. But he was off to the pub and everything, so when I came, all these people were going off to the pub and every-thing. They were dressed up. And I've never, I mean, when I came up, is this what they look like when they go out? You know, is this what they look like when they go to the pub and things? I went, I don't really want to, I don't. I want to go home. That's what I felt like. They were all going out to the pub and it just scared me, you know. I think I've got security and everything. If I went, I don't know what would happen. I suppose I could, if anybody asked me, I guess I could have made the excuse. But I could never do that, because I would feel so guilty after. I don't think I could go to pubs and enjoy myself like they do 'cause of what I've been through, you know, how I've been brought up. The way I've been brought up I can, I mean

I can sort of just go to school and I can enjoy myself and talk to whoever I want, but then I can go home. I mean I'm living sort of an Indian life and an English life as well.

Within the Sikh communities in Leeds, people watch where unmarried teenagers go and what they do, and they gossip about those whose actions "cross the line" or "go too far," transcending the boundaries of Sikh respectability and honor. Gossip can either reinforce or ruin a family's honor. According to Rabinder, a Sikh girl in the sixth form, and her Punjabi Muslim friend Sajdha, fear of community gossip leads parents to be more restrictive.

Rabinder: They're afraid of what other people say.
Sajdha: If they didn't care about, if they really didn't care about the gossip then they would let us do what we like. But I think they do care. I mean they couldn't say, "Let people talk, you can do as you like." I mean they could still keep control over us even if they do give us that much freedom we're asking for.
KH: What happens with gossip? I mean, why is it such a bad thing?
Rabinder: It's sorta like your family's, right, it's like all families are meant to sort of stick together. Then if somebody sort of says something like, "Oh I saw their daughter with him," or something, that's a sudden mark on the family. It's just like that.
Sajdha: Yeah.
KH: What happens when a family is marked?
Rabinder: People don't really like associating with them. I mean, everybody sort of looks down on um. They're not liked, I mean, then the, some people won't let their children be associated with their children, just in case something, "bad influence."
Sajdha: The parents think they haven't got any honor left. I think honor is built up so that you get better places for arranged marriages. 'Cause they look at all your background and what your brothers do and sisters do and your dad and everything. All your relatives.

When people watch and gossip they impose a set of moral, physical, and behavioral constraints that serve as a powerful form of social control—a conservative force for social and cultural reproduction—that bridges the boundaries of the individual family unit. Parents enforce communal norms, teens feel, because of what others will think, not because they themselves believe in them. Sounding like typical teenagers, many I spoke with were frustrated by what they, like this young man, Jatinder, saw as their parents' "moral inconsistency":

All Asian parents will say, we don't really care if you talk to girls or whatever ... it's what other parents say, that's what they're worried about is what other people say. But it's like one big circle because everyone else is worried about what their parents will say. It's a bit like catch 22, really.

Becoming English at School

The majority of the Sikhs at Grange Hill High have been in English schools all their lives. They have grown accustomed to the rhythms, restrictions, and rewards of daily life at school. At school British Sikhs encounter the most pressure as well as the greatest opportunity to "act English." When they enter the school they move into a world removed from the gaze of their parents. Here they feel free to be, as Rabinder phrased it, "what they want to be."

Well, I think at school you're mostly sort of Westernized or English. But when you're at home you're more, like what your parents want you to be. At school it's what you want to be. They can't see what you are here, and they think you are what they see at home. They don't see this side of us. . . . If they came to school to see what I was like, I would not be what I am now. Not because I was afraid of them to see, but because, I don't know, if there's someone watching you.

Their world at school is an English world; they interact with English friends and engage in English activities. Some girls even bring an entirely different outfit to wear in school. Once inside the school walls, they change their clothes to suit their cultural context: on goes the makeup and down and "free" goes the hair. And, most important, at school the boys become friends. Girls can talk to boys and boys to girls, and things can develop, or not, from there.

Harjit and Bobby, two Sikh boys in the sixth form, sense that the sudden freedom they experience at school sometimes overwhelms Asian girls and distract them from their studies. The restrictions placed on girls at home disadvantage them at school.

Bobby: The parents are not there, just the kids. . . . [Some girls] take advantage of it, and they flirt with anyone. And I think that's over the line, because they're really just doing it because they happen to suddenly get a lot of freedom and they don't know what to do with it.

Harjit: I think they have to get out, because they're so deprived of it, they have to use the freedom that they've been given.

Bobby: They go over the top.... If you notice, a lot of these Asian girls when they go into the sixth form find there's so much freedom, than, say, from when they were doing O-levels, 'cause you get free lessons. You get more chance to talk with other people, you know, other boys, other girls ... and they tend to sort of let everything loose all at once. And it's not until later on in the upper sixth when they realize that there are other things much better and they seem to cool down.

Harjit: But sometimes it's too far, it's too late. They've socialized a lot more in school, and when it comes to more socializing than studying, when it comes to the exams, it's too late. I think that's unfair to Asian girls. I mean, to the boys, we are given a certain amount of freedom, and it builds up for us and it's not as much affected towards our exams.

Growing up in Britain, young Sikhs come to understand their parents' cultural views and expectations reflexively. Their engagement with forms of cultural production at school serves to "denaturalize" the cultural routines and rhythms they move within in the context of other cultural fields. Sikh students feel they have become "free to be what they want to be" because they have entered a cultural field in which their parents' influence and authority become questionable and contestable. Viewing British culture from the vantage point of Sikh cultural orientations gives it a similar arbitrary character.

Beyond this freedom to choose what to wear or whom to talk with, Sikh youth sense that other perhaps more profound social boundaries do constrain their social possibilities. Students, particularly minority youth, are never free to construct their self-identities in any way they choose. Schools are primary sites for the reproduction of social inequality and the reassertion of cultural hegemony. At school, British Sikhs are subjected to productive forms of power that are part of the taken-for-granted "order of things." Those who aspire to do well in school have to confront the contradictions between the promises of the liberal ideology of meritocracy and the marginalizing discourse of race and class difference.

The processes that marginalize difference work in subtle ways. At school certain standards are approved and rewarded over others; those demonstrating independent thinking, confident and assertive self-presentation, self-direction, and individual autonomy are highly regarded. Sikh children are trained at home, however, to subsume individual concerns within the greater needs and interests of the family unit and to show their respect to elders in their silences. The social value of their mother tongue was countered for a time by a school policy that scheduled Punjabi lessons after school. The emphasis in university applications on extracurricular activities as a sign of student initiative discriminates against Asian girls whose parents do not allow them to participate in what they define as "non-education related" activities.

The formal school practice of dividing according to "ability" reinforces divisions among the British Sikh students at Grange Hill High. The division of Sikh students into set groupings has two interrelated effects. First, these classes provide the primary context for meeting other students and developing friendships. This, in turn, affects the class and racial composition of friendships, for set groups vary considerably in their racial and class make-up. In the lower and middle sets there are more working-class Afro-Caribbean, Asian, and white students. British Sikh students in these sets tend to form friendship groups that include mainly working-class students, but are also more integrated racially.

Second, students classified at the same level in the set hierarchy spend a good deal of time together in classes and share a similar perspective on school and on the value of schooling. Students develop different subcultural orientations to school, interactive styles, ways of evaluating their fellow students and teachers, and goals for their futures. For British Sikh students, these subcultural styles are associated with different ways of "acting English."

Ways of "acting English" are infused with class distinctions, but resonate with racially marked styles of expression and behavior. British Sikh students in the lower sets are more apt to have Afro-Caribbean friends, and more frequently display "anti-school" or confrontational attitudes and responses to teachers and to rules and authority in general. Teachers and school-identified students define "loud" and "aggressive" Sikh students as "disruptive" or "discipline problems"; other students in the anti-school subculture assume that they are simply "becoming like us."

British Sikhs who stay in all-Asian groups and do not interact with Afro-Caribbean or white students remain socially "invisible" to white students. They are stereotyped as "Asian" and the majority of other students do not attempt to get to know the persons behind the stereotype. For these British Sikhs, "acting English" takes on a set of meanings that reflect interaction patterns between themselves and other Asians—such as talking to boys or girls in an environment where they are free from their parents' gaze. They also embody a sense of "being English" as they "act English" or as they move through the structures and with the rhythms of the school's English middle-class cultural milieu.

Some British Sikhs, particularly among those in the top sets, choose to "assimilate" in behavior, outlook, attitude, and dress to the normalizing pressures of the school's (and society's) dominant middle-class culture. These students tend to make friends more easily with white students, and sometimes share perspectives on social differences with their white middle- or working-class friends.

Kamaljit, who Mrs. Pound referred to as "not seeming at all Asian," lived in Moortown, for her family was socially mobile; she was in the top sets. In choosing friends, she found she felt most comfortable with the white girls in her classes. Other potential friends, such as the Sikh teenagers she encountered at the gurdwara, in her words "just seemed boring." And the Asian girls at school seemed as different to her as they did to her white middle-class friends.

Some of them just stand around and don't say anything, so you just don't get on with them. And some of them just give you funny looks. I don't know why. And so you just don't want to talk to them. I don't know, some Indian girls just get on my nerves. I just can't mix with Indian girls. I think they think too much of themselves most of the time. Like some of the girls in the fourth year, they all hang around together and think they're really good. And, they formed this group, you see. They were pestering this girl saying, "You have to join our group because you are Indian and if you don't we'll beat you up." It's a bit stupid. But now they're all broken up because they can't stand each other.

British Sikh teenagers who become more "English" often sense the subtle forms of racism that mark them as different in the eyes of their white friends. The turban symbolizes this social distance. For adolescent boys who choose to keep the signs of their faith, the turban comes to symbolize the tensions they face in their everyday lives. The decision to wear a turban, for boys like Harpal, emerges from a desire to respect their families and to "belong" in "their own culture."

Ah, it's partly out of respect, and it's partly out of, just because, when I was young I came out of hospital. And whenever we went to anyone's house, nobody knew I even existed, because I didn't use to live at home. And when I was young, I was really pale white, and I used to look like an English, and you couldn't tell the difference. And I used to have my hair cut. And whenever we used to go to anyone's house, everyone used to say, "Oh this kid you brought along." And you couldn't tell that I was with my other two brothers, and so I thought, I want to belong, I want to be together, so I said, I'll wear the turban.

Other Sikh boys are moved by a desire to be accepted as English by their English friends. These young men face the exceedingly difficult decision of whether to cut their hair to attempt to become more English. Baljit shared with me her feelings about her cousin Jaspal's dilemma.

Jaspal talked to me about his mom and dad saying, "I wish I was, I wish I could cut my hair, I wish I could do this, I wish I could do that." And I felt sorry for him, because he's the kind of person that needs to go out and have loads of friends and things. He's just that kind of person. I mean, his mum and dad really love him, and I know he really loves his mom and dad, because he's their only son. He still has this thing that he can't be like his friends, and I think he's . . . he's a bit self-aware or something, I don't know the word, self-conscious or something. He thinks that people think he looks funny or something because he's Indian. But I try to explain to him, "You know, you're really funny. People like you as you are. You don't have to cut your hair and try to look English to be, you know, liked." I think that's one of his problems, really. I mean, I know that he's really happy and everything. But I know he wants to, because he's lived with loads of English people all his life, um, I think he wants to be like them, do what they do.

The boundaries of racial difference, however, are not erased when turbans and hair are removed. British Sikh boys who do not wear turbans share the same haunting suspicion that racial boundaries are impermeable; they presume that in the eyes of some, the white girls they might fancy, there will always be "something against them."

Hardip, the wealthy sixth former who we met in Chapter 4, was one of the more "English" among the Sikhs at Grange Hill High. He fit in well and socialized exclusively with a popular group of friends who included James, Amanda, Lizzy, and Katie. But in spite of his social status he still had trouble attracting girls. In a conversation I had one day with him and his friend Jagjit, they both admitted they were shy around girls they fancied. They, like most Sikh boys, they said, lacked confidence because they assumed white girls would never fancy an Asian boy.

KH: Do you think many Sikh guys date?
Jagjit: I think what they lack is confidence.
Hardip: Yeah, that's true.
Jagjit: They think that they've got something against them. Because I think a lot of girls, whether they be Indian, of course Indian girls, they're not used to going out with boys anyway. . . .
Hardip: [interrupting] A lot of fifth year girls in this school, they're really mad on boys.
Jagjit: . . . their reaction straight away is, no, you know, we can't go out. Whereas English girls, I think, it's going against what their friends and everything

think, to go out with an Indian boy or something. So that's what's against them.

Hardip: A lot of Indian boys lack confidence with girls. They think girls won't go out with them just because they're Indian.

KH: I've heard that English girls are attracted to Indian boys!

Hardip: Really, where's this then?!

KH: An Indian boy told me!! [laughter]

Ambiguity and Agency

As they move across the cultural fields that make up their everyday lives, young Sikhs encounter boundaries of belonging legitimated by discourses of difference. These boundaries separate worlds in which they feel compelled to act "English" or "Indian," and instill in them a sense that the boundaries that divide these worlds can be crossed but not erased. But as they accumulate life experiences and learn from those of others, these young people begin to question seriously, as Baljit does below, what these boundaries might mean to them.

I want to go to university ... my mum's worried ... because, I mean, I've had three cousins, a family, the oldest was a girl, a boy and a girl. Two of them went to university. They met somebody there. They got married—they're English, but they were happy. And before they got married, their parents came to see my parents and said, "Will you come to the wedding?" And my dad said, "It's your daughter and if she's happy and if you're happy with it then why should I mind because it's not my daughter. My daughters, I know, are *definitely not* going to marry somebody English or anything like that. But if you're happy, then why should I mind." And we went and a lot of people did not go. A lot of relatives didn't go, and it was really sad, because he's a really nice person, Jeff, the one she married. He obeyed the Indian wedding, and wore a turban and everything.... And then, [the other son] went to the university. He met Susan. He got married to her. It was the same again, and she's really nice as well. And then, when the youngest got married, they were really hoping that she would marry somebody Indian. But she got married to somebody English. And I don't know, they all got married, Susan wore a sari, and she had an English wedding and an Indian wedding, so it was kind of mixed. He's growing a beard, and every day he learned how to sit cross-legged for like a couple of hours [her voice becomes really animated]. So, um, I mean they're really nice!

I sometimes wonder, if you have an English person—well, if they're white, not English—and they can speak Punjabi better than you, you have some people over, they have a beard, they wear a turban and they are Sikh, and what's the difference between them and us? Sometimes I wonder whether, if you fall in love with them and everything, what can your parents do about it? It's just their color, then, isn't it, and nothing else?...

I mean, somebody said to me, "If somebody Jewish got married to somebody who wasn't Jewish, it would kill my family." And I thought, yes, it would kill my family as well. Because, it's just, I think, every Indian girl's dream is to have her [wedding] day. But a lot of girls nowadays are interested in their career, more than anything else. But, I mean, I've been brought up in a way that I think, I'm bothered about my career, but I want an Indian wedding.... I know that I'm going to have an arranged marriage, and I know that I still have doubts, you know, about falling in love with someone and things like that. I mean, you do, after everything, because you live in England. I've been able to cope up till this, and I've never been out with boys or anything. And I've got friends that are boys and I've never had any problems.

Among the more academically able Sikh students, higher education, particularly at an institution away from home, provides a way out, a context for "getting out" and "enjoying themselves." It also offers a strategic way to delay the inevitable marriage-making ritual. At university, some young people make "love matches" and evade the arranged marriage procedures altogether—provided the potential spouse fits the criteria of caste, family status, and religion. Educational qualifications and economic independence are sources of leverage for young people in negotiating their marital options with their families. For some, like Hardip, this realization provides motivation for taking exams and going on to university.

See, I think in our families if you've got, you know, if you've got a degree or something then your parents will give you more of what you want to do for yourself. They'll let you choose a wife virtually for yourself. But if you're nothing, well, we haven't got that many nothings, that's why I did these subjects. I didn't want to do A-levels. I didn't want to do O-levels [laughs]. They pick, um, all, like my cousin chose all these, the one who's the university student. See Asians really, they really push. Their parents really want their kids to get a degree and a good job and a lot of money.

University life brings a certain kind of freedom, particularly for Sikh girls. But as they found their freedom, I watched many girls get caught up in profoundly difficult personal dilemmas. When they leave home and enter university life, for example, romance becomes tempting, and dating can lead to sex before marriage. For some girls, this act can create serious internal conflicts, causing them to lie both to themselves and to their families. I asked Jaspir how girls manage if they do have sex before marriage, and she told me,

They lie. Internally they're dead. They're dead in the sense that when it comes to actually getting married, they fake it. I know a lot of girls who have said, "Oh, I was a virgin when I got married," since they faked it and pretended it was the first time. And I know a couple of girls who literally blocked it out of their minds. And to this day they think they are virgins, even though we know, and the guys they've done it with know, that they're not. To them, to do that, right, is a big thing and if it doesn't work out, in the sense of never falling in love, the guy leaves them, the only way they can forget about that, they have to block it out, because if they're faced with it everyday they won't be able to cope. Because they've broken a vow, which when they're little, they've been told they can't do. They've got to save it for one person, so they broke it. So they think the only way they can cope is to say, all right, it never happened.

Stories of Asian teenage girls running away to London in search of freedom or independence from "despotic parents" have been favorites with the British media. Familial restrictions do exist, and Asian girls do run away. But for most Sikh girls I spoke with, the option of running away was, in the words of Rabinder and Sajdha, "the worst."

Rabinder: I think that's the worst. That's the worst.

Sajdha: You do respect your parents, we do know it's their honor, but that's the last thing you can do is hurt them in that way. I think of writing notes, "I'm running away, but it's not for a boy" [laughs]. 'Cause usually girls do run away because they want to marry someone who the parents don't want to. But if I ran away, I wouldn't run away for that. I'd run away to get away from them [laughs].

Rabinder: To get your freedom for yourself.

Sajdha: But I wouldn't run away.

Rabinder: You couldn't. I don't think I could, I wouldn't. I couldn't. It's just how I feel for them. I mean, okay, even my relatives, all my relations would suddenly be cut. I mean I'd never have any of them again. I'd be looked down on. I would *hate* that. I couldn't live with it. I mean, okay, I say that they don't understand me, but I couldn't live without my parents. I mean, our parents, even though they don't understand us, but they still mean a lot to us. They are a great deal to us, I mean in their different ways, but they still are our parents.

To successfully have the best of both worlds, young Sikh women have to maintain certain boundaries that if crossed could bring serious consequences—the severing of family ties. Despite their personal dreams, fantasies, or desires, most Sikh boys and girls work hard to protect their family honor. While these efforts often involve deceptions of various kinds, loyalty to one's parents and extended family remains paramount in their hearts and minds. Sikh teenagers consistently told me that they would trust their parents to "assist" their marriages before they would trust an English love match, a form of marriage that seemed, statistically, more apt to lead to divorce.

Hybrid Performances

British Sikhs become more or less English, more or less Indian, or more or less "black" by situationally performing identities and creating lifestyles that differentially articulate race, class, gender, and cultural markers. If a young man from a working-class British Sikh family living in Chapeltown "messes about" with working-class Afro-Caribbean boys in Chapeltown, listens to reggae, wears hip-hop clothes, and works in a factory he constructs himself as more "black" as well as working class. If a Sikh boy were to become a football fanatic, drop out of school, and frequent pubs with working-class white boys, he would seem "more English" but still working class. And then again, if this boy were to spend his time exclusively within the Sikh community in Chapeltown, choose to keep his turban, speak Punjabi in public spaces, and follow his father into the factory, he would be living a working-class Sikh life—he would also be considered "traditional."

The class, racial, and cultural identities of Sikh girls are signified and experienced in different ways. Teenage girls, if they conform to the community's gendered expectations and restrictions, have fewer possibilities for actively constructing "black" or "English" lifestyles. The behavior of Sikh girls and women more generally is central to preserving Sikh cultural traditions and protecting family honor. If a girl's family is closely connected to a Sikh community, the choice to act "black" or "English," particularly in terms of dating, wearing provocative dress, or going to clubs with Afro-Caribbean or English friends, can have painful consequences for her and her family. Girls who grow up in more "modern" middle-class or cosmopolitan households may experience greater freedom to perform publicly a greater range of identities and lifestyle choices.

For all British Sikhs who wish to become middle class or achieve a middle-class status position (in contrast to simply becoming wealthy), however, a certain degree of assimilation is required. To be accepted as middle class, British Sikhs must become more like middle-class English in manner and style—they must become more "modern." To seem "too Indian" or "other" (in dress, language, accent, or demeanor) if one is raised in Britain is to display markers the English view as inferior and attribute to lower-class status.[4] Once British Sikhs have gained middle-class status they can reappropriate certain external signs of their ethnic "folk" tradition; they can wear saris on social occasions, serve an Indian meal to guests, or enjoy Indian classical music. When they are otherwise living a lifestyle accepted as modern and middle class, their selective display of Indian cultural symbols takes on new class-based meanings. They can embrace their "folk tradition" in a middle-class manner.

The Costs of Social Mobility

A large number of second generation British Sikhs have chosen to pursue upward mobility through education. To achieve social mobility, to become members of the British middle class, requires that young Sikhs challenge the barriers of "racialized" class differences and transform themselves— distance themselves from certain signs of "Asianness." But to deny one's Sikh identity in an attempt to become "English" is to attempt to become what one never can be. It is this realization that underlies Devinder's concern about becoming "too modern" or "too un-Asian" in the process of being educated in Britain. Her fellow Asian classmates at the university, like her uncles, she believes, are falling into this trap.

They're all very modern. They've totally lost their religion and their own—you know—they don't think of it the way I do. They're like my uncles, all of them. You see I've seen the trap my uncles led themselves into and I can see these kids doing the same. They're trying to be something they're not without giving in and really being themselves. They're trying to live another life. But then you see, the problem with my family is rather than standing up to it, they—my uncles definitely, they just took the easy way out and tried to change themselves to fit in. My uncle doesn't look Indian. He looks more English, more Greek, as my friends say. I think if you want to achieve real success in this country, you can't let them bully you. I think they respect you more if you stick to your own.

Finding themselves in this contradictory space, many Sikh young people feel they live two lives. At home they are comfortable with their British Sikh selves and the security of family life. But when they step outside this world they see their families through the gaze of their assimilated selves, and they are ashamed of the embarrassment they feel. They encounter what W. E. B. Du Bois metaphorically depicts as "the veil" of racism. In choosing to assimilate, in becoming British and middle class, they face the danger, as Devinder's words painfully depict, of participating in their own subjugation.

I've got real problems because I'd love my friends to meet my parents and my mum can't speak English. And that I feel they're going to think, you know, she's been here so long, why the hell can't she speak English. I could explain it. I'm sure they'd understand, but I'm almost afraid to explain it. I mean, it's not as if I'm not working with Indian clients. I am. And so are they. And half the time when they can't speak English, it's a real joke with a lot of them. You see what I mean. I'm sure they don't mean it that way. But I feel they'd be embarrassed when an Indian lady comes in, dressed in Indian gear, not being able to speak a word of English. It doesn't look right. It just doesn't—it's an embarrassment. Because, they say if people are living in our country surely they should make the effort to learn the language. You see, the thing is, there are too many Indians in this country.

These words capture the hidden costs of social mobility in the face of racism and class inequality. Yet what is also hidden by these words is the cultural creativity and improvisations these young people enact. Their lives embody a creative tension, a counterpoint of sorts that engages the dialectics of power and inequality as well as the dynamics of cultural improvisation and transformation. At the heart of this creative tension is a process of cultural production that Rosaldo (1989) has called "transculturation" and Homi Bhabha (1994) refers to as "translation," a process that enables the creation of new hybrid forms of cultural identity. Acts of translation in the lives of British Sikhs are relational processes of reciprocal cultural exclusion (British from Sikh as well as Sikh from British) and mutual assertions of communal inclusion, each legitimated by reified cultural traditions. Second generation British Sikhs are negotiating these intersecting fields of power and meaning. Through their struggles they will continue to challenge and slowly and subtly reshape the racialized and reified boundaries of "both."

British Sikhs live their lives between the forces of two ideological formations, two invented status communities. But these teenagers possess desires and imaginings and encounter social relations and cultural influences through which they consciously and practically apprehend a world filled with a broader range of possibilities. As they acquire additional life experiences, they deepen their sense of self-awareness and develop forms of self-expression and lifestyles associated with imagined future lives. For those who are choosing the route of social mobility, their journeys are forging a variety of distinctive life paths. On their life journeys, they come to know intimately what is gained and what is sacrificed along the road to success.[5]

8. Consciousness, Self-Awareness, and the Life Path

> Then it dawned upon me with a certain suddenness that I was different from the others; or like, mayhap, in heart and life and longing, but shut out from their world by a vast veil. I had thereafter no desire to tear down that veil, to creep through; I held all beyond it in common contempt, and lived above it in a region of blue sky and great wandering shadows.... [T]he Negro is a sort of seventh son, born with a veil, and gifted with second-sight in this American world—a world which yields him no true self-consciousness, but only lets him see himself through the revelation of the other world. It is this peculiar sensation, this double-consciousness, this sense of always looking at one's self through the eyes of others, of measuring one's soul by the tape of a world that looks on in amused contempt and pity.
>
> —Du Bois (1903/1969: 44–45)

British Sikh teenagers take part in a number of distinctive cultural fields. As they cross the fields of this modern capitalist landscape, they are called to enact or react, embrace or reject the cultural influences that seductively play at the parameters of their conscious awareness. Their practical activity "teaches" them lessons they cannot always articulate, but which "are present in nascent or inchoate form in their consciousness" (see Gramsci 1971, 1988: 323–34). These forms of practical "knowledge" are often sensed or felt but not explicitly "known" (Bourdieu 1977).

When individuals become subject to social forces that distinguish them as different and inferior, they develop what Du Bois refers to above as a "double consciousness" (see also Fanon 1967). Defined as "other," their experience of "otherness" produces a reflexive form of subjectivity, the ability to see themselves through the eyes of the dominant "other."

Antonio Gramsci notes, however, that practical knowledge, for subordinate peoples in particular, provides a consciousness of social life that contradicts this dominant gaze, or as I have described it, the various discourses about difference that produce them as subjects. Everyday "lived" forms of culture, as Willis (1977) suggests, enables subordinate peoples to "see through" or denaturalize reproductive forces in a social order. Whether "penetration" or "resistance" leads to the transformation of relations of inequality, however, is a far more complex matter.

Sikh youth speak of wanting the "best of both worlds," of deciding when to act "English" or "Indian," while they perform identities and practice cultural possibilities that blur the boundaries of both. After high school their lives continue in directions that defy easy classification and refuse to fit into conventional trajectories of immigrant assimilation or marginalization. Their life paths narrate a wide range of immigration stories. Their lifestyles weave together diverse cultural orientations, celebrating the aesthetic sensibilities of the urban cosmopolitan as well as the sentiments of Sikh religious or Punjabi cultural "tradition." Some have remained part of their local communities, while others have moved on to alternative lifestyles. They are crafting a wide range of cultural selves as gays and lesbians, religious practitioners, millionaires, multicultural newscasters, bhangra musicians, and corner shop owners in villages, towns, and cities across the UK. Through acts of translation, they have found new ways to act English, to act Indian, and, more often, to enact the "best of both."

I conclude this study with biographical portraits of people who shared their lives with me, depicting their personal struggles and the life paths they are forging as they strive to be "successful," to challenge inequality, and to find a bit of happiness in their everyday lives.

Becoming Modern Traditional Sikhs

Kulwant and Amarjit are Ramgarhia Sikhs. Kulwant's family is from Punjab, Amarjit's from Kenya. Both came to Britain before they were five. Their families are middle class. Amarjit's family brought economic and cultural capital from East Africa; Kulwant's, since arriving, has financially become quite comfortable. Kulwant is a successful solicitor, Amarjit a radiologist.

Kulwant and Amarjit fell in love as their marriage was being arranged. The couple and their families are very religious and quite active in their respective gurdwaras. Amarjit's family attends the Ramgarhia Board, while Kulwant's family is active in the "main" Sikh temple. Neither Kulwant nor Amarjit has taken *amrit pahul* (nectar of immortality) or, in other words, been baptized into the Khalsa. Yet, they are both Kes-dhari Sikhs (Sikhs who retain the *kes*, or uncut hair) who for the most part keep the five symbols of the Sikh faith. Kulwant wears a turban, except on Saturdays when he plays cricket.

Kulwant worries a great deal about the survival of the Sikh religion in Britain. He reads widely on Sikh history and religion and has taught "Sunday school" classes for teenagers at the temple in an attempt to pass on this knowledge to the next generation. Kulwant is concerned that the essential principles of Sikhism are at risk. The young have little knowledge of the faith and, in his view, show little interest in learning. More profoundly, perhaps, he fears that certain practices among the first generation threaten to "Hinduize" Sikhism (a fear that is hardly new in Sikhism or unique to Sikhs in Britain). Sikh women in particular, he feels, grant supernatural power to ritual acts, sounds, scents, and, most critically perhaps, particular holy people. For Kulwant the essence of Sikhism resides in its textual base, in the teachings of the original ten Sikh Gurus contained in the Sikh holy book, the Guru Granth Sahib. A Sikh's faith, he believes, should be grounded in a rational, literate, and informed understanding of Sikh religious teachings. Kulwant dedicates his free time to reading, teaching, and taking a leadership role at the gurdwara in order to protect the purity of his religious tradition.

Amarjit's everyday life revolves around her family. While tremendously close to her own family, she and Kulwant live with *his* parents. For Amarjit this is a source of great ambivalence. She is fond of and respects her in-laws and values living in an extended family unit—one of the benefits is that her children are learning Punjabi. But having grown up in Britain she is sad that the elderly she lives with and cares for are not *her* relations. While she enjoys the communal nature of family life, the constant flow of relatives and friends through the doors of her in-laws' home, she wishes they would phone before coming and, on arriving, would not expect her to prepare a full-blown Indian meal. Amarjit's ambivalence fuels her fantasies of moving out on their own, of enjoying the kind of domestic privacy she imagines exists in a British nuclear family.

When I visit Amarjit, our days are spent in perpetual motion, preparing meals and traveling from house to house, gurdwara to gurdwara, children in hand, to be with relatives or to join in the festivities at yet another wedding.

Between my visits, her letters tell of new babies born, siblings who have wed, and the deaths of elderly loved ones.

Becoming Cosmopolitan

Devinder was born in Britain. Her parents, too, are quite religious and active in the Sikh temple. They came to England during the early 1960s from a village in Punjab where, as members of the Jat caste, their families were landowning farmers. When her father first arrived he stopped wearing the turban, but following the storming of the Golden Temple in Amritsar in 1984 he began once again to keep the symbols of the faith. Devinder's family is upwardly mobile. Her father started his own small business and as the eldest family member worked to put his brothers (not his sisters) through university while his own children were young.

During my first stay in Britain, Devinder, the eldest among her siblings, was studying dentistry at Leeds University while living at home. She was a successful student and remains a dutiful daughter. Her appearance at the time reflected her respect for the cultural ideals of her family; her hair was long and plaited, her face was free of makeup, and her dress modestly covered her body, usually in a jumper (sweater) and jeans. She never wore a skirt or dress. Though strongly devoted to her family, she is not religious. Outside family events and weddings, she avoids the gurdwara and other Asian-specific spaces where she says she feels awkward and out of place.

Devinder possesses a double consciousness. She is aware of differences between how she views herself and how she and her family are seen through the eyes of the dominant British population. This awareness was deepened by the sense of "release" she felt during a visit to India, where for the first time she felt English *and* did not feel marginalized racially.

Devinder: [W]hen I went to India for my holiday it was really funny because I thought that I'd been released. I could walk in the streets, and I felt a part of it. Everybody looked like me and behaved like me. It's funny because I never thought I was conscious of it, but I felt suddenly as if I was home. It's silly isn't it? I've lived here all my life, so this should be the place. I mean, I was really happy to come back. It was really, really nice to have been there, but I think I was happier just coming back home. But while I was there, I had this feeling, you can't imagine.

KH: Did you feel different, in any way, from the people who were there?

Devinder: Well, yes, I did feel different.... I could see by the way I was dressed they knew that I'd come from England.... That wasn't the difference—that I could speak English and they couldn't. That's not the point. It's just that if I wore an Indian suit, I suppose, and went somewhere, they wouldn't know where I was from. What's the difference?

Devinder's academic success has taken her across racial and class boundaries, deepening and refining in many ways her understanding of how power relations are legitimated by the signification of social difference. In spite of her academic success at university, she had a profound sense that she did not belong in the white middle-class world of her classmates. Her family and her background did not "fit," did not correspond to the taken-for-granted British norm. The pressures of otherness, of living two lives permeated her everyday experiences.

Devinder: I've never had a really close English friend like you, because nobody else would understand. They can't understand the two different—the fact that I can cope with the way my parents are and still be happy at university, and not totally living the way students are supposed to live.... [I'm] two different people. I get into the car to come home, I'm somebody else.
KH: Is that hard?
Devinder: It depends which side of me dominates. Because there are times when the university side dominates, and that interferes with home life. But when I'm at home, like I have been for the last four weeks, it's going to be harder getting used to going back there. Not consciously, but, I suppose, I'm just aware of it because you asked me. I wouldn't normally think of it. I mean, I'll be successful here, but I want a home in India.

When Devinder finished her university course, her parents informally initiated the process of arranging or assisting her marriage. A number of frustrating meetings with potential partners ensued. At the point when her patience was about to give out, her father happened to meet a very interesting young Sikh man at a wedding and invited him home to tea. Raj and Devinder met, were very attracted to one another, discovered they had a great deal in common, dated, fell in love, and married. Like Kulwant and Amarjit, Raj and Devinder are of the same caste. Both their families came from villages in Punjab, and their fathers have established businesses in England. Raj's father in particular has made a great deal of money in manufacturing and export. Raj attended public school, graduated from university, and is employed with the government. He also is not religious and has never kept a turban—though Devinder's younger sisters were quite taken with the romantic image of Raj on his wedding day, standing tall, handsome, and heroic in his turban.

The couple lived for a short time at Raj's parents' estate in an upperclass village in the country outside London, but they soon decided they preferred the city and purchased their own flat in central London. Marriage has transformed Devinder. A few months after the wedding, I went to visit. When she met me at the train I didn't recognize her. Her hair was short, her eyes were enveloped in a lovely shade of blue, and she was dressed in a knee-length navy skirt, white blouse, tailored jacket, navy tights, and heels. Devinder tells me that, except for subtle middle-class forms of racism she senses periodically, she now feels that she somehow "fits in." She and Raj have driven through France and across Ireland. They subscribe to the opera, eat out regularly, and catch all the latest films. And in between they visit their families.

Bridging the Borderland

Jas is from a middle-class family. His father, a Ramgarhia Sikh from Punjab, has a university degree. They are religious and very active in the Sikh temple. During his high school and university years, Jas blended into a very middle-class English world. He never wore a turban or attended the gurdwara. Recently Jas decided to grow his hair and began to wear a turban. This reconnection to his faith came at the same time as his engagement to his white English girlfriend.

These seemingly contradictory developments in Jas's life reflect in part the political transformation he has undergone in the last few years. While completing his MA he became involved in local politics and community organizing, work that he says has "politicized him." While passionate about politics, he remains concerned about the ramifications of his choices. His unease is evident, as he characterizes "getting tunneled" into race work, as well as getting married, as "significant crises."

Jas: I'm getting tunneled into another kind of area called race work. That I find unhappy because it's not what I want to do. Being here has been very very useful, because it's politicized me, it's given me information about how the system works and how individuals in the system work, etc. etc. But now, I'm personally getting labeled into that. And now, there's another significant crisis. I'll probably get, not probably, I am getting married to a white woman....

KH: Are your dad and mom okay with the marriage?

Jas: Yes, now they are, yeah. But, you know, there's all kinds of dilemmas on both sides. You know, it's not just my mom and dad. I think it's ... it's probably worse for my parents, in the sense that in Sikh society marriage brings more friends, gives them more relations.

Imagining raising children with his soon-to-be-wife has prompted Jas to think about being a Sikh in a new light. Marrying a non-Sikh, a non-Asian, has given him a heightened sense of why his "tradition" is important to him.

I've just been on a holiday with my so-called girl friend at the moment, and one of the questions was: What are we going to do with our kids? Are they going to wear a turban? And I, in the ostrich situation, say yes. No questions asked, yes. . . . I will have no choice for them being black or white, they'll have to be both, they'll have to go into both kind of cultures. . . . [T]he minority culture is the culture which I think they will question the most, because they will be like this more, they will question that more, because the majority culture is there anyway. . . . I want to keep the identity going. I want them to be, find out about the faith, where they belong. I want to give them this sense of belonging. They belong here, you know. Their granddad, their grandparents are in Leeds and Manchester, one happens to be Sikh, one happens to be white. They will both love them. They will.

As he identifies what his child will have to confront in relation to racial, cultural, and religious differences, Jas speaks from the perspective of his own experience. Growing up in Britain, he, too, developed a double consciousness, a consciousness that his cultural background would be questioned and could not be taken for granted or simply "lived." He has been forced to think critically about his identity, and he has continued to question, identify with, and challenge the ways of his parents' generation. His words reflect an objective distance, a space of self-awareness about his choice to marry outside his "race" and culture. But simultaneously he has chosen to proclaim, quite visibly, his identity as Sikh. Proud, he still wonders where it will lead.

I still, until we get married she can't get involved with the gurdwara, really. We can't go hand and hand, boyfriend and girlfriend. But I think, you know, I think she would take it on. She's the kind of person who would say, well look, I may not become a Sikh, but I will come to the gurdwara. I'll have to dress up and do something. But she's brilliant. I don't personally recognize that sometimes, because I do this ostrich thing. So, yes I think, I feel more powerful, you know, in having a turban. . . . It makes you do certain things. So like here, dressing up, putting the turban on, makes you take care of how you present yourself. It makes you think, all the time, who you are. There are certain things you wouldn't do in public that you might do otherwise.

Forced when growing up to "think all the time about who you are," Jas has learned to think about who he is in a thoughtful, reflective manner. Becoming politicized and thinking about his tradition through the eyes of his future child have brought Jas back to his community, to an identification with being Sikh, to political activism, and to involvement at the gurdwara.

Battling Racism

Looking back on the many conversations I shared with Jaspir, I can see stark differences in the way she discussed gender issues, the topics she raised, the information she seemed to have, and the emotions I could feel just below the surface of what she could say. It was Jaspir who was thinking about the ramifications of going to nightclubs, and Jaspir who spoke so eloquently about the way girls "died inside" when they lied about premarital sexual experiences. She was older than many of the girls I grew to know; yet her tone separated her even from young women near her age or older. Jaspir seemed quite aware of and concerned with the consequences of boundary transgressions.

Jaspir is the daughter of a very religious Punjabi Ramgarhia family. Her family established a highly successful business. Her father was active in both gurdwara and local city politics. She was a serious, thoughtful, and outspoken college student. We spent hours talking about the dilemmas faced by the second generation, dilemmas about which she was passionately concerned.

After I left Leeds, Jaspir's life path took a painful turn. She had taken a "race" job with a local authority in Yorkshire, a job her father, active on a number of race relations committees, had helped her get. She was engaged in the fight against racism. Jaspir fell in love with a man she met at her job. This would have been difficult enough for her "traditional" family, but the man she chose to love was Afro-Caribbean. And she chose to love him openly, publicly, and against her family's wishes. Her family felt betrayed. She had acted in a way they didn't understand, and her behavior had hurt their standing in the Sikh community. The family disowned Jaspir. When her favorite aunt died, she was not invited to the funeral. Jaspir's act challenged the principles of Sikh family honor, respect, and trust, and she is no longer considered family.

Jaspir's story powerfully portrays the deep racial contradictions that cut through the Sikh status system. In loving a black man, Jaspir acted on the anti-racist ideals for which her father fervently fought, but against the principles of Sikh family honor that he felt were fundamental to his faith. She bravely chose to follow her heart and her politics along a path of resistance, but without her family, she must find that path quite a lonely one.

Becoming American

I remember the first time I saw Ravi. I was sitting in a car with her sister and brother-in-law waiting for her to appear from her medical school lab at Leeds University. We were heading out on the motorway to visit Ravi's sister's family in Cardiff, Wales. "There she is. Finally!" her brother-in-law announced in frustration. I looked up to see a strikingly beautiful young woman with lush black hair in a spotted fake-fur coat, short blue skirt, black lace tights, and funky black and white loafers. She hopped in back with me, and we talked all the way to Wales. She complained about school, said she disliked medicine on the whole, and quietly mentioned her white boyfriend Ben. They were living together and considering marriage but her family had not quite adjusted to the idea yet.

Although not at all religious, Ravi is from a very religious Ramgarhia Sikh family who came to Britain from Kenya. Her father and uncles wear a turban, her brother does not. Ravi's parents were both educated in the British colonial educational system and had professional careers, both in Kenya and in England.

During the days we spent with her sister, Ravi and I continued to talk incessantly as we decompressed, her from university, me from fieldwork, over wine, samosas, and crisps (potato chips). We shared personal stories of the trials and tribulations of student life, and she taught me all about Leeds—which clubs were "in" and where I could find the best clothes bargains or Chinese food to die for. She was and remains totally "hip." Her interests and obsessions, activities and travels seldom take her into purely Asian social worlds. She thinks of herself as British, and in situations that become racialized a black woman. She has been forced to confront racism and sexism often during her medical schooling and in the initial stages of her career. She takes these irritations in stride, avoids incidents when she can, and continues to frame her life, individualistically, around her pleasures and her accomplishments.

We met a few times at O'Hare Airport when she was flying through to her residency in Barbados or to see relatives in California. One summer I received an invitation to her wedding at a Unitarian church in New York City. I was in Britain at the time and could not attend. All Ravi's relatives— her parents, sisters and brothers, nieces and nephews, and aunts and uncles— flew to New York from Britain and California for the wedding, which, her sister reported, the couple forgot to have videotaped. Ravi and Ben have settled in Manhattan, where they are both practicing medicine.

In forging her life path, Ravi has found ways to subvert the dominant pressures of family honor and British racism, partially, perhaps, by removing herself completely from the Sikh community in Leeds as well as from Britain itself. Her family has adjusted to her choices and accepted Ben into the fold. Ravi's two older sisters, in contrast, chose to marry Sikh men they were introduced to through more "traditional" arrangements. One husband wears a turban; the other does not. Cultural change is taking distinctive forms among as well as within British Sikh families.

British Sikhs are paving life paths through everyday acts of translation. They are producing new identities and fashioning novel lifestyles, from the overtly cosmopolitan to the decidedly more traditional. Their stories highlight what many postmodern analyses of hybrid identity formation too often seem to ignore—the constraints and personal costs associated with cultural mixing, with making choices that directly challenge boundaries of belonging. Through their struggles, old boundaries are slowly becoming blurred, just as new relations of inequality are continuing to emerge, particularly in the form of class differences that increasingly divide the British Asian population. As they raise their children and enjoy their grandchildren, second generation British Sikhs will continue to reflect on the nature of their culture and their identity in England, and they will make choices at each new life stage that reconfigure their relationship to both.

Epilogue:
An Unfinished Story

The immigration stories in this account go back to an England under the sway of Thatcherism, a political context that was in many ways different from Tony Blair's England today. I wish I could frame my study as a historical ethnography depicting a social world found now only in the increasingly dusty archives of Britain's problematic past. But as I completed the manuscript in Philadelphia in the summer of 2001 I was haunted by images in the media of violent encounters among Muslim Asian youth, British National Party supporters, and the police erupting across cities in the north of England—Oldham, Burnley, Bradford, and even Leeds. Their acts continue to write the history of postwar racial conflict in Britain, making my book more relevant than I ever wanted it to be.

But the racial violence of the summer of 2001 diverged from the struggles of the past. British Sikhs as well as Hindus seem to have been largely absent from these events. A large proportion of the Sikh, Hindu, and Muslim Asian population has achieved a comfortable level of economic success. But other segments of the Asian population, low-income Pakistani and Bangladeshi citizens in particular, are among Britain's urban poor. They live in racially segregated, socially isolated neighborhoods with high concentrations of poverty and unemployment that on the surface seem very like those inhabited by the "truly disadvantaged" Americans described by William Julius Wilson (1987) in his now classic work.

Yasmin Alibhai-Brown, a British journalist, wrote a commentary on the riots in Bradford that appeared in the *Independent*. Her account captures a sense of the complex social and economic disparities of late capitalism that fueled the flames of racial hatred expressed in these most recent urban uprisings. She writes,

I have to confess that I didn't think Bradford would follow Oldham and Burnley in the bonfires of lunacies sweeping through towns of Northern England this sticky summer. But it has, and once again this city has become the symbol of ethnic tensions, brutal racism, failed integration and miserably inadequate inner-city policies. Hundreds of young Muslim men, maddened (sometimes said as though this was the only reason) by the growing presence of the National Front and the British National Party, took to the streets and were met by white racist thugs looking for a bloody good fight. In the end, the mobs turned against the police. The usual slogans and explanations—deprivation, racism, Islamaphobia, the far right—are already in circulation. Repair kits—regeneration, training, additional resources, possibly a report by a major commission—will soon follow....

Things are more complicated than we think.... Most Asian men, even young hot-headed Muslims, do not act this destructively even if they are victims of deprivation, racism and neo-Nazism. If anything Asian men have found it difficult to gain respect in this society because they are seen as weaklings.... Many of the young Muslim men do not know who they are. Abused as "Pakis" all their lives, their parents and others have driven them to embrace a Pakistani identity that is a negation of their Britishness. Many in the older generation tell me that the youngsters are "too British, too much full of rights ... Bloody fools ... In Pakistan the police would kill them on sight." If you talk to white locals, the same confusions about Identity and self-esteem emerge. They hate it that their Bronte-land has become a Balti-land, even though most of them have never even watched a televised version of *Jane Eyre* and could not survive a week without curry. Both groups feel like aliens in the knowledge economy, which is passing them by, and in a society where you are what you own. Pimping and drugs offer prospects of control and money, which is why so many of these white and Asian rioters are involved in such activities.[1]

As I have yet to study these worlds directly, I will not take the analogy between the truly disadvantaged in the United States and Britain any further for fear of misrepresenting situations that are clearly as historically distinctive as they are similar. But it is clear that, somewhere in the complex interplay of globalizing capital and the racialization of inequality, similar forms of structural poverty are making it increasingly difficult for segments of the British Asian population to follow the paths to mobility that I describe in this account. But that, indeed, is another chapter, a story that is yet to be told.

This book will enter a world greatly transformed by the September 11, 2001 attacks on the World Trade Center and the Pentagon. In the aftermath of the horror of 9/11, Sikhs found themselves targets of hate crimes in Britain and in the United States, rooted in the racialization of global terrorism. The "war on terrorism" has produced its own forms of terror in the lives of those, like Sikhs, who have been implicated however mistakenly as "other." We have yet to discover what impact the reconfiguration of global politics will have on national politics of citizenship and difference in the United Kingdom and throughout the world. I hope that my account will offer some insight to those who continue to challenge the increasingly complex relations of racial, religious, and class inequality in this era of globalization.

Notes

Chapter 1. Introduction: A Different Immigration Story

1. The names and insignificant details about individuals as well as the name of the high school have been changed to ensure anonymity and protect confidentiality. Places, locations, and organizations, however, have been correctly identified.

2. I use the term "South Asian" to refer to people who have migrated from the South Asian subcontinent to various parts of the world and "Asian" or "British Asian" to refer more specifically to South Asians in Britain. "Asian" is the term used in Britain to refer to citizens of South Asian origin, regardless whether they originally migrated from Pakistan, India, Bangladesh, or East Africa (the homelands of the majority of South Asians in Britain). I also refer to second generation Sikhs as "British Sikhs" to emphasize their citizenship and identification as British.

3. Generation, of course, is a slippery analytic term in immigration research. To simplify, I refer to the "first generation" as those who came to Britain as adults and the "second generation" as those who either arrived when they were children (under thirteen) or were born in Britain.

4. This account follows the lead of a number of innovative studies in political anthropology concerned with state level processes, including Greenhouse and Greenwood (1998), Ferguson (1994), Malkki (1995), Stephens (1995), Coronil (1997), Litzinger (2000), Paley (2001), and Comaroff and Comaroff (2001).

5. Men and women keep the Five Ks, but among Punjabi Sikhs only men wear turbans. Amrit-dhari Sikhs, who have undergone baptism by the double-edged sword (*khande-da-amrit*) into the Khalsa (brotherhood), are required to adhere to a code of conduct, the *Rahit Maryada*, which includes keeping the Five Ks. Amrit-dhari Sikhs have traditionally been distinguished from Sahaj-dhari Sikhs who have not been baptized. This distinction was instituted after the tenth Guru, Gobind Singh, first elected a segment of the Sikhs to undergo baptism into the Khalsa. Kes-dhari Sikhs (those who keep *kes*) are Sahaj-dhari Sikhs who keep the five symbols of the faith. Other Sahaj-dhari Sikhs choose to cut their hair and to practice Sikhism without keeping the symbols. According to McLeod, only about 15 percent of Sikhs are Amrit-dhari and another 70 percent "heed the principal requirements of the *rahit*" (McLeod 1999: 64; see also Lal 1999). See Oberoi (1994) for a historical account of the making of Sikh tradition.

6. As Gilroy (1987) suggests in the title of his study, "There Ain't No Black in the Union Jack," the notion that black people could be British or English has been nearly an oxymoron in British nationalist consciousness. "Blackness," historically, has been associated with colonial subjects in exotic lands far away, and with

colonial people of color generally. The idea of ex-colonial subjects of color becoming British is threatening both to nostalgic notions of imperial glory and, as I will argue, to the basis of British national identity itself.

7. This account of the experiences of Sikhs in Britain parallels Gilroy's (1987, 1990, 1993, 1995) location of identity formation among Afro-Caribbeans in Britain in the politics of race and nation as well as within the broader context of diasporic cultural connections.

8. A number of works focus specifically and comparatively on issues of immigration, citizenship, and nationalism across European nations (Modood and Werbner 1997; Werber and Modood 1997; Cesarani and Fulbrook 1996; Ålund and Granqvist 1995).

9. Essentialism is a position that accepts the notion that social groups share a pregiven or preconstituted identity. Feminist theorists, however, have argued for "the rhetorical use of the essentialist claim, sometimes in terms of 'strategic essentialism.'" Judith Butler prefers to think in terms of "the invocation of identity as a strategic provisionality," a view that continues to subject the concept to a political challenge concerning its usefulness (Butler 1995: 130–31). Theories of cultural hybridity, in turn, stress that identities are multiple, contingent, and often contradictory, and hence must be negotiated by individuals as they move across different social situations.

10. The literature on globalization in anthropology has focused a great deal of attention on how "production, consumption, communities, politics, and identities become detached from local places" (Kearney 1995: 552). Kearney (1995) and more recently Tsing (2000) provide insightful critical overviews of anthropological approaches to studying issues of globalization and transnationalism.

11. In this vein, classic theories of race and ethnic relations grounded in traditional Marxist (Castles and Kosack 1973; Sivanandan 1976), Weberian (Rex 1970; Rex and Moore 1967) or "culturalist" (Ballard and Driver 1977; Banks and Lynch 1986) perspectives have been challenged for representing race, ethnicity, or social class as fixed, bounded, and enduring collectivities (see Mac an Ghaill 1999).

12. Stanley Aronowitz has challenged that "we must stop pretending that there is no possible class discourse, even as we firmly reject its antecedent expressions.... We were right to throw out the reductionist 'class analysis' that was the theoretical basis of both the Old Left and, with variations, much of the New Left. This version of social and political theory virtually excluded all other considerations, or regarded them as displacements of the class struggle. In the course of this rightful rejection, however, class was occluded from the lexicon of radical terms on the basis of its pernicious history.... To say that there are no longer master discourses of history precludes neither history nor its agents" (1995: 123–24). Cornel West reinforces this view, stating that "The crucial role that class plays.... Now that has something to do with resources, something to do with the way identity politics is articulated, given this tremendous sense of desperation and despair among people who are victims of cutbacks and slowdowns and taxes taken out of their pockets.... Can you imagine the attempt to talk about the articulation of Black

identities versus upper-class identities without talking about resources? It makes no sense. It's radically ahistorical.... [W]hen you talk about identity it's got to be linked to material conditions in terms of what kinds of assets and resources people have" (Butler 1995: 139).

13. This study also draws from other anthropological formulations of the role of nationalist ideologies in plural societies, namely Fox (1990) and Foster (1991).

14. I cannot do justice here to the rich and extensive literature on South Asians overseas (La Brack 1979; Gibson 1988; Clarke, Peach, and Vertovec 1990; Werbner 1990; Modood 1992; Dasgupta 1998; Singh and Barrier 1999; Kumar 2000). Under the auspices of "diaspora" studies, one line of research has focused particularly on social phenomena that transcend local contexts, "deterritorialized" networks, relations, organizations, and forms and forces of cultural production that enable local South Asian populations across the globe to imagine themselves as or become conscious of belonging to a transnational community with common ties to a "homeland" (Barrier and Dusenbery 1989: Women of South Asian Descent Collective 1993; Bahri and Vasudeva 1996; see particularly Tatla 1999). While breaking important new ground, many have argued that research into "diaspora" as a transnational entity is still largely undertheorized (Cohen 1997: x; Vertovec 1997: 277). Others have warned that, while "diaspora" may be a useful analytic construct, its use can lead one to accept the existence, for example, of a "Sikh diaspora" as a "relatively unproblematic social fact," to adopt a category of practice as a category of analysis (Dusenbery 1995: 17). Sikh historians W. H. McLeod (1989) and Karen Leonard (1989) have challenged scholars to consider whether and when it is appropriate to speak of a Sikh diaspora, for the meaning and significance of being a Sikh have changed over time and across nation-states. Drawing from her historical research on early Punjabi migration to the farming regions of central California, Leonard has explained the problem quite succinctly: "It has become common to talk of the Sikh diaspora, but there is some question whether or not 'Sikh' is the most appropriate category for analysis of these emigrants from South Asia. While the overwhelming majority of the Punjabi pioneers in early twentieth century California were indeed Sikhs, my research indicates that religion was less salient than other characteristics of these men. It was in fact a Punjabi diaspora, and to go back and emphasize Sikhs and Sikhism does violence to the historical experiences of the immigrants and their descendants" (1989: 120).

15. Frequently undertheorized or underanalyzed in studies of South Asian migration are the class and status group differences among members of overseas South Asian populations as well as "the racialization of [these] immigrant groups within nation-state borders" (Visweswaran 1997: 22). A central contribution of this study, then, is the approach it provides to understanding identity formation among South Asians in the context of the racialization of class and cultural differences, which I argue is central to the ongoing struggles of nationalism and race relations in postimperial Britain.

16. My analysis of the normative constraints surrounding the cultural production of different lifestyles draws from Weber's (1978) notion of status groups as

well as more recent work on status "distinctions" (Bourdieu 1979, 1984) and status reckoning within plural societies (see B. Williams 1991). For an overview of traditional approaches to the study of lifestyle and status groups, see Zablocki and Kanter (1976).

17. For analyses of theories of social reproduction, see Bowles and Gintis (1976), Bourdieu (1973), Bourdieu and Passeron (1977), Giroux (1983), Wexler (1987), and Willis (1981). Ethnographic studies of youth that draw on theories of social and cultural reproduction include MacLeod (1987), Foley (1990), Holland and Eisenhart (1990), and Levinson, Foley, and Holland (1996).

18. My use of the concept of ideology is similar to what the Comaroffs, following Raymond Williams (1977: 109), have defined as "an articulated system of meanings, values, and beliefs of a kind that can be abstracted as [the] 'world-view' of any social grouping. Borne in explicit manifestos and everyday practices ... this worldview may be more or less internally systematic, more or less assertively coherent in its outward forms. But, as long as it exists, it provides an organizing scheme for collective symbolic production" (Comaroff and Comaroff 1991: 24).

19. As Brackette Williams has argued, "hegemonic homogenization of the content of national cultures combines economic and political domination with ideological justification that explains these forms of domination as the 'natural' outcomes of differences in the intellectual capabilities of races and in the relative quality of the cultures they produce consequent to these intellectual variations" (1991: 437–38).

20. I hesitate in using the category "white," for it reinscribes the significance of racial differences among the students at Grange Hill High. However, the alternatives are no better, as "English" would imply that nonwhite students are not English and "Anglo-English" is simply clumsy.

21. Afro-Caribbean students are present at Grange Hill High, but in very small numbers. I interviewed and grew to know a few of them, particularly three students who were in the sixth form.

22. In recording this history I am drawing liberally from Roger Ballard's (1989) account of the stages of Sikh migration to Britain. His research and that of Catherine Ballard in Leeds, particularly their accounts of the experiences of first generation Sikhs, provide important background information to my own study. See, for example, R. Ballard and C. Ballard (1977); C. Ballard (1978, 1979); R. Ballard (1982, 1987, 1989). For historical accounts of South Asian immigration to Britain, see Hiro (1971), Fryer (1984), Vadgama (1984), and Visram (1986).

23. Figures and tables are reproduced as published in the Office for National Statistics volumes, *Ethnicity in the 1991 Census*. Specific citations appear with the figures and tables.

24. The British census does not gather data that would allow the breakdown of ethnic groups by religion, "mother tongue," or region of origin. A "country of birth" question, however, does make it possible to differentiate between Indian families who lived in East Africa (if they or their children were born there) and

those who came directly from the subcontinent. Yet people of East African origin may identify themselves as "Indian" rather than "Other-Asian" and, if they are born in the UK, there would be no way to identify them as of East African heritage (see Ratcliffe 1996: 8).

25. Owen points out that "the coding scheme yielded a more precise measure of the broad ethnic categories, but at the considerable cost of yielding only vague information about the characteristics of people with parents from different ethnic groups" (1996: 89). This is evident particularly with regard to interpreting the categories referred to as "other." The category "Other-Asians" seems to have been chosen by Asian people who could identify their origins within the standard categories, such as people who identify themselves as Vietnamese or Filipino or Sri Lankan. A smaller segment of "Other-Asians" included Indo-Caribbean or East African Asians, though, Owen surmises, "the form of the question invites Indo-Caribbean people to identify themselves as either Black-Caribbean or Indian, and most East African Asians appear to have identified themselves as Indian (1996: 89). The "Black-Other" category included people who identified themselves as "British" (32.5 percent), half of whom, according to Owen, "were persons of mixed parentage" since no separate categories for mixed parentage were included in the 1991 census. Owen attributes the substantial numbers in this category, however, to the presence of other groups such as Black U.S. military personnel. The "Other-Other" category (290,000 people, 0.5 percent of the population) included the most diverse range of peoples, for example, North Africans, Arabs, and Iranians. This category, states Owen, also "obscures relatively large groups of people of mixed Black and White, Asian and White, and other mixed parentage (together 153,000 or 53.6 percent of the category" (1996: 89–90).

26. Numbers for Leeds are taken from figures provided in Rees and Phillips (1996: 275–76).

Chapter 2. From Subjects to Citizens

1. This theory of postnationalism is developed within a political science literature addressing the nature of citizenship in the global era. As I discuss in chapters that follow, anthropologists such as Arjun Appadurai have used the concept of postnationalism to refer to different but related global processes. Appadurai similarly calls anthropologists to "think ourselves beyond the nation" (1996: 158), for "the nationalist genie, never perfectly contained in the bottle of the territorial state, is now itself diasporic. . . . It is increasingly unrestrained by ideas of spatial boundary and territorial sovereignty . . . Where soil and place were once the key to the linkage of territorial affiliation with state monopoly of the means of violence, key identities and identifications now only partially revolve around the realities and images of place. . . . In the Sikh demands for Khalistan . . . images of a homeland are only part of the rhetoric of popular sovereignty and do not necessarily reflect a territorial bottom line" (160–61). I implicitly draw on Appadurai's powerful notion

of a diasporic "postnational" nationalism in Chapter 5 when I consider the diasporic nationalist imaginings of British Sikhs.

2. Another example of the postnationalist view of citizenship is found in Jacobson (1997). For a critical treatment of postnationalism, see Joppke (1998).

3. Hansen, for one, in his analysis of citizenship and immigration in postwar Britain, concurs with this argument. He writes, "The British case frustrates—totally—the expectations of globalization theory. Unless it is dismissed as *sui generis*, the UK makes clear that globalized markets are consistent with closed borders. Strict migration control on the Commonwealth crystallized in the early 1970s and rules on family reunification were tightened in the 1980s and 1990s. These, of course, are the decades in which globalization accelerated. International norms and instruments have exercised little if any constraining influence on UK migration policy" (2000: 23).

4. In parts of England in the wake of waves of devolution, the "Englishness" of this "British" heritage is increasingly emphasized. In 2000 the annual survey of social attitudes conducted by the National Centre for Social Research in Britain found that during the first two years of Blair's government, as power devolved to Scotland and Wales, the percentage of people expressing allegiance to England over Britain increased from 7 percent to 17 percent. Among these "Little Englanders," more than a third "freely admitted to being racially prejudiced, compared with 17 percent of those who continued to assert their Britishness" (*The Guardian*, "The Rise of Little Englanders," November 28, 2000; <www.guardian.co.uk>).

5. See Hechter's analysis of England's relationship to its "internal colonies" (1975).

6. During the 1960s and '70s, British MP Enoch Powell became famous for his inflammatory rhetoric. In his noted "rivers of blood" speech, Powell warned that a major social crisis would come to pass if black migration was not ended. He became the hero of working-class racist movements such as the National Front.

7. *The Guardian*, January 31, 1978 (quoted from Solomos 1993: 187).

8. Gilroy and others from the Centre for Contemporary Cultural Studies (including Stuart Hall and John Solomos) associate modern British race relations with a state of crisis resulting from Britain's postcolonial decline. The political obsession with defining "who is" and "who is not" essentially British, they argue, has been fueled by a need to impose order on a social world perceived to be falling apart (Solomos et al. 1982: 28).

9. One of the articles reads: "Britain should be formally recognised as a multicultural society whose history needs to be 'revised, rethought or jettisoned', says a report that has been welcomed by ministers. Minorities are left out of the island story and they associate Britishness with the Empire and colonialisation, says the Commission on the Future of Multi-Ethnic Britain. The inquiry was set up three years ago by the Runnymede Trust ... and launched by Jack Straw, Home Secretary. Philip Johnston, "Straw Wants to Rewrite Our History" (*Daily Telegraph*; <www.news.telegraph.co.uk>).

10. Quoted from "Straw Attacks 'Unpatriotic' Left" (*Independent*, October 12,

2000; <www.independent.co.uk>). See also "Straw Backs Britishness for Britain" (*The Times*, October 11, 2000; <www.thetimes.co.uk>).

11. Mick Hume, "True Brit?" *The Times*, October 12, 2000;<www.thetimes.co.uk>)

12. Yasmin Alibhai-Brown, journalist and member of the Commission on the Future of Multi-Ethnic Britain, describes the intense reactions she received in the wake of the controversy in "Why Does Questioning the Nature of Britishness Raise So Much Fury?" (*Independent*, October 18, 2000; <www.independent.co.uk>). The 23 members of the Commission included a large number of academic experts on various aspects of race and ethnic relations in Britain, among them Stuart Hall, Muhammad Anwar, Sally Tomlinson, and Tariq Modood (an adviser), as well as broadcast journalist Trevor Phillips. The commission was racially diverse and included representatives from the police, social work agencies, community organizations, and the media as well as researchers. Set up in January 1998, the Commission conducted extensive research including a review of the literature, soliciting written submissions and reports, site visits, focus groups, interviews, meetings, and seminars. A full discussion of the consultation process and a list of all who participated is presented in the report (see Parekh 2000: 350–71).

13. Maya Jaggi, "First Among Equalizers" (*The Guardian*, October 21, 2000; <www.guardian.co.uk>).

14. Quoted from (Foreign Secretary) "Robin Cook's Chicken Tikka Masala Speech" (*The Guardian*, April 19, 2001; <www.guardian.co.uk>). See also "Tony Blair's Britain speech" (*The Guardian*, March 28, 2001), and on a much lighter note Jonathan Glancey's amusing series "On Redesigning the Union Jack" <www.guardian.co.uk/galleryguide/0,6191,184378,00.html>.

15. Roy Hattersley, "Definitions of a Notional Identity" (*The Guardian*, November 13, 2000; <www.guardian.co.uk>).

16. The terms "minority" and "majority" are used as "folk" or emic categories, not as analytic categories. The terms index the asymmetrical relations of power that divide peoples of a nation rather than any simple numerical dominance of one population over another. In fact, I argue here that "minority" statuses are themselves social constructs that actually produce and position the "groups" of which they speak.

17. A full analysis of the political history surrounding the successive immigration acts is not possible here. I consider immigration law as one among several sites in the public sphere in which "minority" categories and statuses have been produced. For historical accounts, see Paul (1997), Spencer (1997), Layton-Henry (1992), Miles (1989), Bevan (1986), MacDonald (1983, 1969) and Foot (1965). Hansen (2000) gives close scrutiny to the divergent ideological arguments and positions that surrounded the eventual passage of increasingly racialized immigration acts. Scholars to date, he argues, have not granted this political complexity sufficient attention.

18. The first independent dominions, the "Old Dominions," included Australia, Canada, New Zealand, and South Africa. These were joined by Southern

Rhodesia (now Zimbabwe) and what came to be called the New Dominions, India, Pakistan (later divided into Pakistan and Bangladesh), and Ceylon (now Sri Lanka).

19. Since 1955, however, steps had been taken by the governments of India and Pakistan to restrict emigration by withholding passports (Hansen 2000: 84). Hansen presents documentary evidence from the period that suggests that some politicians viewed West Indian and Asian migration differently; West Indians (who were still colonial peoples) were thought to be "more British," hard working and, therefore, more desirable as immigrants (84–87).

20. The link here with processes of decolonization is critical. The Colonial Office had taken a very different position in relation to Commonwealth migration, arguing for more generous quotas for category C vouchers. However, these were the days of the end of Empire, and the historical changes underway were undermining the authority of the Colonial Office. It was merged with the Commonwealth Relations Office in 1966 and closed in 1967. The Commonwealth Relations Office was itself merged with the Foreign Office in 1968 (Hansen 2000: 127).

21. Kenya achieved independence in 1963 and passed its own nationality laws. Those of African descent and others whose families had historically lived in the country were granted automatic citizenship. Others had two years to apply for Kenyan citizenship. Kenyan nationality laws forbade dual citizenship; therefore Asians and Europeans were required to choose whether to maintain their CUKC citizenship or become Kenyan citizens. Fewer than 20,000 from the 185,000 Asians and 42,000 Europeans residing in Kenya applied for Kenyan citizenship. In 1967 the Kenyan Immigration Act instituted a work permit requirement for those without Kenyan citizenship. British Asian citizens in Kenya then began to migrate to Britain. Nearly 1,000 per month were arriving in 1967 (Hansen 2000: 159); in February 1968, 10,000 largely skilled and middle-class Kenyan Asians entered Britain (Hayter 2000: 53). This triggered fears of an immigration crisis.

22. For a detailed analysis of the steps that led up to the passage of the 1968 Commonwealth Immigration Act, see Hansen (2000: 153–78).

23. The British Nationality Act of 1981 for the first time allowed that mothers could pass on their British citizenship to children born outside the UK.

24. Hayter also points out that on the day the Immigration Act of 1971 became law, January 1, 1973, Britain joined the European Economic Community, which opened the nation's doors to some 200 million Europeans who have the right to enter and settle in the UK (2000: 55).

25. Individuals possessing British Dependent Territories Citizenship were those who were residents of the remaining colonies, the majority in Hong Kong, but also in Bermuda, the British Virgin Islands, and Gibraltar. Those who qualified for British Overseas Citizenship were largely individuals like those remaining in East Africa and Malaysia who were in actuality stateless. As Hansen explains, these two categories "essentially granted one of two impoverished legal identities to any former CUKC without local citizenship" (2000: 214).

26. This account cannot do justice to the range of issues that have emerged

in the politics surrounding the formation of immigration acts and policies (see in particular Hansen 2000 and Spencer 1997 for treatment of these issues). In keeping with the focus of this study, I have looked primarily at the construction of racial and national identities, but these laws and policies have also managed migration on the basis of gender and generational categories as well as, more recently, the category "asylum seeker" or "refugee."

27. Quoted in Cashmore (1984: 13).

28. This history, of course, is far more complex than the treatment it received within these deliberations. The turban, as I noted earlier, is not one of the five symbols of the Sikh faith and is only worn by observant Sikh men and not by women. The history of the turban and its significance to certain groups of Sikhs is complex and a source of great controversy. An analysis of this history is beyond the scope of this present work but has been given notable attention by Sikh historians (see Oberoi 1994; McLeod 1999).

29. This is quoted in Banton (1989: 155). This article and Cashmore (1989) discuss the test case for criteria set down in *Mandla v. Dowell Lee*. These stipulations were applied in *Dawkins v. Crown Suppliers*, a case brought to court by the Commission for Racial Equality on behalf of rasta Trevor Dawkins, who was refused a job as a driver at the Government Transport Division's Property Services Agency because he would not cut his dreadlocks. The court declared Rastafarians, in Cashmore's words, "Britain's latest official 'ethnic group.'" Therefore, the "no dreads" ban is illegal in Britain (except where short hair can be proved to be necessary for effectively carrying out a job).

30. My discussion of the transport disputes is informed by Beetham (1970), a study of the effects of local politics on two such disputes in Manchester and Wolverhampton. Due to local contingencies, the two cases played out in very different ways.

31. Following the resolution of the Manchester controversy, Sikhs won similar disputes in Birmingham and Wolverhampton. Sikhs who wear turbans were granted special (in this case religious) exemption from wearing motorcycle helmets under the Motor-Cycle Crash Helmets (Religious Exemption) Act of 1976, Chapter 62. The Act reads, "Be It Enacted by the Queen's most Excellent Majesty, by and with the advice and consent of the Lords Spiritual and Temporal, and Commons, in this present Parliament assembled, and by the authority of the same, as follows: 1. In section 32 of the Road Traffic Act 1972 there shall be inserted after subsection (2) the following new subsection: '(2A) A requirement imposed by regulations under this section (whenever made) shall not apply to any follower of the Sikh religion while he is wearing a turban.' 2. This Act may be cited as the Motor-Cycle Crash-Helmets (Religious Exemption) Act 1976."

32. There are, however, numerous definitions of communitarianism and positions that fall loosely under this rubric; see Etzioni (1995). As Etzioni suggests, "definitional questions have plagued communitarian thinking," but theorists associated with this tradition share a "commitment to exploring the ways in which contemporary political theory can better address questions of community, virtue, and

moral discourse in the public square" (1995: 2). These views, at their most basic level, provide a critique of the excesses of liberalism.

33. The liberal construction of the public/private dichotomy has a long and complex history, one that reaches across several political traditions and versions of liberalism. A full analysis of this history is not possible here (see Calhoun 1997; Weintraub and Kumar 1997).

34. For a more extensive analysis of the "Honeyford Affair," see Halstead (1988).

35. The term "moral panic" was used by Stanley Cohen (1972) to describe public reaction to the emergence in postwar Britain of various forms of youth culture. As Cohen explains the phenomenon, "Societies appear to be subject, every now and then, to periods of moral panic. A condition, episode, person or group of persons emerges to become defined as a threat to societal values and interests; its nature is presented in a stylized and stereotypical fashion by the mass media; the moral barricades are manned by editors, bishops, politicians and other right-thinking people; socially accredited experts pronounce their diagnoses and solutions; ways of coping are evolved or (more often) resorted to; the condition then disappears, submerges or deteriorates and becomes more visible.... Sometimes the panic passes over and is forgotten, except in folklore and collective memory; at other times it has more serious and long-lasting repercussions and might produce such changes as those in legal and social policy or even in the way the society conceives itself" (1972: 9).

36. As Calhoun cautions, however, "this does not mean that the flowering of innumerable potential publics is in and of itself a solution to this basic problem of democracy. On the contrary, democracy requires discourse across lines of basic difference. But this discourse can be conceptualized—and nurtured—as a matter of multiple intersections among heterogeneous publics, not only as the privileging of a single overarching public. Nationalist thought, however, commonly rejects such notions of multiple and multifarious publics as divisive. The presumption that the nation is a unitary being is a staple of nationalist thought" (1997: 81).

37. S. Hall attributes the ideological power of this form of populist "common sense" to its resonance with strands of British popular morality: "Thatcherism has effectively exploited a traditional space in popular ideologies: the moralism endemic in conservative 'philosophies.' The language of popular morality has no necessary class-belongingness: but it is also true that traditional and uncorrected common sense is a massively conservative force, penetrated thoroughly—as it has been—by religious notions of good and evil, by fixed conceptions of the unchanging and unchangeable character of human nature, and by ideas of retributive justice" (1990b: 142).

38. The phrase "Education for All" has specific roots within the history of British educational policy evoking R. H. Tawney's 1922 essay in which he set down his argument for providing access for "all" (meaning previously excluded working-class children), to secondary education. Like Tawney's position, the proposals of the Swann Report are firmly founded on liberal democratic principles of justice and equality for all.

39. Chantal Mouffe advances a powerful critique of what she calls "extreme pluralism" or the valorization of all differences: "What such a pluralism misses is the dimension of the political. Relations of power and antagonisms are erased, and we are left with the typical liberal illusion of a pluralism without antagonism.... To deny the need for a construction of collective identities and to conceive democratic politics exclusively in terms of a struggle of a multiplicity of interest groups or of minorities for the assertion of their rights is to remain blind to the relations of power. It is to ignore the limits imposed on the extension of the sphere of rights by the fact that some existing rights have been constructed on the very exclusion or subordination of others" (Mouffe 1996: 247).

40. New Right conservatives provided the most vocal criticisms largely aimed at Race Awareness Training (RAT), the most extreme of the anti-racist education approaches. RAT sought to uncover racism in curricula, in language use, and, more disturbingly for some, in the attitudes and practices of white teachers and administrators. RAT strategies, and by implication all anti-racist interventions, were represented as fascist and fanatical. Together with the tabloid press, conservative critics orchestrated a moral panic around particular "loony left councils," reporting that they were "banning black dustbin liners, insisting on renaming black coffee 'coffee without milk', and censoring the performance of 'Ba-ba black sheep' in the classroom," all of which, according to Rattansi, "turned out to be complete fabrications" (1992: 13). Anti-racist education was politicizing schooling. Frank Palmer (1986), in the title of his book, characterized this as an "assault on education and value." Schools were being transformed "from centres of learning into instruments of political revolution—ideological power-stations calculated to promote a cynical, if not openly hostile, outlook on British society and all major British institutions, including the forces of law and order. Such an outlook, thriving upon a failure to distinguish education from indoctrination, could easily encourage civil strife and racial discord" (Palmer 1986: 2).

41. The most astonishing feature of the Education Reform Act's history is how Thatcher and Baker were able to impose such radical changes in so short a period of time and against a great deal of opposition. This was accomplished by swift actions that were to take the nation by surprise. They were able to outmaneuver much of the opposition by circumventing traditional procedures, such as the publishing of white papers for consultation and debate. Simon reports that, instead, "The main series of consultation papers, affecting schools, were ... made available at the end of July. Responses were asked for in all cases within two months— by the end of September. This narrowed time-scale led to an almost unanimous cry of protest by those most directly involved. How could parents (with children at home), governors, teachers' organizations and others meet effectively during the summer months to consider and articulate their responses?" (Simon 1991: 539). This process, Simon notes, was quite different from the consultation procedures conducted over passage of other significant pieces of education reform legislation. In crafting both the 1918 and the 1944 Education Acts, government consultations had been conducted over the course of two to three years: "All organisations had

had the opportunity to express their views, to publish them, to meet with and negotiate directly with the ministers concerned." This was not the case with the 1988 Act.

Chapter 3. The Politics of Language Recognition

An earlier version of this chapter appeared as "Asserting 'Needs' and Claiming 'Rights': The Cultural Politics of Community Language Education in England." *Journal of Language, Identity and Education* 1, 2 (2002). Reprinted by permission.

1. "Minority" and "majority," as I have noted before, are problematic terms, since in certain national contexts the "majority" of people speak "minority" languages. Several recent works in the field of sociolinguistics have looked more closely at the problematic nature of constructs of "linguistic majority" and "linguistic minority" and implications for language policy (cf. Heller 1999; Pennycook 1998; Coulmas 1998).

2. Blommaert (1999: 431–34) provides a useful analysis of processes through which language quality is often assessed and languages become ranked within national hierarchies.

3. In an important and insightful recent ethnography, Heller (1999) describes how "hyper-modernity is transforming relations of power and the bases of identity in the Western world" in ways that give value to the linguistic repertoires of linguistic minorities (French speaking Canadians in her study) that is "radically different from the value they had when a centralizing nation-state and a primary resource extraction based economy defined it" (4). What is emerging is a new basis of legitimacy for "minority language" speakers, "one founded not on authenticity and tradition, but rather on pluralism, on the extensiveness of the minority's social networks and on the quality of the linguistic resources the minority possesses" (5). This shift, she argues, calls linguistic minorities to abandon the old politics of identity as they take their new positions as members of an emerging bilingual, even multilingual elite. While I agree with Heller that globalization is reconfiguring the logic of language hierarchies worldwide (a phenomenon I discuss in relation to Britain at the end of this chapter), I do not see these processes as putting an end to forms of cultural domination or the identity politics that emerge to challenge them. As many have argued (cf. J. L. Comaroff 1996; N. Fraser 1997; May 2000: 371), multiple contradictory forms of politics are emerging in the wake of developments associated with global political and economic realignments, politics that are bringing forth a new appreciation for cultural and linguistic pluralism in some nations and the reassertion of homogenizing nationalist projects in others. Heller's emphasis on the emergence of a new bilingual elite is appropriate in the case of Canadian French speakers in the global economy. But other linguistic minorities fight on for recognition, for forms of bilingualism such as speaking Punjabi in England or Ebonics/African American Vernacular English in the United States (Collins 1999) remain devalued within the global economic order.

4. For a more detailed overview of the history of education language policy in England, see Thompson, Fleming, and Byram (1996), Bourne (1997), and Stubbs (1991).

5. This is an analysis of language policy debates in England, not in Britain. Only England and Wales fall under the auspices of the secretary of state for education and science (the Ministry of Education for Britain), and in Welsh matters such as the teaching of the Welsh language in schools, the secretary of state for Wales is granted primary authority. The Welsh Language Act of 1993 is actually the only legally based language policy in the United Kingdom, an act passed to ensure that Welsh and English should be treated equally in public businesses and in the administration of justice within Wales (Thompson, Fleming, and Byram 1997: 106–7). With the exception of the Welsh Act, Britain has never passed laws designating language rights, and Welsh has legal status only within the borders of Wales. One other exception, however, was the Polish Resettlement Act of 1947, which set in place special language provisions for Polish ex-soldiers who settled in Britain after World War II (Rassool 1997).

6. Section 11 of the 1966 Local Government Act states that local authorities can apply to the British Home Office (national government) for 75 percent of the costs of employing extra staff for educational and other purposes in areas with large numbers of Commonwealth immigrants for whom special provision is required because of differences in language or customs. At the time of the campaign, this policy was still in full effect. Since 1993 there has been a restructuring of Section 11 funding procedures. This funding, which had been available only to Commonwealth immigrants, is now available to all ethnic groups including refugees. In 1994 the Home Office instituted cutbacks in the Section 11 budget. Funding to Local Educational Authorities (LEAs) decreased to 57 percent in 1994–95 and to 50 percent in 1995–96. Local authorities had to decide whether they were able to increase their budgets beyond their original contribution of 25 percent (for a discussion of these changes see Rassool 1997).

7. My assessment of class differences among Sikh families is based on my knowledge of residential patterns and local perceptions. The school's catchment area included low-income neighborhoods such as Chapeltown as well as the middle-class neighborhood surrounding the school. Members of the Sikh communities and school faculty shared a perception that Sikh students who lived in these neighborhoods were from different class backgrounds. These students had also attended different primary schools before entering Grange Hill High.

8. During the period when I carried out my initial field research, the traditional O- and A-level exams were still in existence. In 1988 O-levels were replaced by General Certificate of Education exams (GCEs).

9. Italics in interview quotations indicate my emphasis.

10. An imagined multilingual Britain has in fact appeared in recent language policy discourse. In the Foreword to the Nuffield Report (2000), "Languages: The Next Generation," Chairmen of the Inquiry Sir Trevor McDonald and Sir John Boyd call for developing multilingualism in Britain: "in a complex and disparate world in

which modern communications have transformed personal contact across boundaries, is English really enough? In our view it is not. Capability in other languages—a much broader range than hitherto and in greater depth—is crucially important for a flourishing UK.... The UK needs a change of policy and practice to fit us for the new millennium" (2000: 4–5).

Chapter 4. "Becoming like Us"

1. A number of recent ethnographic studies in the anthropology of education have contributed original and analytically powerful frameworks for understanding the interrelationships among global, national, and local political processes through the analysis of educational policies and practices. Among these works, several stand out as exemplary, including Ngwane (2001), Lukose (2000), and Luykx (1999).

2. As Foucault explains, "The workshop, the school, the army were subject to a whole micro-penalty of time (lateness, absences, interruptions of tasks), and of activity (inattention, negligence, lack of zeal), of behavior (impoliteness, disobedience), of speech (idle chatter, insolence), of the body ('incorrect' attitudes, irregular gestures, lack of cleanliness), of sexuality (impurity, indecency)" (1995: 178).

3. The Norwood Report (1943), the report of the Norwood Committee on Secondary School Curricula and Examinations, was one of three official government reports published in 1943 and 1944 on issues related to postwar education. In accordance with assumptions common at the time about the "natural" basis of Intelligence levels, the Norwood Committee came out in support of different types of secondary schools for different types of students. Contrasts were made between students "interested in learning for its own sake," who were thought best suited for the grammar schools; those "whose interests and abilities lie markedly in the field of applied science or applied art," who were designated to modern schools; and, finally, the pupil "who deals more easily with concrete things than with ideas," or students who were thought best suited for technical (or vocational) schools (Lawson and Silver 1973: 422). During the 1950s, an increasing number of sociological studies found that the selection process for grammar school attendance greatly favored middle-class children (Rubinstein and Simon 1969: 61).

4. The late 1950s and early '60s saw increased attention toward assessing the performance of existing comprehensive schools and establishing numerous others, particularly in certain areas of Britain and Wales, notably London, the West Riding (West Yorkshire), Staffordshire, Manchester, and Swansea (Rubinstein and Simon 1969: 70).

5. The "authoritative" voices in this account are often male. I interviewed and got to know as many white middle-class females as I did males; however, among female students issues of "race" or ethnic difference seldom came up, in formal interviews or in everyday conversation. The boys, knowing that I was doing a study of Asian students, were always eager to express themselves and often asked me to interview them, teasing me that they had converted and were soon to have

an arranged marriage. But the boys' interest in talking about racial politics went beyond these performative gestures; conversations among boys both inside and outside classrooms more regularly turned to politics and often to issues of race. The differences I found between the ways boys and girls talked about and related to issues of racial difference suggest that racial attitudes and forms of expression vary according to gender as well as class. It was the dominant middle-class males who were most concerned with and spoke most openly and spontaneously about issues of national identity, cultural differences, and conflicts that arise when immigrants choose not to assimilate but to assert "their cultures" instead.

6. Some teachers were committed to rectifying this problem and were creating curricula that aimed to enrich the academic learning of students relegated to the bottom sets.

7. Over the centuries various types of "civilizing missions" have targeted a range of populations both within the boundaries of Britain and beyond—people who were seen as "uncouth savages" or "barbarian races" in need of English uplifting. After suppressing the Jacobite revolt of 1745, the state attempted to pacify and civilize the Scottish Highlanders by introducing the Protestant religion, a sense of loyalty to the king, and an ethic of industry. The Highlanders "were signified as a culturally alien Other, whose distinctive dress, language, manner and mode of material subsistence were interpreted as marks of the membership of a distinct and inferior 'race'" (Miles 1993: 92–93). During the nineteenth century, the "dangerous class" of "urban savages"—the desperately poor who inhabited England's industrializing cities—were frequently the target of projects of "moral regulation" (see Corrigan and Sayer 1985). Viewed as lacking morals and a work ethic, they were "thought to be degenerate, uncivilised and perhaps uncivilisable," so different in "breeding" that many believed they were a different kind of human being or "a race apart" (Miles 1993: 94; Lorimer 1978: 110, 210; Corrigan and Sayer 1985).

Chapter 5. Mediated Traditions

1. Benedict Anderson's formulation has provided a useful starting point for a range of studies exploring the nation as an imagined community (Appadurai 1996; Ivy 1995). My account also draws from Handler (1988) and Cohn (1987) in considering processes through which forms of culture become objectified.

2. Margaret Eisenhart (1995) provides a brief overview of how anthropologists have applied cognitive theories of cultural models in analyses of identity formation. My point here is quite different. In discussing the various ways that culture and identity are imagined, I am considering not simply different "cultural models" (e.g., of marriage or romance) but distinctive ways "models" or concepts of culture (e.g., as tradition, "ethnic," or hybrid) are themselves symbolically constructed. My analysis resonates with recent work by Pauline Turner Strong and Barrik Van Winkle, who examine different types of discourse (which they refer to as "official" and "unofficial") that signify Washoe Indian identity in contrasting ways (1996: 558).

3. As Hamid Naficy has documented in his study of television production and consumption among Iranian exiles in Los Angeles, television in particular is "a vehicle through which the exilic subculture and its members, collectively and individually, construct themselves in the new environment. Television for them not only reflects but also constitutes and transforms the community" (1993: 90).

4. I borrow Greg Urban's (1993, 2001) concept of metaculture to refer to these forms of referential talk about culture. In this account I do not explicitly differentiate different levels of culture, as does Urban in his analysis of what he calls alpha and omega aspects of culture. Rather I am concerned with how the contrast between concepts of culture and community in different media discourse can serve to "denaturalize" culture as lived, making it possible to think about culture as an object.

5. See Oberoi (1994) for a fine history of the making of modern Sikh identities. Oberoi's historical work considers the emergence of two different views of Sikhism, the Tat Khalsa and Sanatan traditions. He argues that the Sanatan Sikh tradition was pluralist in orientation: "it presented its adherents with a wide variety of choices to determine what they did with their rites, festivals, body management, language and social organization" (1994: 421). The Tat Khalsa, on the other hand, "disowned this pluralist tradition and enunciated an orderly, pure, singular form of Sikhism." The Tat Khalsa view is the one found in these religious pamphlets. A full discussion of this complex and controversial history is beyond the parameters of this book. My point here is simply to consider the different cultural processes in Britain through which distinctive orientations toward Sikh identity are being produced and circulated.

6. The process of entextualization described here is literally "textual." Entextualization, however, does not refer exclusively to the making of material "texts" as linguists define "texts" as any type of ritualized or patterned talk or discourse. The entextualization of culture in material texts or in any other form involves processes that serve to "frame" culture in a particular way. As Silverstein and Urban explain, to entextualize culture is "to seem to give it a decontextualized structure and meaning, that is, a form and meaning that are imaginable apart from the spatiotemporal and other frames in which they [in this sense religious beliefs and practices] can be said to occur. Such an autonomously meaningful object becomes a trope for culture, understood in the sense of an ensemble of shared symbols and meanings, so that we should not be surprised at its appeal for students of culture. For if a text has a despatialized and detemporalized meaning—in short, a deprocessualized one—then that meaning can be clearly transmitted across social boundaries such as generations, without regard for the kinds of recontextualizations it might undergo. . . . [T]his utility of texts is precisely what the natives (including us) see as well. They engage in processes of entextualization to create a seemingly shareable, transmittable culture" (1996: 1–2).

7. In an excellent study, Brian Axel (2000) explores the iconography of violence, relating it to the making of a Sikh "diaspora."

8. See Chapter 1, n. 5.

9. <www.sikh.net/home.htm>.

10. <www.sikh.net/sikhism/ardas.htm>.

11. Indian films, as Marie Gillespie's (1993) study shows, are also vehicles through which families are re-creating and representing tradition in the lives of second generation British Asians.

12. Veena Das in an article on Indian soap operas raises a number of subtle theoretical issues concerning the challenges the production and consumption of television images and narratives pose to anthropological theories of culture. She makes a similar point about how tele-documentaries and talk shows have created a public culture, an intertextual space in which "new kinds of speech can be generated, breaking certain codes of silence" surrounding domestic issues in India (1995: 184).

13. Manjit, like many Sikh girls as well as boys, is not opposed to arranged marriages. Young Sikhs often find comfort in having their parents involved in finding good marriage partners, but they want the right to make the final choice from among those their parents view as appropriate. Young people may also meet at university or in the workplace and ask their parents to arrange a marriage for them. These "assisted marriages" are typically viewed as having a better chance at lasting than a "love match."

14. It is not possible to provide an adequate account here of the tragic history of Operation Bluestar and the assassination of Prime Minister Indira Gandhi. For a closer analysis of these events and the Khalistani movement more generally see Tatla (1999).

15. British films such as *My Son the Fanatic* and *East Is East*, focusing on intergenerational cultural and religious conflicts in British Asian families, demonstrate the continued relevance of this theme.

16. Sanjay Sharma, John Hutnyk, and Ashwani Sharma raise concern about Gillespie's depiction of Apache Indian's hybrid music style as "subversive." Being hybrid, they argue, is not the same as being subversive. Much "play" with signifiers is highly apolitical, and forms of expressive culture that are consciously political in a discursive sense are often disconnected from forms of political action in the world (1996: 3).

17. Paul Gilroy (1987: 217), bell hooks (1990), and Stuart Hall (1992) each discuss the significance of this process of empowerment. Hall refers to this engagement as the "politics of representation" (see also 1980, 1990/1996).

Chapter 6. "You Can't Be Religious and Be Westernized"

1. I draw from Cohn (1987) as well as Kapferer (1988) and Handler (1988) in analyzing cultural reification and ethnic identity formation.

2. Cultural capital refers to forms of knowledge, manners, and aesthetic sensibilities transmitted tacitly in families of a particular class background and taught more formally in school. Bourdieu posits that economic capital is "the root of all

the other types of capital." But the measure of all equivalences among types of capital is labor-time. "It has been seen," he writes, "that the transformation of economic capital into social capital presupposes a specific labor, i.e., an apparently gratuitous expenditure of time, attention, care, concern. ... [I]f the best measure of cultural capital is undoubtedly the amount of time devoted to acquiring it, this is because the transformation of economic capital into cultural capital presupposes an expenditure of time that is made possible by possession of economic capital. More precisely, it is because the cultural capital that is effectively transmitted within the family itself depends not only on the quantity of cultural capital, itself accumulated by spending time, that the domestic group possesses, but also on the usable time (particularly in the form of the mother's free time) available to it (by virtue of its economic capital, which enables it to purchase the time of others) to ensure the transmission of this capital and to delay entry into the labor market through prolonged schooling, a credit which pays off, if at all, only in the very long term" (1997: 54). In other words, it is the withdrawal from economic necessity that allows for the cultivation of forms of social as well as cultural capital.

3. Roger Ballard explains that the move into manufacturing began years ago when market traders and wholesalers "realized that it would be easy to produce the clothes they sold, given that they had a ready and relatively skilled labor force in their own close female kin." What have become large and profitable manufacturing firms were initiated as tiny back-room establishments. Many firms cut costs by hiring out sewing to Asian women, both Sikh and Punjabi Muslim women, who frequently are not allowed to work for wages outside the home (1989: 215–16).

4. The business activities of Asians in Britain has been addressed in many studies of first generation British Asians. Pnina Werbner (1984, 1987, 1990) has written extensively on the Pakistani population in Manchester. Roger Ballard (1987) has carried out research with Sikh and Pakistani communities in Britain as well as in the Punjab and Pakistan. He has documented aspects of the "political economy of migration" looking at Pakistani and Sikh diaspora networks. For additional perspectives on South Asian and other ethnic entrepreneurs in Britain, see Ward and Jenkins (1984), Westwood and Bhachu (1988).

5. Parminder Bhachu in her book *Twice Migrants* concentrates solely on the community of East African Sikh settlers in Southall, London. Hers is a traditional ethnography rich in detail about the community's social organization and ritual practices, particularly marriage procedures and the dowry system.

6. Alan James has an informative section on sports and games played by Sikh children and adults during the early period of settlement in his book *Sikh Children in Britain* (1974: 25–29).

7. Bains (1988) and Baumann (1996) each describe similar processes of "ethnic mobilization," or interest group politics within Asian communities in Southall.

8. Sewa Singh Kalsi has written extensively about caste divisions in the Sikh population in Britain (1992, 1999). Due to the sensitive nature of this controversial

topic, I rely heavily on his work and on the words of members of different Sikh communities to explain why caste remains significant to first generation Sikhs in Britain.

9. The Punjabi dictionary gives the meaning of *kaum* as nation, creed, caste, tribe, sect, or clan. But the Punjabi word for national is *kaumi*; *kaumiat* means nationality, and *kaumkarn karna* to nationalize. David Lelyveld in his book about Aligarh, the Anglo-Oriental College, and Muslim solidarity in British India, discusses a dichotomy between the Muslim *qaum*, a people of common descent, and the *ummah*, the community defined by religious belief rather than birth. In Muslim beliefs, "An individual's submission (*Islam*) to God's will was to override bonds of kinship; an ultimate equality of believers would undercut old patron-client ties among Arab kin-defined groups" (1978: 27–28). This resonates with Sikh notions of the caste quam and the *khalsa* or *panth* (the community of the devout). According to Lelyveld, the word "qaum" was redefined in nineteenth-century British India by leaders such as Sayyid Ahmad, a founder of Aligarh College. In their political interchanges with British rulers, members of the political elite developed a vocabulary influenced by British notions of legitimate social classifications and, moreover, by their desires to stimulate communal solidarities, to evoke "imagined communities" transcending localized kin-based affiliations. The term "qaum" provided this association: "Sayyid Ahmad redefined the meaning of 'qaum.' The word had been a loose one for any group defined by a concept of common ancestry—tribe, caste, lineage, family. Now it referred to the Muslims of British India, not just north India but places as far flung as eastern Bengal.... Sayyid Ahmad continually emphasized that he was acting not out of self-interest but for the sake of the *quami bhala'i* and *qaumi hamdardi*, the qaum's welfare and sense of fellow feeling. The term replaced the concept of ummah or ahl'i Islam, the people who had submitted to God, and *mazhab*, the category of a religious group, sect, or school. It referred now to "Indian Muslims," an ethnic group. The closest English equivalent to qaumi hamdardi would have been patriotism; later the word "communalism" was coined to represent the concept" (1978: 143).

10. Many other "traditional" marriage rules have become preferences and are not enforced in Britain. Clan exogamy (including cognates and agnates) is prohibited but only in relation to direct clans of the mother and father. Bhachu (1985) found that in fact East African Sikhs have shallow genealogies, only two to three generations in depth. Regional endogamy is also preferred but not required.

11. The questionnaire is the same for the dating site and the marriage site, with the exception that "sex" is categorized as "Male" or "Female" on the dating form, and "Groom" and "Bride" on the marriage database form.

12. Arjun Appadurai (1990: 18–19) notes how women in particular become "pawns in the heritage politics of the household" as migrant families adjust to the "traumas of deterritorialization" and to the conflicting pressures of work, leisure, and domestic life. He writes that the women "are forced to enter the labor force in new ways on the one hand, and continue the maintenance of familial heritage on the other. Thus the honor of women becomes not just an armature of stable (if

inhuman) systems of cultural reproduction, but a new arena for the formation of sexual identity and family politics, as men and women face new pressures at work, and new fantasies of leisure."

Chapter 7. "There's a Time to Act English and a Time to Act Indian"

Earlier versions of portions of this chapter appeared in "There's a Time to Act English and a Time to Act Indian': The Politics of Identity Among Sikh Adolescents in England," in *Children and the Politics of Culture*, ed. Sharon Stephens (Princeton, N.J.: Princeton University Press, 1995). Reprinted by permission.

1. Michel de Certeau elaborates on the distinction between places and spaces in (1984: 117).

2. My use of the concept of cultural field diverges from Bourdieu's sense of the term, in that I emphasize the normative or regulatory aspects of practices that also tend to be "learned," in Lave and Wenger's (1991) sense, in situated activities within "communities of knowledge and practice" (1991: 29). My notion of cultural field is a hybrid concept that brings together Bourdieu's powerful concept of field, Foucault's sense of regulatory practices, Butler's emphasis on performativity, and Lave and Wenger's emphasis on the situated nature of socially constituted learning in practice.

3. Butler's theory of performativity has opened the way for "agency" in poststructuralist formulations of productive power (following on aspects of Foucault's later work). In explaining how gender binaries come to be subverted, she writes, "The subject is not determined by the rules through which it is generated because signification is not a founding act, but rather a regulated process of repetition that both conceals itself and enforces its rules precisely through the production of substantializing effects. In a sense, all signification takes place within the orbit of the compulsion to repeat; "agency," then, is to be located within the possibility of a variation on that repetition. If the rules governing signification not only restrict, but enable the assertion of ... new possibilities for gender that contest the rigid codes of hierarchical binarisms.... [I]t is only within the practices of repetitive signifying that a subversion of identity becomes possible" (1990: 145).

4. This applies to the second generation born and raised in Britain—those who if they are to belong are required to seem "British." Cosmopolitan elites from India and Pakistan can seem upper or middle class while at the same time seeming "foreign" or "not British."

5. In an important ethnographic study of African American student success, Signithia Fordham (1996) describes the costs of success for students a society represents as "other" and racially inferior. Her study, building upon John Ogbu's "macro" labor market framework for explaining "minority school failure," argues that success among African Americans is seen as "acting white." This also resonates with the stories I am depicting here. She goes on, however, to argue that academically successful African Americans perceive their school performance as a form

of "resistance" through conforming to the dominant expectations of the school. They are succeeding, she argues, in order to "resist" or counter dominant views of African Americans as academically inferior. Although her approach clearly captures many of the concerns of socially mobile African Americans' and British Sikhs as well, I believe her analysis is overly reductionistic. While she makes note of the multiple and contrasting cultural influences in student lives, she relies on a dichotomous model of "avoidance" or "conformist" resistance. Students either succeed or fail and both choices are explained as forms of resistance. Hence all experiences of academic success are simply viewed as "resistance," which drastically oversimplifies the range of ways students of color experience becoming successful in academic terms. Moreover, as Herve Varenne and Ray McDermott (1998) argue, the tendency among anthropologists of education to reduce minority student experiences to school "success" or "failure" reinforces this problematic and narrow view of school experiences and ignores other ways young people become "successful" and identify themselves in affirming ways. This, as Spencer et al. (2001) suggest, limits our ability to understand sources of "resiliency" in the lives of disadvantaged youth.

Chapter 8. Consciousness, Self-Awareness, and the Life Path

Earlier versions of portions of this chapter appeared in "British Sikh Lives Lived in Translation," in *Everyday Life in South Asia*, ed. Sarah Lamb and Diane Mines (Bloomington: University of Indiana Press, 2002). Reprinted by permission.

Epilogue: An Unfinished Story

1. Yasmin Alibhai-Brown, "The Fear and Alienation That Lie Behind the Explosion of Violence," *The Independent*, July 10, 2001; <www.independent.co.uk>.

Works Cited

Agnihotri, Rama Kant. 1987. *Crisis of Identity: The Sikhs in England*. New Delhi: Bahri Publications.

Ahmad, Noshin. 1999. "Hijabs in Our Midst." In *Young Britain: Politics, Pleasures and Predicaments*, ed. Jonathan Rutherford. London: Lawrence and Wishart.

Althusser, Louis. 1971. "Ideology and the Ideological State Apparatuses." In *Lenin and Philosophy and Other Essays*. Trans. Ben Brewster. New York: Monthly Review Press.

Ålund, Aleksandra. 1996. "The Stranger: Ethnicity, Identity and Belonging." In *The Future of the Nation-State: Essays on Cultural Pluralism and Political Integration*, ed. Sverker Gustavsson and Leif Lewin. London: Routledge.

Ålund, Aleksandra, and Raoul Granqvist, eds. 1995. *Negotiating Identities: Essays on Immigration and Culture in Present-Day Europe*. Amsterdam: Rodopi.

Anderson, Benedict. 1983. *Imagined Communities: Reflections on the Origin and Spread of Nationalism*. London: Verso.

Anwar, Mohammad. 1998. *Between Cultures: Continuity and Change in the Lives of Young Asians*. London: Routledge.

Apache Indian. 1993. Apache Indian (Don Raja). Island Records. (Disk)

Appadurai, Arjun. 1990. "Disjuncture and Difference in the Global Cultural Economy." *Public Culture* 2, 2 (spring): 1–24.

———. 1991. "Global Ethnoscapes: Notes and Queries for a Transnational Anthropology." In *Recapturing Anthropology: Working in the Present*, ed. Richard G. Fox. Santa Fe, N.M.: School of American Research Press.

———. 1996. *Modernity at Large: Cultural Dimensions of Globalization*. Minneapolis: University of Minnesota Press.

Aronowitz, Stanley. 1995. "Reflections on Identity." In *The Identity in Question*, ed. John Rajchman. New York: Routledge.

Axel, Brian Keith. 2000. *The Nation's Tortured Body: Violence, Representation, and the Formation of a Sikh "Diaspora"*. Durham, N.C.: Duke University Press.

Bahri, Deepika, and Mary Vasudeva, eds. 1996. *Between the Lines: South Asians and Postcoloniality*. Philadelphia: Temple University Press.

Bains, Harwant S. 1988. "Southall Youth: An Old-Fashioned Story." In *Multi-Racist Britain*, ed. Philip Cohen and Harwant S. Bains. London: Macmillan.

Bakrania, Falu. 2002. "Re-Fusing Identities: Young British Asians and the Politics of Popular Music." PhD dissertation, Stanford University.

Balibar, Etienne. 1991a. "Is There a 'Neo-Racism'?" In *Race, Nation, Class: Ambiguous Identities*, ed. Etienne Balibar and Immanuel Wallerstein. London: Verso.

————. 1991b. "Race, Nation, Class." In *Race, Discourse and Power in France*, ed. Maxim Silverman. Aldershot: Avebury.

Ballard, Catherine. 1978. "Arranged Marriages in the British Context." *New Community* 6, 3 (summer): 181–96.

————. 1979. "Conflict, Continuity and Change." In *Minority Families in Britain*, ed. Verity Saifullah Khan. London: Macmillan.

Ballard, Roger. Unpublished manuscript. "The Ethnic Minorities in Leeds: An Analysis of the 1981 Census." University of Leeds.

————. 1982. "South Asian Families." In *Families in Britain*, ed. Robert N. Rapaport, Michael Patrick Fogarty, and Rona Rapaport. London: Routledge and Kegan Paul.

————. 1987. "The Political Economy of Migration: Britain, Pakistan and the Middle East." In *Migration, Labour and the Social Order*, ed. Jeremy S. Eades. ASA Monographs 25. London: Tavistock.

————. 1989. "Differentiation and Disjunction Amongst the Sikhs in Britain." In *The Sikh Diaspora: Migration and the Experience Beyond Punjab*, ed. N. Gerald Barrier and Verne A. Dusenbery. Columbia, S.C.: South Asia Publications.

————. 1996. "The Pakistanis: Stability and Introspection." In *Ethnicity in the 1991 Census*. Vol. 2, *The Ethnic Minority Populations of Great Britain*, ed. Ceri Peach. London: HMSO.

Ballard, Roger, and Catherine Ballard. 1977. "The Sikhs: The Development of South Asian Settlements in Britain." In *Between Two Cultures: Migrants and Minorities in Britain*, ed. James L. Watson. Oxford: Blackwell.

Ballard, Roger, and G. Driver. 1977. "The Ethnic Approach." *New Society* 16 (June): 543–45.

Banerji, Sabita, and Gerd Baumann. 1990. "Bhangra 1984–8: Fusion and Professionalization in a Genre of South Asian Dance Music." In *Black Music in Britain*, ed. Paul Oliver. Buckingham: Open University Press.

Banks, James, and James Lynch, eds. 1986. *Multicultural Education in Western Societies*. London: Holt, Rinehart and Winston.

Banton, Michael. 1989. "Are Rastafarians an Ethnic Group?" *New Community* 16 (October): 153–57.

Barker, Martin. 1981. *The New Racism*. London: Junction Books.

Barrier, N. Gerald, and Verne A. Dusenbery, eds. 1989. *The Sikh Diaspora: Migration and the Experience Beyond Punjab*. Columbia, S.C.: South Asia Books.

Bauman, Zygmunt. 1991. *Modernity and Ambivalence*. Ithaca, N.Y.: Cornell University Press.

Baumann, Gerd. 1996. *Contesting Culture: Discourses of Identity in Multi-Ethnic London*. Cambridge: Cambridge University Press.

Beck, Ulrich, Anthony Giddens, and Scott Lash. 1994. *Reflexive Modernization: Politics, Tradition and Aesthetics in the Modern Social Order*. Cambridge: Polity Press.

Beetham, David. 1970. *Transport and Turbans: A Comparative Study in Local Politics.* London: Oxford University Press.

Benhabib, Seyla. 1999. "Civil Society and the Politics of Identity and Difference in a Global Context." In *Diversity and Its Discontents: Cultural Conflict and Common Ground in Contemporary American Society*, ed. Neil J. Smelser and Jeffrey C. Alexander. Princeton, N.J.: Princeton University Press.

Berrington, Ann. 1996. "Marriage Patterns and Inter-Ethnic Unions." In *Ethnicity in the 1991 Census.* Vol. 1, *Demographic Characteristics of the Ethnic Minority Populations*, ed. David Coleman and John Salt. London: HMSO.

Bevan, Vaughan. 1986. *The Development of British Immigration Law.* London: Croom Helm.

Bhabha, Homi K. 1990. "Interview with Homi Bhabha: The Third Space." In *Identity: Community, Culture and Difference*, ed. Jonathan Rutherford. London: Lawrence and Wishart.

———. 1994. *The Location of Culture.* New York: Routledge.

Bhachu, Parminder. 1985. *Twice Migrants: East African Sikh Settlers in Britain.* London: Tavistock.

Blommaert, Jan. 1999. "The Debate Is Open/The Debate Is Closed." In *Language Ideological Debates*, ed. Jan Blommaert. Berlin: Mouton de Gruyter.

Bourdieu, Pierre. 1973. "Cultural Reproduction and Social Reproduction." In *Knowledge, Education, and Cultural Change: Papers in the Sociology of Education*, ed. Richard Brown. London: Tavistock.

———. 1977. *Outline of a Theory of Practice.* London: Cambridge University Press.

———. 1979. "The Sense of Honor." In *Algeria 1960.* Trans. Richard Nice. Cambridge: Cambridge University Press.

———. 1984. *Distinction: A Social Critique of the Judgement of Taste.* Trans. Richard Nice. Cambridge, Mass.: Harvard University Press.

———. 1987. "What Makes a Social Class? On the Theoretical and Practical Existence of Groups." *Berkeley Journal of Sociology* 32: 1–18.

———. 1997. "The Forms of Capital." In *Education: Culture, Economy, and Society*, ed. A. H. Halsey, Hugh Lauder, Phillip Brown, and Amy Stuart Wells. Oxford: Oxford University Press.

Bourdieu, Pierre, and J. C. Passeron. 1977. *Reproduction in Education, Society, and Culture.* Beverly Hills, Calif.: Sage.

Bourdieu, Pierre, and Loïc J. D. Wacquant. 1992. *An Invitation to Reflexive Sociology.* Chicago: University of Chicago Press.

Bourne, Jill. 1997. "'The Grown-Ups Know Best': Language Policy-Making in Britain in the 1990s." In *Language Policy: Dominant English, Pluralist Challenges*, ed. William Eggington and Helen Wren. Amsterdam: John Benjamins.

Bowles, Samuel, and Herbert Gintis. 1976. *Schooling in Capitalist America: Educational Reform and the Contradictions of Economic Life.* New York: Basic Books.

Brah, Avtar. 1996. *Cartographies of Diaspora: Contesting Identities.* London: Routledge.

Brewer, R. 1986. "A Note on the Changing Status of the Registrar General's Classification of Occupations." *British Journal of Sociology* 37: 131–40.

Briggs, Asa. 1968. *Victorian Cities.* Harmondsworth: Penguin.

Briggs, Charles L. 1996. "The Politics of Discursive Authority in Research on the 'Invention of Tradition.'" *Cultural Anthropology* 11, 4: 435–69.

Briggs, Charles L., and Richard Bauman. 1992. "Genre, Intertextuality, and Social Power." *Journal of Linguistic Anthropology* 2: 131–72.

Bright, Charles, and Michael Geyer. 1987. "For a Unified History of the World in the Twentieth Century." *Radical History Review* 39: 69–91.

Broadhead, Ivan. 1990. *Leeds.* Otley: Smith Settle.

Brubaker, Rogers. 1996. *Nationalism Reframed: Nationhood and the National Question in the New Europe.* Cambridge: Cambridge University Press.

Buckingham, David. 1993. Introduction to *Reading Audiences: Young People and the Media.* Manchester: Manchester University Press.

Butler, Judith. 1990. *Gender Trouble: Feminism and the Subversion of Identity.* New York: Routledge.

———. 1993. *Bodies That Matter: On the Discursive Limits of "Sex".* New York: Routledge.

———. 1995. "Discussion." In *The Identity in Question,* ed. John Rajchman. New York: Routledge.

———. 1997. *The Psychic Life of Power: Theories in Subjection.* Stanford, Calif.: Stanford University Press.

Calhoun, Craig. 1997. "Nationalism and the Public Sphere." In *Public and Private in Thought and Practice: Perspectives on a Grand Dichotomy,* ed. Jeff Weintraub and Krishan Kumar. Chicago: University of Chicago Press.

Cameron, Deborah. 1995. *Verbal Hygiene.* London: Routledge.

Cashmore, E. Ellis. 1984. *Dictionary of Race and Ethnic Relations.* 2nd ed. London: Routledge.

———. 1989. "The Dawkins Case: Official Ethnic Status for Rastas." *New Community* 16 (October): 158–60.

Castles, Stephen, and Godula Kosack. 1973. *Immigrant Workers and Class Structure in Western Europe.* London: Oxford University Press/Institute of Race Relations.

Centre for Contemporary Cultural Studies. 1982. *The Empire Strikes Back: Race and Racism in 70s Britain.* London: Hutchison.

Cesarani, David, and Mary Fulbrook, eds. 1996. *Citizenship, Nationality and Migration in Europe.* London: Routledge.

Chambers, Ross. 1990. *Room for Maneuver: Reading (the) Oppositional (in) Narrative.* Chicago: University of Chicago Press.

Chomsky, Noam. 1979. *Language and Responsibility: Based on Conversations with Mitson Ronat.* London: Harvester.

Clarke, Colin, Ceri Peach, and Steven Vertovec. 1990. "Introduction: Themes in the Study of the South Asian Diaspora." In *South Asians Overseas: Migration and Ethnicity*. Cambridge: Cambridge University Press.

Cohen, Robin. 1997. *Global Diasporas: An Introduction*. London: University College London Press.

Cohen, Stanley. 1972. *Folk Devils and Moral Panics: The Creation of the Mods and Rockers*. London: MacGibbon and Kee.

Cohn, Bernard S. 1987. *An Anthropologist Among the Historians and Other Essays*. Delhi: Oxford University Press.

Collins, James. 1999. "The Ebonics Controversy in Context: Literacies, Subjectivities and Language Ideologies in the United States." In *Language Ideological Debates*, ed. Jan Blommaert. Berlin: Mouton de Gruyter.

Comaroff, Jean, and John Comaroff. 1991. *Of Revelation and Revolution: Christianity, Colonialism, and Consciousness in South Africa*. Vol. 1. Chicago: University of Chicago Press.

———, eds. 2001. *Millennial Capitalism and the Culture of Neoliberalism*. Durham, N.C.: Duke University Press.

Comaroff, John L. 1996. "Ethnicity, Nationalism, and the Politics of Difference in an Age of Revolution." In *The Politics of Difference: Ethnic Premises in a World of Power*, ed. Edwin N. Wilmsen and Patrick McAllister. Chicago: University of Chicago Press.

Comaroff, John L., and Jean Comaroff. 1992. *Ethnography and the Historical Imagination*. Boulder, Colo.: Westview Press.

Coronil, Fernando. 1997. *The Magical State: Nature, Money, and Modernity in Venezuela*. Chicago: University of Chicago Press.

Corrigan, Philip. 1987. "In/Forming Schooling." In *Critical Pedagogy and Cultural Power*, ed. D. W. Livingstone. New York: Bergin and Garvey.

Corrigan, Philip, and Derek Sayer. 1985. *The Great Arch: English State Formation as Cultural Revolution*. Oxford: Blackwell.

Coulmas, Florian. 1998. "Language Rights—Interests of State, Language Groups and the Individual." *Language Sciences* 20, 1: 63–72.

Das, Veena. 1995. "On Soap Opera: What Kind of Anthropological Object Is It?" In *Worlds Apart: Modernity Through the Prism of the Local*, ed. Daniel Miller. London: Routledge.

Dasgupta, Shamita Das, ed. 1998. *A Patchwork Shawl: Chronicles of South Asian Women in America*. New York: Routledge.

Davies, B. 1990. "Agency as a Form of Discursive Practice: A Classroom Scene Observed." *British Journal of Sociology of Education* 11, 3: 341–61.

de Certeau, Michel. 1984. *The Practice of Everyday Life*. Trans. Steven Rendall. Berkeley: University of California Press.

DES (Department of Education and Science). 1975. *A Language for Life: Report of the Committee of Inquiry Appointed by the Secretary of State for Education and Science* (The Bullock Report). London: HMSO.

————. 1990. *Modern Foreign Languages for Ages 11 to 16: National Curriculum: Proposals of the Secretary of State for Education and Science* (The Harris Report). London: HMSO.

Dewan, Veeno. 1989. "Tabla! How Low Can You Go—The Birth of Asian Rap." *I-D* (February): 20–23.

Dirks, Nicholas B., Geoff Eley, and Sherry B. Ortner. 1994. Introduction to *Culture/Power/History: A Reader in Contemporary Social Theory*, ed. Nicholas B. Dirks, Geoff Eley, and Sherry B. Ortner. Princeton, N.J.: Princeton University Press.

Domínguez, Virginia R. 1992. "Invoking Culture: The Messy Side of 'Cultural Politics.'" *South Atlantic Quarterly* 91, 1: 19–42.

Douglas, Mary. 1966. *Purity and Danger: An Analysis of Concepts of Pollution and Taboo*. London: Routledge and Kegan Paul.

Du Bois, W. E. B. 1903/1969. "Of Our Spiritual Strivings." In *The Souls of Black Folk*. New York: Signet.

Durkheim, Emile. 1977. *The Evolution of Educational Thought: Lectures on the Formation and Development of Secondary Education in France*. Trans. Peter Collins. London: Routledge and Kegan Paul.

Dusenbery, Verne A. 1995. "A Sikh Diaspora? Contested Identities and Constructed Realities." In *Nation and Migration: The Politics of Space in the South Asian Diaspora*, ed. Peter van der Veer. Philadelphia: University of Pennsylvania Press.

————. 1996. "Socializing Sikhs in Singapore: Soliciting the State's Support." In *The Transmission of Sikh Heritage in the Diaspora*, ed. Pashura Singh and N. Gerald Barrier. New Delhi: Manohar.

————. 1997. "The Poetics and Politics of Recognition: Diasporan Sikhs in Pluralist Polities." *American Ethnologist* 24, 4: 738–62.

Edgell, Stephen. 1993. *Class: Key Concept in Sociology*. New York: Routledge.

Eisenhart, Margaret. 1995. "The Fax, the Jazz Player, and the Self-Story Teller: How Do People Organize Culture?" *Anthropology and Education Quarterly* 26, 1: 3–26.

Eller, Jack David. 1999. *From Culture to Ethnicity to Conflict: An Anthropological Perspective on International Ethnic Conflict*. Ann Arbor: University of Michigan Press.

Etzioni, Amitai, ed. 1995. *New Communitarian Thinking: Persons, Virtues, Institutions, and Communities*. Charlottesville: University Press of Virginia.

Fanon, Frantz. 1967. *Black Skin, White Masks*. Trans. Charles Lam Markmann. New York: Grove Weidenfeld.

Featherstone, Mike, ed. 1990. *Global Culture: Nationalism, Globalization and Modernity*. London: Sage.

Ferguson, James. 1994. *The Anti-Politics Machine: "Development," Depoliticization and Bureaucratic Power in Lesotho*. Minneapolis: University of Minnesota Press.

Foley, Douglas E. 1990. *Learning Capitalist Culture: Deep in the Heart of Tejas*. Philadelphia: University of Pennsylvania Press.

Foot, Paul. 1965. *Immigration and Race in British Politics*. Harmondsworth: Penguin.

Fordham, Signithia. 1996. *Blacked Out: Dilemmas of Race, Identity, and Success at Capital High*. Chicago: University of Chicago Press.

Foster, Robert J. 1991. "Making National Cultures in the Global Ecumene." *Annual Review of Anthropology* 20: 235–60.

Foucault, Michel. 1972. *The Archeology of Knowledge*. Trans. A. M. Sheridan Smith. New York: Pantheon.

———. 1995. *Discipline and Punish*. Trans. Alan Sheridan. New York: Vintage.

———. 1982. "The Subject and Power." In *Michel Foucault: Beyond Structuralism and Hermeneutics*, ed. Hubert L. Dreyfus and Paul Rabinow. Chicago: University of Chicago Press.

———. 1991a. "Politics and the Study of Discourse." In *The Foucault Effect*, ed. Graham Burchell, Colin Gordon, and Peter Miller. Chicago: University of Chicago Press.

———. 1991b. "Governmentality." In *The Foucault Effect*, ed. Graham Burchell, Colin Gordon, and Peter Miller. Chicago: University of Chicago Press.

Fox, Richard G. 1990. Introduction to *Nationalist Ideologies and the Production of National Cultures*, ed. Richard G. Fox. American Ethnological Association Monograph Series 2. Washington, D.C.: American Anthropological Association.

Fraser, Derek, ed. 1980. *A History of Modern Leeds*. Manchester: Manchester University Press.

Fraser, Nancy. 1989. "Struggle over Needs." In Fraser, *Unruly Practices: Power, Discourse, and Gender in Contemporary Social Theory*. Minneapolis: University of Minnesota Press.

———. 1992. "Rethinking the Public Sphere: A Contribution to the Critique of Actually Existing Democracy." In *Habermas and the Public Sphere*, ed. Craig Calhoun. Cambridge, Mass.: MIT Press.

———. 1997. "From Redistribution to Recognition? Dilemmas of Justice in a 'Postsocialist' Age." In Fraser, *Justice Interruptus: Critical Reflections on the "Postsocialist" Condition*. New York: Routledge.

Fryer, Peter. 1984. *Staying Power: The History of Black People in Britain*. London: Pluto Press.

Fun^Da^Mental. 1994. Dog-Tribe. Nation. (Disk)

Gal, Susan. 1989. "Language and Political Economy." *Annual Review of Anthropology* 18: 345–67.

Gibson, Margaret A. 1988. *Accommodation Without Assimilation: Sikh Immigrants in an American High School*. Ithaca, N.Y.: Cornell University Press.

Giddens, Anthony. 1990. *The Consequences of Modernity*. Stanford, Calif.: Stanford University Press.

Gillborn, David. 1995. *Racism and Antiracism in Real Schools: Theory, Policy, Practice*. Buckingham: Open University Press.

Gillespie, Marie. 1993. "The Mahabharata: From Sanskrit to Sacred Soap. A Case Study of the Reception of Two Contemporary Televisual Versions." In

Reading Audiences: Young People and the Media, ed. David Buckingham. Manchester: Manchester University Press.

———. 1995. *Television, Ethnicity and Cultural Change*. London: Routledge.

Gilroy, Paul. 1987. *"There Ain't No Black in the Union Jack": The Cultural Politics of Race and Nation*. London: Hutchinson.

———. 1990. "One Nation Under a Groove: The Cultural Politics of 'Race' and Racism in Britain." In *Anatomy of Racism*, ed. David Theo Goldberg. Minneapolis: University of Minnesota Press.

———. 1992. "The End of Anti-Racism." In *"Race," Culture and Difference*, ed. James Donald and Ali Rattansi. London: Sage.

———. 1993. *The Black Atlantic: Modernity and Double Consciousness*. Cambridge, Mass.: Harvard University Press.

———. 1995. "Diaspora Crossings: Intercultural and Trans-National Identities in the Black Atlantic." In *Negotiating Identities: Essays on Immigration and Culture in Present-Day Europe*, ed. Aleksandra Ålund and Raoul Granqvist. Amsterdam: Rodopi.

Giroux, Henry A. 1983. *Theory and Resistance in Education: A Pedagogy for the Opposition*. South Hadley: Bergin and Garvey.

Goldberg, David Theo. 1993. *Racist Culture: Philosophy and the Politics of Meaning*. Oxford: Blackwell.

Gopinath, Gayatri. 1995. "'Bombay, U.K., Yuba City': Bhangra Music and the Engendering of Diaspora." *Diaspora* 4, 3: 303–21.

Gordon Paul, and Francesca Klug. 1986. *New Right, New Racism: Race and Reaction in the United States and Britain*. London: Searchlight.

Goulbourne, Harry. 1991. *Ethnicity and Nationalism in Post-Imperial Britain*. Cambridge: Cambridge University Press.

Gramsci, Antonio. 1971. *Selections from the Prison Notebooks*. Ed. and trans. Quinten Hoare and Geoffrey Nowell Smith. New York: International Publishers.

———. 1988. "Philosophy, Common Sense, Language and Folklore." In *An Antonio Gramsci Reader: Selected Writings, 1916–1935*. Ed. David Forgacs. New York: Schocken.

Greenhouse, Carol J., and Davydd J. Greenwood. 1998. "Introduction: The Ethnography of Democracy and Difference." In *Democracy and Ethnography: Constructing Identities in Multicultural Liberal States*, ed. Carol J. Greenhouse with Roshanak Kheshti. Albany: State University of New York Press.

Gupta, Akhil, and James Ferguson, eds. 1997. *Culture, Power, Place: Explorations in Critical Anthropology*. Durham, N.C.: Duke University Press.

Gutmann, Amy. 1992. Introduction to Charles Taylor, *Multiculturalism and "The Politics of Recognition"*, ed. Charles Taylor. Princeton, N.J.: Princeton University Press.

Habermas, Jürgen. 1996. "Three Normative Models of Democracy." In *Democracy and Difference: Contesting the Boundaries of the Political*, ed. Seyla Benhabib. Princeton, N.J.: Princeton University Press.

Hall, Kathleen. 1995. "'There's a Time to Act English and a Time to Act Indian':

The Politics of Identity Among British-Sikh Teenagers." In *Children and the Politics of Culture*, ed. Sharon Stephens. Princeton, N.J.: Princeton University Press.

———. 1999. "Understanding Educational Processes in an Era of Globalization." In *Issues in Educational Research: Problems and Possibilities*, ed. Ellen Condliffe Lagemann and Lee S. Shulman. San Francisco: Jossey-Bass.

Hall, Stuart, ed. 1980. "Encoding/Decoding." In *Culture, Media, Language: Working Papers in Cultural Studies*. London: Unwin Hyman.

———. 1990a. "Cultural Identity and Diaspora." In *Identity: Community, Culture and Difference*, ed. Jonathan Rutherford. London: Lawrence and Wishart.

———. 1990b. *The Hard Road to Renewal: Thatcherism and the Crisis of the Left*. London: Verso.

———. 1990/1996. "Cultural Identity and Cinematic Representation." In *Black British Cultural Studies: A Reader*, ed. Houston A. Baker, Jr., Manthia Diawara, and Ruth H. Lindeborg. Chicago: University of Chicago Press.

———. 1992. "New Ethnicities." In *"Race," Culture and Difference*, ed. James Donald and Ali Rattansi. London: Sage.

———. 1996. "The Question of Cultural Identity." In *Modernity: An Introduction to Modern Societies*, ed. Stuart Hall, David Held, Don Hubert, and Kenneth Thompson. Oxford: Blackwell.

Halstead, Mark. 1988. *Education, Justice and Cultural Diversity: An Examination of the Honeyford Affair.* London: Falmer Press.

Handler, Richard. 1988. *Nationalism and the Politics of Culture in Quebec*. Madison: University of Wisconsin Press.

Hannerz, Ulf. 1990. "Cosmopolitans and Locals in World Culture." In *Global Culture: Nationalism, Globalization and Modernity*, ed. Mike Featherstone. London: Sage.

———. 1996. *Transnational Connections: Culture, People, Places*. London: Routledge.

Hansen, Randall. 2000. *Citizenship and Immigration in Post-War Britain: The Institutional Origins of a Multicultural Nation*. Oxford: Oxford University Press.

Harvey, David. 1989. *The Conditions of Postmodernity: An Inquiry into the Origins of Cultural Change*. London: Blackwell.

Hayter, Teresa. 2000. *Open Borders: The Case Against Immigration Controls*. London: Pluto Press.

Hebdige, Dick. 1979. *Subculture: The Meaning of Style*. London: Methuen.

Hechter, Michael. 1975. *Internal Colonialism: The Celtic Fringe in British National Development, 1536–1966*. Berkeley: University of California Press.

Heller, Monica. 1999. *Linguistic Minorities and Modernity: A Sociolinguistic Ethnography*. London: Longman.

Helweg, Arthur Wesley. 1986. *Sikhs in England*. Delhi: Oxford University Press.

———. 1999. "Transmitting and Regenerating Culture: The Sikh Case." In *Sikh Identity: Continuity and Change*, ed. Pashaura Singh and N. Gerald Barrier. New Delhi: Manohar.

Hiro, Dilip. 1971. *Black British, White British*. Harmondsworth: Penguin.

Hobsbawm, Eric, and Terence Ranger. 1983. Introduction to *The Invention of Tradition.*, ed. Hobsbawm and Ranger. Cambridge: Cambridge University Press.

Holland, Dorothy C., and Margaret A. Eisenhart. 1990. *Educated in Romance: Women, Achievement, and College Culture*. Chicago: University of Chicago Press.

Holland, Dorothy, William Lachicotte, Jr., Debra Skinner, and Carole Cain. 1998. *Identity and Agency in Cultural Worlds*. Cambridge, Mass.: Harvard University Press.

Honeyford, Ray. 1988. *Integration or Disintegration? Towards a Non-Racist Society*. London: Claridge Press.

hooks, bell. 1990. *Yearning: Race, Gender, and Cultural Politics*. Boston: South End Press.

Hornberger, Nancy H. 2000. "Bilingual Education Policy and Practice in the Andes: Ideological Paradox and Intercultural Possibility." *Anthropology and Education Quarterly* 31, 2: 173–201.

Housee, Shirin, and Mukhtar Dar. 1996. "Re-Mixing Identities: 'Off' the Turn-Table." In *Dis-Orienting Rhythms: The Politics of the New Asian Dance Music*, ed. Sanjay Sharma, John Hutnyk, and Ashwani Sharma. London: Zed Books.

Huq, Rupa. 1996. "Asian Kool? Bhangra and Beyond." In *Dis-Orienting Rhythms: The Politics of the New Asian Dance Music*, ed. Sanjay Sharma, John Hutnyk, and Ashwani Sharma. London: Zed Books.

Hustlers HC. 1994. On a Ride. Nation. (Disk)

Irvine, Judith. 1997. "Language and Community: Introduction." *Journal of Linguistic Anthropology* 6, 2: 123–25.

Ivy, Marilyn. 1995. *Discourses of the Vanishing*. Chicago: University of Chicago Press.

Jacobson, David. 1997. *Rights Across Borders: Immigration and the Decline of Citizenship*. Baltimore: Johns Hopkins University Press.

James, Alan G. 1974. *Sikh Children in Britain*. Oxford: Oxford University Press.

Joppke, Christian. 1998. "Immigration Challenges the Nation-State." In *Challenges to the Nation-State: Immigration in Western Europe and the United States*. Oxford: Oxford University Press.

Kalsi, Sewa Singh. 1992. *The Evolution of a Sikh Community in Britain: Religious and Cultural Change Among the Sikhs of Leeds and Bradford*. Community Religions Project Monograph Series. Leeds: University of Leeds.

———. 1999. "The Sikhs and Caste: The Development of Ramgarhia Identity in Britain." In *Sikh Identity: Continuity and Change*, ed. Pashaura Singh and N. Gerald Barrier. New Delhi: Manohar.

Kapferer, Bruce. 1988. *Legends of People, Myths of State: Violence, Intolerance, and Political Culture in Sri Lanka and Australia*. Washington, D.C.: Smithsonian Institution Press.

Kaur, Raminder, and Virinder S. Kalra. 1996. "New Paths for South Asian Identity and Musical Creativity." In *Dis-Orienting Rhythms: The Politics of the New Asian Dance Music*, ed. Sanjay Sharma, John Hutnyk, and Ashwani Sharma. London: Zed Books.

Kearney, Michael. 1995. "The Local and the Global: The Anthropology of Globalization and Transnationalism." *Annual Review of Anthropology* 24: 547–65.

Khan, Aisha. 1995. "Homeland, Motherland: Authenticity, Legitimacy, and Ideologies of Place Among Muslims in Trinidad." In *Nation and Migration: The Politics of Space in the South Asian Diaspora*, ed. Peter van der Veer. Philadelphia: University of Pennsylvania Press.

King, Anthony D., ed. 1997. *Culture, Globalization, and the World-System: Contemporary Conditions for the Representation of Identity*. Minneapolis: University of Minnesota Press.

Kondo, Dorinne K. 1990. *Crafting Selves: Power, Gender, and Discourses of Identity in a Japanese Workplace*. Chicago: University of Chicago Press.

Kumar, Amitava. 2000. *Passport Photos*. Berkeley: University of California Press.

Kureishi, Hanif. 1989a. "London and Karachi." In *Patriotism: The Making and Unmaking of British National Identity*, ed. Raphael Samuel. London: Routledge.

———. 1989b. "England, Your England." *New Statesman and Society*, July 21 1989, 29.

Kymlicka, Will. 1995. *Multicultural Citizenship: A Liberal Theory of Minority Rights*. Oxford: Oxford University Press.

La Brack, Bruce. 1979. "Sikhs Real and Ideal: Discussion of Text and Context in the Description of Overseas Sikh Communities." In *Sikh Studies: Comparative Perspectives on a Changing Tradition*, ed. Mark Juergensmeyer and N. Gerald Barrier. Berkeley, Calif.: Graduate Theological Union.

Laclau, Ernesto. 1988. "Metaphor and Social Antagonisms." In *Marxism and the Interpretation of Culture*, ed. Cary Nelson and Lawrence Grossberg. Urbana: University of Illinois Press.

Lal, Bhai Harbans. 1999. "Sahajdhari Sikhs: Their Origin and Current Status Within the Panth." In *Sikh Identity: Continuity and Change*, ed. Pashaura Singh and N. Gerald Barrier. New Delhi: Manohar.

Lave, Jean, and Etienne Wenger. 1991. *Situated Learning: Legitimate Peripheral Participation*. Cambridge: Cambridge University Press.

Lavie, Smadar, and Ted Swedenburg. 1996. Introduction to *Displacement, Diaspora and Geographies of Identity*, ed. Smader Lavie and Ted Swedenburg. Durham, N.C.: Duke University Press.

Lawson, John, and Harold Silver. 1973. *A Social History of Education in England*. London: Methuen.

Layton-Henry, Zig. 1992. *The Politics of Immigration: Immigration, "Race" and "Race" Relations in Post-War Britain*. Oxford: Blackwell.

Lee, Benjamin. 1993. "Going Public." *Public Culture* 5, 2: 165–78.

Lelyveld, David. 1978. *Aligarh's First Generation: Muslim Solidarity in British India*. Princeton, N.J.: Princeton University Press.

Leonard, Karen. 1989. "Pioneer Voices from California: Reflections on Race,

Religion and Ethnicity." In *The Sikh Diaspora: Migration and the Experience Beyond Punjab*, ed. N. Gerald Barrier and Verne A. Dusenbery. Columbia, S.C.: South Asia Publications.

———. 1992. *Making Ethnic Choices: California's Punjabi Mexican Americans.* Philadelphia: Temple University Press.

Leung, Constant, Roxy Harris, and Ben Rampton. 1997. "The Idealised Native Speaker, Reified Ethnicities, and Classroom Realities." *TESOL Quarterly* 31, 3: 543–60.

Levine, Donald N. 1985. *The Flight from Ambiguity: Essays in Social and Cultural Theory.* Chicago: University of Chicago Press.

Levinson, Bradley A., Douglas E. Foley, and Dorothy C. Holland, eds. 1996. *The Cultural Production of the Educated Person: Critical Ethnographies of Schooling and Local Practice.* Albany: State University of New York Press.

Litzinger, Ralph A. 2000. *Other Chinas: The Yao and the Politics of National Belonging.* Durham, N.C.: Duke University Press.

Lorimer, Douglas A. 1978. *Colour, Class and the Victorians: English Attitudes to the Negro in the Mid-Nineteenth Century.* Leicester: Leicester University Press.

Lowe, Lisa. 1996. *Immigrant Acts: On Asian American Cultural Politics.* Durham, N.C.: Duke University Press.

Lukose, Ritty A. 2000. "Learning Modernity: Education and Youth Culture in Kerala, South India." PhD dissertation, University of Chicago.

Luykx, Aurolyn. 1999. *The Citizen Factory: Schooling and Cultural Production in Bolivia.* Albany: State University of New York Press.

Lyotard, Jean François. 1984. *The Postmodern Condition: A Report on Knowledge.* Manchester: Manchester University Press.

Mac an Ghaill, Máirtín. 1999. *Contemporary Racisms and Ethnicities: Social and Cultural Transformations.* Buckingham: Open University Press.

Macdonald, Ian A. 1969. *Race Relations and Immigration Law.* London: Butterworths.

———. 1983. *Immigration Law and Practice in the United Kingdom.* London: Butterworths.

MacLeod, Jay. 1987. *Ain't No Makin' It: Leveled Aspirations in a Low-Income Neighborhood.* Boulder, Colo.: Westview Press.

Maira, Sunaina. 1999. "Identity Dub: The Paradoxes of an Indian American Youth Subculture (New York Mix)." *Cultural Anthropology* 14, 1: 29–60.

Maira, Sunaina, and Rajini Srikanth, eds. 1996. *Contours of the Heart: South Asians Map North America.* New York: Asian American Writers' Workshop.

Malkki, Lisa H. 1995. *Purity in Exile: Violence, Memory, and National Cosmology Among Hutu Refugees in Tanzania.* Chicago: University of Chicago Press.

Martin-Jones, Marilyn, and Monica Heller. 1996. "Introduction to the Special Issues on Education in Multilingual Settings: Discourse, Identities and Power. Part II: Contesting Legitimacy." *Linguistics and Education* 8: 127–37.

May, Stephen. 1999. "Introduction: Towards Critical Multiculturalism." In *Critical*

Multiculturalism: Rethinking Multicultural and Antiracist Education. London: Falmer Press.

———. 2000. "Uncommon Languages: The Challenges and Possibilities of Minority Language Rights." *Journal of Multilingual and Multicultural Development* 21, 5: 366–85.

———. 2001. *Language and Minority Rights: Ethnicity, Nationalism, and the Politics of Language.* White Plains, N.Y.: Longman.

McDonald, Sir Trevor, and Sir John Boyd. 2000. *Languages: The Next Generation: The Final Report and Recommendations of the Nuffield Language Inquiry* (The Nuffield Report). London: Nuffield Foundation.

McLaren, Peter. 1994. *Life in Schools: An Introduction to Critical Pedagogy in the Foundations of Education.* White Plains, N.Y.: Longman.

McLeod, W. H. 1976. *The Evolution of the Sikh Community.* London: Oxford University Press.

———. 1989. "The First Forty Years of Sikh Migration: Problems and Possible Solutions." In *The Sikh Diaspora: Migration and the Experience Beyond Punjab,* ed. N. Gerald Barrier and Verne A. Dusenbery. Columbia, S.C.: South Asia Publications.

———. 1999. "The Turban: Symbol of Sikh Identity." In *Sikh Identity: Continuity and Change,* ed. Pashuara Singh and N. Gerald Barrier. New Delhi: Manohar.

McRobbie, Angela. 1994. *Postmodernism and Popular Culture.* London: Routledge.

McRobbie, Angela, and Jenny Garber. 1976. "Girls and Subcultures." In *Resistance Through Rituals: Youth Subcultures in Post-War Britain,* ed. Stuart Hall and Tony Jefferson. London: Hutchinson.

Miles, Robert. 1989. "Nationality, Citizenship, and Migration to Britain, 1945–1951." *Journal of Law and Society* 16, 4 (winter): 426–42.

———. 1993. *Racism After "Race" Relations.* London: Routledge.

Miller, Daniel. 1995. "Introduction: Anthropology, Modernity and Consumption." In *Worlds Apart: Modernity Through the Prism of the Local,* ed. Miller. London: Routledge.

Modood, Tariq. 1992. *Not Easy Being British: Colour, Culture and Citizenship.* Stoke-on-Trent: Runnymede Trust and Trentham Books.

Modood, Tariq, and Pnina Werbner, eds. 1997. *The Politics of Multiculturalism in the New Europe: Racism, Identity and Community.* London: Zed Books.

Moore, Henrietta L. 1999. "Anthropological Theory at the Turn of the Century." In *Anthropological Theory Today,* ed. Moore. Cambridge: Polity Press.

Morgan, C. J. 1980. "Demographic Change, 1771–1911." In *A History of Modern Leeds,* ed. Derek Fraser. Manchester: Manchester University Press.

Morley, Dave. 1980. "Texts, Readers, Subjects." In *Culture, Media, Language: Working Papers in Cultural Studies,* ed. Stuart Hall. London: Unwin Hyman.

Morris, Rosalind, C. 1995. "All Made Up: Performance Theory and the New Anthropology of Sex and Gender." *Annual Review of Anthropology* 24: 567–92.

Mouffe, Chantal. 1996. "Democracy, Power and the 'Political.'" In *Democracy and*

Difference: Contesting the Boundaries of the Political, ed. Seyla Benhabib. Princeton, N.J.: Princeton University Press.

Naficy, Hamid. 1993. *The Making of Exile Cultures: Iranian Television in Los Angeles*. Minneapolis: University of Minnesota Press.

Nesbitt, Eleanor. 1999. "Sikhs and Proper Sikhs: The Representation of Sikhs in Curriculum Books and Young British Sikhs' Perceptions of their Identity." In *Sikh Identity: Continuity and Change*, ed. Pashaura Singh and N. Gerald Barrier. New Delhi: Manohar.

Ngwane, Zolani. 2001. "The Politics of Campus and Community in South Africa: An Historical Ethnography of the University of Fort Hare." PhD dissertation. University of Chicago.

Oberoi, Harjot. 1994. *The Construction of Religious Boundaries: Culture, Identity and Diversity in the Sikh Tradition*. Chicago: University of Chicago Press.

Ong, Aihwa. 1999. "Cultural Citizenship as Subject Making: Immigrants Negotiate Racial and Cultural Boundaries in the United States." In *Race, Identity and Citizenship: A Reader*, ed. Rodolfo D. Torres, Louis F. Miron, and Jonathan Xavier Inda. Oxford: Blackwell.

Ong, Aihwa, and Donald M. Nonini, eds. 1997. *Underground Empires: The Cultural Politics of Modern Chinese Transnationalism*. New York: Routledge.

Ó Riagáin, Pádraig, and Niamh Nic Shuibhne. 1997. "Minority Language Rights." *Annual Review of Applied Linguistics* 17: 11–29.

Owen, David. 1996. "Size, Structure and Growth of the Ethnic Minority Populations." In *Ethnicity in the 1991 Census*. Vol. 1, *Demographic Characteristics of the Ethnic Minority Populations*, ed. David Coleman and John Salt. London: HMSO.

Paley, Julia. 2001. *Marketing Democracy: Power and Social Movements in Post-Dictatorship Chile*. Berkeley: University of California Press.

Palmer, Frank. 1986. *Anti-Racism: An Assault on Education and Value*. London: Sherwood Press.

Parekh, Bhikhu. 2000. *The Future of Multi-Ethnic Britain: The Parekh Report*. Runnymede Trust. London: Profile Books.

Parsons, Talcott. 1959. "The School Class as a Social System: Some of Its Functions in American Society." *Harvard Educational Review* 29, 4: 292–318.

Paul, Kathleen. 1997. *Whitewashing Britain: Race and Citizenship in the Postwar Era*. Ithaca, N.Y.: Cornell University Press.

Peach, Ceri. 1996. Introduction to *Ethnicity in the 1991 Census*. Vol. 2, *The Ethnic Minority Populations of Great Britain*, ed. Ceri Peach. London: HMSO.

Pennycook, Alastair. 1998. "The Right to Language: Towards a Situated Ethics of Language Possibilities." *Language Sciences* 20, 1: 73–87.

Phillipson, Robert, ed. 2000. *Rights to Language: Equity, Power, and Education*. Mahwah, N.J.: Lawrence Erlbaum.

Rampton, Ben. 1995. *Crossing: Language and Ethnicity Among Adolescents*. London: Longman.

Rampton, Ben, Roxy Harris, and Constant Leung. 1997. "Multilingualism in England." *Annual Review of Applied Linguistics* 17: 224–41.

Rassool, Naz. 1997. "Language Policies for a Multicultural Britain." In *Language Policy and Political Issues in Education*, ed. Ruth Wodak and David Corson. Dordrecht: Kluwer Academic.

Ratcliffe, Peter. 1996. "Social Geography and Ethnicity: A Theoretical, Conceptual and Substantive Overview." In *Ethnicity in the 1991 Census*. Vol. 3, *Social Geography and Ethnicity in Britain: Geographical Spread, Spatial Concentration and Internal Migration*, ed. Peter Ratcliffe. London: HMSO.

Rattansi, Ali. 1992. "Changing the Subject? Racism, Culture and Education." In *"Race," Culture and Difference*, ed. James Donald and Ali Rattansi. London: Sage.

———. 1994. "'Western' Racisms, Ethnicities and Identities in a 'Postmodern' Frame." In *Racism, Modernity and Identity on the Western Front*, ed. Ali Rattansi and Sallie Westwood. Cambridge: Polity Press.

Rees, Philip, and Deborah Phillips. 1996. "Geographical Spread: The National Picture." In *Ethnicity in the 1991 Census*. Vol. 3, *Social Geography and Ethnicity in Britain: Geographical Spread, Spatial Concentration and Internal Migration*, ed. Peter Ratcliffe. London: HMSO.

Reich, Robert. 1992. *The Work of Nations: Preparing Ourselves for Twenty-First Century Capitalism*. New York: Random House.

Rex, John. 1970. *Race Relations in Sociological Theory*. London: Weidenfeld and Nicolson.

———. 1989. "Equality of Opportunity, Multiculturalism, Anti-racism and 'Education for All.'" In *Education for All: A Landmark in Pluralism*, ed. Gajendra K. Verma. London: Falmer Press.

Rex, John, and David Mason. 1986. *Theories of Race and Ethnic Relations*. Cambridge: Cambridge University Press.

Rex, John, and Robert Moore. 1967. *Race, Community and Conflict, a Study of Sparkbrook*. London: Oxford University Press for the Institute of Race Relations.

Ricento, Thomas. 2000. "Historical and Theoretical Perspectives in Language Policy and Planning." *Journal of Sociolinguistics* 4, 2: 196–213.

Robinson, Vaughan. 1990. "Boom and Gloom. The Success and Failure of Britain's South Asians." In *South Asians Overseas: Migration and Ethnicity*, ed. Colin Clarke, Ceri Peach, and Steven Vertovec. Cambridge: Cambridge University Press.

———. 1996. "The Indians: Onward and Upward." In *Ethnicity in the 1991 Census*. Vol. 2, *The Ethnic Minority Populations of Great Britain*, ed. Ceri Peach. London: HMSO.

Rosaldo, Renato. 1989. *Culture and Truth: The Remaking of Social Analysis*. Boston: Beacon Press.

Rowse, Alfred Leslie. 1990. *The Field: Magazine for the Country* 272, 7028 (May).

Rubenstein, David, and Brian Simon. 1969. *The Evolution of the Comprehensive School, 1926–1972*. London: Routledge and Kegan Paul.

Said, Edward W. 1981. *Covering Islam: How the Media and the Experts Determine How We See the Rest of the World*. New York: Pantheon.

Saifullah Khan, V. 1979. "Work and Network: South Asian Women in South London." In *Ethnicity at Work*, ed. Sandra Wallman. London: Macmillan.

Sassen, Saskia. 1996. *Losing Control? Sovereignty in an Age of Globalization*. New York: Columbia University Press.

Sharma, Sanjay. 1996. "Noisy Asians or 'Asian Noise'?" In *Dis-Orienting Rhythms: The Politics of the New Asian Dance Music*, ed. Sanjay Sharma, John Hutnyk, and Ashwani Sharma. London: Zed Books.

Sharma, Sanjay, John Hutnyk, and Ashwani Sharma. 1996. Introduction to *Dis-Orienting Rhythms: The Politics of the New Asian Dance Music*, ed. Sanjay Sharma, John Hutnyk, and Ashwani Sharma. London: Zed Books.

Sidhu, G. S. 1977/1985. *The Sikh Woman*. Southall: Sikh Missionary Society.

Sikh Missionary Society. 1972/1985. *A Spur to Sikh Youth*. Southall: Sikh Missionary Society.

Silverstein, Michael, and Greg Urban. 1996."The Natural History of Discourse." In *The Natural History of Discourse*. Chicago: University of Chicago Press.

Simmel, Georg. 1971. "The Stranger." In Simmel, *On Individuality and Social Forms: Selected Writings*. Chicago: University of Chicago Press.

Simon, Brian. 1991. *Education and the Social Order, 1940–1990*. New York: St. Martin's Press.

Singh, Pashaura, and N. Gerald Barrier, eds. 1999. *Sikh Identity: Continuity and Change*. New Delhi: Manohar.

Sivanandan, Ambalavaner. 1976. *Race, Class and the State: The Black Experience in Britain*. London: Race and Class Publications/Institute of Race Relations.

Smelser, Neil J., and Jeffrey C. Alexander, eds. 1999. *Diversity and Its Discontents: Cultural Conflict and Common Ground in Contemporary American Society*. Princeton, N.J.: Princeton University Press.

Solomos, John, Bob Findlay, Simon Jones, and Paul Gilroy. 1982. "The Organic Crisis of British Capitalism and Race." In *The Empire Strikes Back: Race and Racism in 70s Britain*, ed. Centre for Contemporary Cultural Studies. London: Hutchinson.

Solomos, John. 1993. *Race and Racism in Britain*. 2nd ed. London: Macmillan.

Soysal, Yasemin Nuhoglu. 1994. *Limits of Citizenship: Migrants and Postnational Membership in Europe*. Chicago: University of Chicago Press.

Spencer, Ian R. G. 1997. *British Immigration Policy Since 1939: The Making of Multi-Racial Britain*. London: Routledge.

Spencer, Margaret B., E. Noll, J. Stoltzfus, and V. Harpalani. 2001. "Identity and School Adjustment: Revisiting the 'Acting White' Assumption." *Educational Psychologist* 36, 1: 21–30.

Spitulnik, Debra. 1997. "The Social Circulation of Media Discourse and the Mediation of Communities." *Journal of Linguistic Anthropology* 6, 2: 161–87.

Stambach, Amy. 2000. *Lessons from Mount Kilimanjaro: Schooling, Community, and Gender in East Africa*. New York: Routledge.

Stephens, Sharon, ed. 1995. *Children and the Politics of Culture*. Princeton, N.J.: Princeton University Press.

Strong, Pauline Turner, and Barrik Van Winkle. 1996. "'Indian Blood': Reflections on the Reckoning and Refiguring of Native North American Identity." *Cultural Anthropology* 11, 4: 547–76.

Stubbs, Michael. 1991. "Educational Language Planning in England and Wales: Multicultural Rhetoric and Assimilationist Assumptions." In *A Language Policy for the European Community: Prospects and Quandaries*, ed. Florian Coulmas. Berlin: Mouton de Gruyter.

Swann, Lord. 1985. *Education for All: The Report of the Committee of Inquiry into the Education of Children from Ethnic Minority Groups*. London: HMSO.

Tatla, Darshan Singh. 1999. *The Sikh Diaspora: The Search for Statehood*. London: University College London Press.

Taylor, Arthur J. 1980. "Victorian Leeds: An Overview." In *A History of Modern Leeds*, ed. Derek Fraser. Manchester: Manchester University Press.

Taylor, Charles. 1992. *Multiculturalism and "The Politics of Recognition"*. Princeton, N.J.: Princeton University Press.

Tebbit, Norman. 1990. "Fanfare." *The Field: Magazine for the Country* 272, 7028 (May).

Thompson, Linda, Michael Fleming, and Michael Byram. 1996. "Languages and Language Policy in Britain." In *Language Policies in English-Dominant Countries: Six Case Studies*, ed. Michael Herriman and Barbara Burnaby. Clevedon: Multilingual Matters.

Tilly, Charles. 1998. *Durable Inequality*. Berkeley: University of California Press.

Tollefson, James. 1991. *Planning Language, Planning Inequality: Language Policy in the Community*. London: Longman.

Troyna, Barry. 1989. "'A New Planet'? Tackling Racial Inequality in All-White Schools and Colleges." In *Education for All: A Landmark in Pluralism*, ed. Gajendra K. Verma. London: Falmer Press.

Troyna, Barry, and Bruce Carrington. 1990. *Education, Racism and Reform*. London: Routledge.

Tsing, Anna. 2000. "The Global Situation." *Cultural Anthropology* 15, 3: 327–60.

Turner, Terence. 1994. "Anthropology and Multiculturalism: What Is Anthropology that Multiculturalists Should be Mindful of It?" In *Multiculturalism: A Critical Reader*, ed. David Theo Goldberg. Cambridge, Mass.: Blackwell.

Urban, Greg. 1993. "Culture's Public Face." *Public Culture* 5, 2: 213–38.

———. 2001. *Metaculture: How Culture Moves Through the World*. Minneapolis: University of Minnesota Press.

Vadgama, Kusoom. 1984. *India in Britain: The Indian Contribution to the British Way of Life*. London: Robert Royce.

van der Veer, Peter, ed. 1995. *Nation and Migration: The Politics of Space in the South Asian Diaspora*. Philadelphia: University of Pennsylvania Press.

Varenne, Herve, and Ray McDermott. 1998. *Successful Failure: The School America Builds*. Boulder, Colo.: Westview.

Vertovec, Steven. 1995. "Hindus in Trinidad and Britain: Ethnic Religion, Reification, and the Politics of Public Space." In *Nation and Migration. The Politics of Space in the South Asian Diaspora*, ed. Peter van der Veer. Philadelphia: University of Pennsylvania Press.

———. 1997. "Three Meanings of 'Diaspora,' Exemplified Among South Asian Religions." *Diaspora* 6, 3: 277–99.

Visram, Rozina. 1986. *Ayahs, Lascars and Princes: Indians in Britain, 1700–1947*. London: Pluto Press.

Visweswaran, Kamala. 1997. "Diaspora by Design: Flexible Citizenship and South Asians in U.S. Racial Formations." *Diaspora* 6, 1: 5–29.

Walkerdine, Valerie. 1990. *Schoolgirl Fictions*. London: Verso.

Ward, Robin, and Richard Jenkins, eds. 1984. *Ethnic Communities in Business: Strategies for Economic Survival*. Cambridge: Cambridge University Press.

Weber, Max. 1946. *From Max Weber*. Ed. H. H. Gerth and C. Wright Mills. New York: Oxford University Press.

———. 1978. "Class, Status Groups and Parties." In *Max Weber: Selections in Translation*. Ed. W. G. Runciman, trans. E. Matthews. Cambridge: Cambridge University Press.

Weintraub, Jeff, and Krishan Kumar, eds. 1997. *Public and Private in Thought and Practice: Perspectives on a Grand Dichotomy*. Chicago: University of Chicago Press.

Werbner, Pnina. 1984. "Business of Trust: Pakistani Entrepreneurship in the Manchester Garment Trade." In *Ethnic Communities in Business: Strategies for Economic Survival*, ed. Robin Ward and Richard Jenkins. Cambridge: Cambridge University Press.

———. 1987. "Enclave Economies and Family Firms: Pakistani Traders in a British City." In *Migrants, Labour and Social Order*, ed. Jeremy S. Eades. ASA Monographs 25. London: Tavistock.

———. 1990. *The Migration Process: Capital, Gifts, and Offerings Among British Pakistanis*. New York: St. Martin's Press.

Werbner, Pnina, and Tariq Modood, eds. 1997. *Debating Cultural Hybridity: Multi-Cultural Identities and the Politics of Anti-Racism*. London: Zed Books.

Westwood, Sallie, and Parminder Bhachu, eds. 1988. *Enterprising Women: Ethnicity, Economy and Gender*. London: Routledge.

Wexler, Philip. 1987. *Social Analysis of Education: After the New Sociology*. London: Routledge and Kegan Paul.

Williams, Brackette F. 1989. "A Class Act: Anthropology and the Race to Nation Across Ethnic Terrain." *Annual Review of Anthropology* 18: 401–44.

———. 1991. *Stains on My Name, War in My Veins: Guyana and the Politics of Cultural Struggle*. Durham, N.C.: Duke University Press.

Williams, Raymond. 1977. *Marxism and Literature*. London: Oxford University Press.

Willis, Paul. 1977. *Learning to Labor: How Working Class Kids Get Working Class Jobs*. New York: Columbia University Press.

———. 1981. "Cultural Production Is Different from Social Reproduction Is Different from Reproduction." *Interchange* 12, 2: 48–67.

Wilson, William Julius. 1980. *The Declining Significance of Race: Blacks and Changing American Institutions*. Chicago: University of Chicago Press.

———. 1987. *The Truly Disadvantaged: The Inner City, the Underclass, and Public Policy*. Chicago: University of Chicago Press.

Women of South Asian Descent Collective, ed. 1993. *Our Feet Walk the Sky: Women of the South Asian Diaspora*. San Francisco: Aunt Lute Books.

Woolard, Kathryn A., and Bambi B. Schieffelin. 1994. "Language Ideology." *Annual Review of Anthropology* 23: 55–82.

Wuthnow, Robert. 1999. *Democratic Liberalism and the Challenge of Diversity in Late-Twentieth-Century America*. Princeton, N.J.: Princeton University Press.

Zablocki, Benjamin D., and Rosabeth Moss Kanter. 1976. "The Differentiation of Life-Styles." *Annual Review of Sociology*: 269–98.

Index

Acknowledgments

Creative projects, even anthropological ethnographies, emerge from the recesses of our minds and hearts, nurtured by our experiences and by the people who enter our lives. Many events and people in my life have laid the foundations for what appears in this text. My desire to understand the basis of social inequality, the processes of educational class mobility, and, more precisely, how young people make sense of racial and class differences is deeply rooted in two powerfully constitutive experiences in my life. Racialized class boundaries were impossible to ignore, but seldom discussed, in the world where I grew up, the red-lined white and middle-class city of San Leandro, California on the border of the equally black and poor neighborhoods of East Oakland. Racism, economic disparity, and segregation became words for realities I had lived and desperately needed to understand and challenge. My interest in social mobility is intertwined, intimately, with my own personal struggles along the academic path to social mobility. Though I am white, I, like many of the young people I write about here, was the first person in my family to test the myth of meritocracy and to climb the educational ladder of class mobility.

At the University of Chicago I was to learn an academic discourse for making sense of my experiences with race and class. Entering into the elite cultural world of this wonderful research university also showed me quite clearly how relations of social inequality are reproduced. My life was powerfully reconfigured by the ideas and mentors I encountered in this rich intellectual environment. It was in a class on Urban Poverty with William Julius Wilson that the questions motivating this study first began to take shape. Over the years, Bill Wilson has continued to be a role model and inspiration, teaching me what it means, truly, to maintain one's vision, personal commitments, and scholarly integrity as a public intellectual. I was privileged to have Bernard Cohn as my advisor. Never directive, Barney opened minds. Ever creative and always far ahead of his time, Barney's imaginative orientation to anthropology drew those of us who worked with him far away from conventional ways of conceptualizing social life. A fundamentally "student-centered" mentor, he sensed and reinforced each student's unique vantage point and intellectual gifts. He nurtured my interest in South Asia and in Britain and showed me what Foucault could contribute to the study of educational processes. While Barney's presence in this book is a subtle one, John and Jean Comaroff's influence is quite apparent throughout. John and Jean taught me how to think about the interplay of culture, power, and identity in modern capitalist societies. Their unique blend of marxist/post-structuralist/historical political anthropology gave my personal vision of social inequality a voice, and John and Jean themselves gave me the encouragement I needed, often when I needed it most, to believe in that voice and what I had to say as a scholar. I am deeply indebted to them, personally and intellectually. As I have become a mentor to my own students, I have developed an even greater appreciation for the time, energy, and attention they gave to each of us, and for what we in turn received. I owe a great deal to Raymond T. Smith for teaching me how to think anthropologically about race, nationalism, and class in "plural" societies, and to the late David Schneider for first igniting in me a passion for theory, and, more profoundly, perhaps, for always being there.

Many others will also see their influence reflected in the pages of this study. Sharon Stephens left this world long before any of her friends wanted to let her go, but if she could read this she would recognize how much she has meant to me. Jean Lave, Ray McDermott, Frederick Erickson, Doug Foley, Shirley Brice Heath, Dorothy Holland, and Bud Mehan, great friends and mentors all, each have powerfully shaped my approach to studying education anthropologically. My thinking about the South Asian diaspora and about immigration more generally, has emerged in dialogue with Arjun Appadurai's creative rethinking of the anthropology of modernity and globalization. My scholarship owes a major debt to Arjun and to Carol Breckenridge for their pioneering work in developing the field of public culture, and, more personally, for their interest in and encouragement of my work over the years. Roger Ballard, who had done extensive work with members of the Sikh community in Leeds, agreed to supervise the initial

Fulbright funded project. The richness of my original field research owes a great deal to his guidance.

I wish to express my gratitude to a number of my colleagues at the University of Pennsylvania. Michael Katz, most significantly, has given me his constant and fervent support as an advisor, critic, and friend. In Eli Anderson I have found a true urban ethnographer-comrade with whom I can creatively reflect. The development of this project has benefited greatly from the critical insights of colleagues who have given generously of their time to read and comment on my work. Stanton Wortham, Ritty Lukose, and Barbara Savage actually made it through the entire manuscript, at least once, and provided incredibly incisive feedback. Barbara walked before me on the tenure track, showing me that calm is an option. Stanton and Ritty, fellow anthropologists and partners in the Education, Culture, and Society Program at the Graduate School of Education, are the most wonderful colleagues one could ever hope to have. I would also like to thank a number of other colleagues who have read and provided insightful comments on different pieces of this work, in particular Rebecca Freeman, Marvin Lazerson, John Puckett, Peggy Sanday, Kathy Schultz, and Jeanne Stanley. My work on this project has also been sustained by the sincere interest and enthusiastic support I have received from colleagues Lisa Bouillion, Yuko Butler, Chuck Dwyer, Ann Farnsworth-Alvear, Susan Fuhrman, Vivian Gadsden, Peg Goertz, Joan Goodman, Nancy Hornberger, Tom Kecskemethy, Peter Kuriloff, Jim Larkin, Ray Lorion, Susan Lytle, Torch Lytle, Rebecca Maynard, Ruth Neild, Norm Newberg, Julia Paley, Tere Pica, Janine Remillard, Jeff Shultz, Elaine Simon, Larry Sipe, Diana Slaughter-Defoe, Harris Sokoloff, Margaret Beale Spencer, Howard Stevenson, Janet Theophano, Ken Tobin, and Greg Urban. It is my students, however, who have taught me the importance of what I do as an intellectual. I want to thank each of my students for their inspiration, challenging questions, and fresh perspectives. I am especially grateful for the contributions of my research assistants Emily Greytak and Regina Smardon. I also with to thank Michele Belliveau, Amy Blank, Bryan Brayboy, Maia Cucchiara, Joseph Cytrynbaum, Aiden Downey, Pritha Gopalan, Raymond Gunn, and Clare Ignatowski for their valuable feedback on drafts of this manuscript. Finally, many members of the staff at GSE have given their time and expertise to the production of this book. I would like to acknowledge Ruth Ebert for her superb copy-editing, Lessie Boyd and Janean Williams for their invaluable assistance with the tables, and Maureen Cotterill, Elizabeth Dean, and Rona Rosenberg for their administrative support.

I have had the good fortune to cross paths with a number of remarkable scholars who have been a part of this project in ways not always easy to "acknowledge." For their inspiration, encouragement, and guidance, my thanks go to Andrew Apter, Rebecca Bryant, Fernando Coronil, Virginia Dominguez, Van Dusenbery, Jane Fajans, Bill Felstiner, Ray Fogelson, "Greta" Gibson, Ron Inden, Catherine Lacey, Ellen Lagemann, Sarah Lamb, Bradley Levinson, Karen Leonard, Mary Ludwig, McKim Marriott, Diane Mines, Ralph Nicholas, Moishe Postone, Marshall Sahlins, Dan Segal, Julie Skurski, Amy Stambach, Brian Street, Pauline Turner Strong, Terry Turner, Bonnie Urcioli, Dirk van der Elst, and Brackette Williams.

Over the past few years, many dear friends (academics and non-academics alike) have learned far more about this book than any of them really wanted or needed to know. For their friendship, patience, and moral support, I thank Nadia Abu el-Haj, Maureen Anderson, Meg Armstrong, Misty Bastian, Anna Beresin, Cliff Boardman, Tony Bryk, Barbara Craig, Wendy Espeland, Lillian Faderman, Peg Faith, Noma Field, Jane Gordon, Sharon Greenberg, Donna, Andy, and Ella Kirschner, Ethel Goldsmith, Tim Hacsi, Mindie Lazarus-Black, Hicks Marlow, Neil Midgely, Elizabeth Moje, Allen and Tatiana Peters, Lisa Rosen, Nick and Clare Rudall, Barbara Sahlins, Henry, Henry, and Wilson Smith, Eeva Tuominen, John Warren, Margaret Weiner, Angharad Williams, Karen von Winbush, and Drexel Woodson. I would also like to express gratitude to family and dear friends who are with me no longer, but whose love sustained me in this effort, namely Enid and Harold Rudall, Julian Goldsmith, and Lucille Strauss.

My family has provided a world away from academe, a place here I could go to laugh and feel loved and give love in return. With their wonderful humor and their practical wisdom, they have never ceased to remind me that there are more important things in life than work, anthropology, or my career. I want to express my love and deep appreciation to my sister, Debbie, my brother-in-law, Craig, my nephews, Stephen and Daniel Coe, my mother, Ruth Hall, and my mother-in-spirit, Leta Schmidt. I dedicate this book to my late grandmother, Ruth Templeton, who taught me what dedication really means.

Research and writing of the book were facilitated by generous funding from a number of sources—a Fulbright Fellowship, a Spencer Foundation Dissertation Fellowship, a Chapin Hall Center for Children Postdoctoral fellowship, a Spencer Foundation/National Academy of Education Postdoctoral Fellowship, and a University of Pennsylvania Research Foundation Grant. In his gentle and gracious way, Peter Agree, Anthropology Editor at the University of Pennsylvania Press, throughout the publishing process, has provided sound professional advice and a solid foundation of encouragement and support. I am grateful to Peter, to Managing Editor Alison Anderson, and to the staff at the Press for their invaluable contributions to the production of this work. A very special thank you is reserved for Carol Greenhouse whose brilliant comments and creative suggestions as an outside reader contributed to making this a far better book. A second reader, who remains anonymous, also provided very valuable comments and my thanks go to her as well.

My greatest debt, however, is to the people in Leeds, England, who granted me the privilege of entering their lives. I am deeply grateful. I thank you for allowing me to learn from you and for trusting me to represent your lives in this account. The staff at Grange Hill High opened their lives and their classroom doors, and many became quite engaged in my efforts to understand the nature of social and cultural difference in their school. The students brought me into their worlds, shared their dilemmas and frustrations, honestly and openly, and, through their constant teasing, made sure that I never took myself, or my research, too seriously. Finally, to each of my very dear British Sikh friends—I offer this study, with the hope that it will contribute something of meaning to your lives. Thank you for making this project possible and for enriching my life in so many ways.